BENEDICT
of BAVARIA

BENEDICT
of BAVARIA

An Intimate Portrait of the Pope and His Homeland

BRENNAN PURSELL

CIRCLE
PRESS

Cataloging-Publication Data is on file with the Library of Congress

ISBN: 1-933271-17-5

PRINTED IN THE UNITED STATES OF AMERICA

8 7 6 5 4 3 2 1

FIRST EDITION

This book is dedicated to my cherished wife,

Irmgard Pursell,

one of Bavaria's loveliest daughters.

TABLE *of* CONTENTS

"Purcell's intimate knowledge of Bavaria lends itself beautifully to this straightforward and easy to read biography of Pope Benedict. If you want to go beyond the headlines and the talking heads to know the real Benedict, this is the place to start."

DR. PIA DE SOLENNI, MORAL THEOLOGIAN
AND CULTURAL COMMENTATOR

"Brennan Pursell is a rare find: he combines intellectual rigor with lively, enjoyable prose, and a mature love for the Church with a keen and respectful understanding of contemporary culture's most pressing issues. If you only read one book on Pope Benedict XVI, this is the one to pick."

FATHER JOHN BARTUNEK, LC, BEST-SELLING AUTHOR OF
INSIDE THE PASSION AND *THE BETTER PART*

"In this very readable book, Brennan Pursell has given all those interested in getting to know the real Pope Benedict the means to understand him from the inside. Pursell ably connects the formative seeds of Joseph Ratzinger's upbringing—his family, his deeply Catholic Bavarian culture, his teachers, as well as his up-close encounter with the evil of Nazism—to the abundant fruit he has borne as a theologian, bishop, Vatican prefect, and pope. This book will nourish both those who know a lot about Pope Benedict and those who know almost nothing."

FATHER ROGER LANDRY, EXECUTIVE EDITOR OF *THE ANCHOR*

ACKNOWLEDGEMENTS

Hearty thanks go to Hanns and Inge Finkenzeller, my research assistants in Germany, to colleagues and administrators at DeSales University for their wise advice and stalwart support, and especially to Juilene McKnight, the living Celtic muse, who edited unsparingly, and Larry Chapp, who checked for faulty theology. My agent, Natalia Aponte, guided the project from its inception, and Circle Press general manager Claudia Volkman saw it to fruition. Fathers Barry O'Toole, LC, John Bartunek, LC, and Cliff Ermatinger, LC, I must thank for spiritual guidance, as well as Father George Salzmann, OSFS, and the Benedictines at Metten, without whom none of this would ever have happened. Finally, I thank my wife, Irmgard, for her support and forbearance during the months of research and writing, and for a meticulous reading in English and German at the end.

$\mathcal{A}$UTHOR'S $\mathcal{N}$OTE

I had two goals in writing this book. The first is to acquaint you with Joseph Ratzinger in the context of his homeland, the Free State of Bavaria, in the southeast of Germany, a place I have come to know well through extensive travel and study over the last dozen years. I want you to know where this rare genius of a man comes from and to understand the culture that formed him.

My second goal is to help you to understand Pope Benedict XVI *on his own terms*. I am writing as a historian, not a journalist, which basically means that I read and researched far more than I wrote. I relied less on the mass media coverage of his career than on the dozens of books, articles, chapters, homilies, speeches, and addresses he has given over the last five decades. I believe that the Pope's own writings are the best source for learning who he is, how he thinks, what he says, what he has done, and what he is going to do. This portrayal also draws heavily on the interviews and testimonies from people in Germany who have known him for years, material I have translated myself.

A note regarding the citations: Each chapter's endnotes will refer to the correct page in the published English translations of the Pope's works, but I have taken the liberty of making translations of my own from the original German text. Discrepancies should be minimal.

INTRODUCTION

"In my vocation, I belong to the whole world,
but my heart beats Bavarian."

– Pope Benedict XVI

Some might say serendipity brought me to Bavaria, but according to others, it was the will of the Almighty.

So how does a young hedonist from the San Francisco suburbs find his way into a Benedictine monastery in the Bavarian forest, convert to Catholicism, and then fall in love with a little old man named Joseph Ratzinger? I hardly know where to begin, though I should, because it happened to me.

I was brought up in a well-adjusted, loving family, experiencing a happy childhood that was pretty much devoid of religion. My mother, a psychologist (raised Catholic), and my father, a businessman (raised Protestant), imparted an appreciation for the Golden Rule to me and my siblings but had a conditional attitude toward Christianity. We sang Christian carols with the extended family and friends at Christmas, but few members of our family truly believed the words of what we were actually saying. Attendance at religious services was rare and done for the sake of general education. When it came to abortion, contraception, euthanasia, the death penalty, women as priests, divorce, and gay marriage, my parents were and are as non-Catholic as the next suburban upper middle-class, American couple.

Don't get me wrong: I love my parents dearly and am enormously grateful for all that they are and do. They are totally committed to each other; for years, friends of mine would meet them and say with a stunned expression, "Wow, look at them, they're in love!" Next to their marriage and children, every other consideration—career, status, friends, you name it—comes in a distant second.

But for me, something was missing.

Going to high school in the San Francisco Bay Area in the early 1980s was an extended exposure to the fleeting delights of drugs, alcohol, and sex—thankfully more indirect than direct. But studying at Stanford University—to this day a monument to relativism and the relentless pursuit of profit—was a time of wanton indulgence. The university's drug policy at the time was "Just say know," in mockery of First Lady Nancy Reagan's slogan. Irreverence reigned supreme among the student body and I loved it, much more than I did my fellow man. If I had read any Nietzsche, I would have been a devotee. I lived the life of a twentieth-century Apollonian: a sun worshipper, a lover of nature and light, of music, drama, health, and physical power and beauty.

By the end of two years, I was struck with the sense that something was wrong, that I was wasting my time. One sunny day after a game of volleyball, the thought came to me: *I should rush a fraternity, change my major, and reorder my life so that my first car will be a Jaguar.* Almost immediately, I felt like someone flung ice water in my face: *You are headed down the wrong path.* That same afternoon I told my advisor that I was going to take a year off from school. I spent it in India, tutoring the children of a rich, dysfunctional family. When I came back, I was imbued with Indian mysticism, particularly in the relativistic belief that all religions are more or less the same manifestations of faith in an unknowable, ineffable, arbitrary god.

When I resumed my studies, it was at Oxford as part of Stanford's extensive overseas program. At that time in my life I prided myself in the knowledge that just about everyone in the world was dull, ignorant, and ugly—myself included, of course. Such sentiments are still shocking in their arrogance. I remember a broad-shouldered Catholic girl telling me, "You put on airs." My response? I berated her for not admitting her own worthlessness as readily as I did my own.

During this time one of my favorite things to do was to find every old stone church I could find, in England and in places I visited on the Continent, stroll around, then go inside and sit down for a while. I don't know why I gravitated to them. They had to be empty; the presence of people ruined the spiritual ambience for me. The sensation of timelessness, the unearthly light, the occasional remnant of incense, and especially organ music struck me as majestic and transporting.

After a year I returned to California and school, graduating as a half-baked misanthrope, thoroughly self-possessed, overconfident, moody, and foulmouthed. By the time I moved to the East Coast to start graduate school at Harvard, I was a self-professed pagan. It just seemed the easiest, most rational, and convenient answer to life's greatest questions. "Black days" accompanied the stress, the sleeplessness, the exhaustion, the panic, and the relentless pressure of graduate study. They made me even more bitter and obnoxious, my easy-going Californian relativism becoming a fuming cynicism.

Something pulled me to Mass. I didn't know or ask why. I would just go to St. Paul's in Harvard Square and sit through the liturgy, taking comfort somehow in things that I barely understood. It was the only place where I found a measure of peace.

It was actually through the historical study of the Protestant Reformation at Harvard (that temple to proud, politically correct postmodernism) that I learned about Roman Catholicism. Whenever we read Luther, Calvin, and the rest of the Reformers, I always found myself sympathizing with the Catholics. Each of the Reformers came up with a uniquely brilliant interpretation of the Bible, but the weight of history always seemed tilted on the side of the Catholic Church. If the Church was as totally corrupt as the Reformers claimed, when exactly did she go down the path of falsehood? Which Council had gotten it wrong? The Reformers showed no agreement on this, or anything else, for that matter. While Scripture supplied support for all competing arguments, the Church could always fall back on her age-old continuity in doctrine and sacrament. "That is," I told myself, "if one can believe in such things."

One grey autumn day on the steps of St. Paul's one of the chaplains greeted me, asked my name, and offered his assistance if I ever needed it. In that moment I remembered what a traveler had told me in India. "Mate, you have to spend time in a monastery. Time stops, the world vanishes, you get peace. Gotta give it a go."

So I asked the chaplain, somewhat curtly, if he knew how I might be able to get into a monastery in Germany. My ulterior motive was to improve my German. He snatched a pen from his breast pocket and scribbled down my contact information. For the next few months I heard nothing. Then one bright, snowy morning in February, after a black day and a night of drinking to expunge it, the ringing of my phone rattled my aching head. I was standing in my room in a green bathrobe, fresh from the shower, dripping a small puddle on the linoleum floor. I answered against my will.

"Yeah, who is it?"

"Ah! Brennan! It's Father George from St. Paul's, and in two hours a friend of mine who knows the Abbot Primate of Bavaria is going to get on a plane to head back across the pond. Do you want to meet him now?"

Forty-five minutes later it was all set.

I spent the summer of 1994 in Metten, a beautiful Benedictine monastery at the foot of the low mountains that make up the backbone of the Bavarian forest. The monks were perfectly hospitable; they let me come and go, pray, eat, and sleep as I pleased, no restrictions applied. The prior, Pater Adalbert Seipolt, a well known children's writer in Germany, was generous with his time and attention. I can't tell you how much I learned from him that summer.

For hours each day, I sat in the reading room adjacent to the splendid, baroque library—they even gave me my own key! I pored over works by St. Augustine and the other Church Fathers. More than anything else, it was St. Ambrose's explanations of the sacraments that threw open the doors. "Ah! *That's* what baptism means! So *that's* what the Eucharist really is!" The liturgies in the monastery church and chapel were simple, devout, and beautiful, and many hours worth of silent prayer sealed the deal.

But how does one write about spiritual experience without cheapening it somewhat or rendering it a bit banal? In general, I can only describe the sensation there, in the solitude of true, comforting peace, as a kind of "lifting."

I've never looked back, never regretted my conversion, not for a minute. The black days never returned, and my prayer life is still growing—again, how does one describe this?—richer, deeper, a joy that is more intense and a peace that is more fulfilling.

There's more to that summer in Metten: I met my wife, Irmgard, there, though at the time I didn't know it. When I returned to Germany a year later to burrow through a number of archives, we fell prey to a classic Shakespearean gag. The gregarious Bavarian gentleman who had made the arrangements for me to go to Metten chortled at me in his gravelly voice, "You know that pretty redhead you met last summer? She heard you were coming and said that she simply *has* to see you." It was a shameless falsehood. Next he called her on the phone, fed her a similar lie, and then invited us over to her place for dinner that evening, something no Bavarian with a sense of probity should do.

From that evening on I was a goner. Now, after a decade of marriage and raising children, I would like to think that I know a thing or two about Bavaria, its people, and its vibrant, distinctive Catholic culture.

Some facts about Bavaria before we continue: It is the largest of the sixteen states in the Federal Republic of Germany, comprising the entire southeastern quarter of the country. It is one of the richest and most populous, and usually ranks among the best when it comes to education and various economic indicators. When Americans think of everything good and fun about Germany—oompah bands, *Lederhosen*, fine sausages, oversized pretzels, exquisite beer served in hefty glass mugs, fairy-tale castles, Alpine skiing, beautiful countryside, exquisite cars, and, of course, *Oktoberfest*—they are thinking of Bavaria, whether they realize it or not.

The state has its own political party, the Christian Socialists, who partner with the Christian Democrats in a "Union" that represents the vast majority of Germany's conservatives. The Bavarian dialect, spoken in the central and southern parts of the state, is so far from the German learned in school that it basically entails another language. I am always relieved when I meet Germans in Bavaria who are left just as flabbergasted at certain phrases as I am. The Bavarian capital, Munich, a city of more than a million, is Germany's premier city in the south in terms of industry, finance, the media, and tourism. And year after year, Munich's international airport is rated the best in all of Europe.

Finally, most of Bavaria is *Catholic*. Churches, cloisters, and cathedrals, built and decorated in the gothic, baroque, and rococo styles are so numerous that it is difficult to drive ten minutes in any direction without spotting another spire. Crucifixes and miniature chapels dot the countryside, and you can expect to find a large cross on every mountaintop. You will learn more about Bavaria's Catholic identity throughout the rest of this book. Suffice it to say, I love Bavaria with the passion of a convert.

And now we come to Joseph Ratzinger, His Holiness, Pope Benedict XVI, the first Bavarian Pope in about one thousand years.

My love for the Pope began as the highest regard for the mind and spirit of Cardinal Ratzinger, the author of dozens of books, all of which contain magisterial arguments written in effortless prose, not only in German, but in the English translations published by Ignatius Press. His theology is the clearest and the most compelling I have ever encountered, and his grasp of history and the nature of humankind is just as persuasive. It is difficult to resist being attracted to the person who moves, inspires, and uplifts you even in print, don't you think?

Furthermore, concerned sympathy has increased this love. At eighty years old, he has suffered two small strokes, and despite the adoring crowds that routinely fill St. Peter's Square, he has the daunting task of leading an organization marked as much by dissension as by unity, in the face of cultures that are largely hostile to all things Catholic. But this is normal in history. The Church is always dealing with one crisis or another.

The mainstream media set its sights on Benedict XVI before he ever appeared on the balcony at St. Peter's. Puerile phrases like "God's Rottweiler" and "Panzer-Cardinal" have plagued this mild, Mozart-loving man for many a year. It may well be that he has begun his pontificate as the most maligned Pope in modern history.

And yet, how fitting. The man is *German*, isn't he? What do most people know about Germany beyond Hitler and the Holocaust? On U.S. college campuses, the primary scholarly interest in Germany is focused on the history of the Nazis and also Martin Luther, and rarely does it venture any further. Hollywood and the History Channel continue to bombard us with reminders that the Germans are the authors of the worst evil ever perpetuated by mankind, the great enemy of the greatest generation, a people crippled—then, now, and forever—by a national defect in character.

Be that as it may, there is more than this one side.

The goal of this book is to present another view of Pope Benedict XVI, a better, fuller picture than you would find in the yellow press. Historians are supposed to be impartial about the subject of their research, and I frankly do not see how that is possible when it concerns things of great importance, like people. So I will strive for fairness instead. When I err, it will be on the side of sympathy rather than criticism. Wherever possible, I have tried to let the man speak for himself.

If asked to sum up this book in a single sentence, I would say this: Joseph Ratzinger, Pope Benedict XVI, despite the extraordinary brilliance of his mind and the universality of his vocation, is deep down still a simple son of his homeland. There is a reason why he has said many times, "My heart beats Bavarian."

FROM SMALL-TOWN BAVARIA: MARKTL AM INN

"My roots remain, I am a Bavarian."

—*Pope Benedict XVI, at his first papal audience*

On April 19, 2005, Joseph Cardinal Ratzinger became Pope Benedict XVI after one of the quickest conclaves in modern history, requiring only four rounds of voting in a total of twenty-four hours. Thereafter, millions, even billions of souls who had never heard of the man began to wonder who he was and what kind of pope he would be.

Before the voting even began, the word was that Cardinal Ratzinger, the Dean of the College of Cardinals, the Prefect of the Sacred Congregation for the Doctrine of the Faith, the presiding celebrant at the funeral mass of Pope John Paul II, was the leading choice, a marked man. The corporate media transmitted waves of critique, as provocative as one would expect from an entertainment industry. American audiences were warned about the former Nazi-turned-theological-*Gestapo*, "God's Rottweiler." Newspapers proclaimed that he had been a member of Hitler Youth, that he had manned antiaircraft units targeting American bombers, which seemed to justify the old epithet, the "Panzer-Cardinal." Even when a few feature articles bothered to mention that Ratzinger had always loathed Nazism and its multitude of heinous crimes, the authors dutifully added that the teenager had failed to make a public demonstration of such views during the 1940s. It was all rather depressing, but the overwhelming majority of the 115 voting members of the College of Cardinals were not to be intimidated.

After Pope Benedict gave his first apostolic blessing, there seemed to be no end to the woes. This man, it was said in tones of false regret, bashed innocent homosexuals, fired the liberal editor of a Jesuit magazine, and even hurled an anathema at Harry Potter. Some media friendly Catholic priests and theologians expressed their grave disappointment and discomfort. The subtext of this commentary was obvious. All those teeming hordes in St. Peter's Square, what on earth could those people be rejoicing about? The happiness in their faces was unassailable proof of their extremism.

Who is Joseph Ratzinger? Who is the man who is the 265th Pope of the Catholic Church? In 2001, when an interviewer asked him to describe himself, he answered, "I feel more like a simple man than a cardinal. I have my home in Germany, in a small village, with people who work in agriculture, in craftsmanship, and there I feel at home."[1] People who want to learn about Pope Benedict XVI would do well to ignore most of what is said about him on network television. Let's begin at the beginning, by traveling to the place of his birth.

⚜ MARKTL AM INN

Until April 2005 almost no one in Germany, let alone the rest of the world, knew anything about Marktl am Inn, a typical example of small-town, rural Bavaria, close to the border with Austria. Compactly settled in four quarters divided by two crossing roads, Marktl is today the home of 2,700 souls, a humble settlement alongside the Inn River, surrounded by dense forests of pine, spruce, beech, and other deciduous trees.

Just passing through, you might get the impression that there is absolutely nothing going on. There is no main drag, no mall, no entertainment center, no amusement park. But the inhabitants have a small library and community center, a community-run kindergarten for up to seventy-five children, an elementary and a middle school, a fire department and other emergency services, a recycling center, and last but not least, a cemetery. The residents' healthcare is overseen by eight doctors, two physical therapists, and a pharmacy. And if they want to have fun, Marktl offers fishing, swimming, golfing, bowling, indoor go-carting, and a studio for silk painting. Little Marktl even has its own local history museum, with 1,700 items displayed in eleven rooms telling the story of the town across the millennia. Marktl is too small to be officially designated as a town or even a village; for nearly six hundred years it has been a "market community."

Archaeological findings indicate that people have been living in the region since the Stone Age. The oldest coin was minted, apparently by a druid, some two thousand years ago during the era when Celts dominated the region. Marktl, like so many settlements in Germany, laid its foundations during the Middle Ages, built its oldest church by the end of the thirteenth century, and received recognition and rights as a market from the local lord by the fifteenth. The town was destroyed once by fire in 1701, and once by flood in 1899. Napoleon Bonaparte passed through the community in 1805, marking the extent of Marktl's appearance on the historical stage.

When Joseph Ratzinger and his family lived in Marktl in the late 1920s, the community was even smaller and much poorer than it is now. Bavaria was the same as she had been for centuries, a landlocked farming region; in the countryside, humble living was the norm. After World War I, unemployment was high in Bavaria's southeast, reflecting the crippled German economy largely due to the immense reparations payments to France and Britain. The bitter political divisions of the Weimar Republic were also present in Marktl, but for the Ratzinger family there were "many beautiful memories of friendship and neighborly aid, memories of small family celebrations and of church life."[2] The bonds of family and community weathered national crises. These days, Marktl is remarkably similar to the way it was then: a quiet, modest market town serving the farming community that surrounds it. A place to cross the river.

Constructed in 1745, the house where the Pope was born was meant to last, true for thousands of such dwellings in Bavaria. A broad, sloping, tiled roof protects the upper and ground levels from rain, sleet, and snow. Wooden shutters on either side of each window serve the same purpose. Despite the building's age, the walls look relatively new, thanks to a recently applied layer of cheery yellow and white stucco. Heavy double doors open to the interior, and an enclosed courtyard is located around back. In the 1920s it served as Marktl's police station, with the local commissioner and his family living in an upstairs apartment.

On Holy Saturday, April 16, 1927, Maria, wife of Josef Ratzinger, safely delivered her third child and second son at home around 4:30 in the morning. The Easter baptismal liturgy was set to begin four hours later, and the newborn's parents said, "Well, the boy's here already."[3] Braving frigid temperatures and piles of unwelcome spring snow, Josef and Maria trudged the two hundred or so yards from one side of the market square to the other, carrying their swaddled newborn into St. Oswald's Church. There the baby was baptized, probably by the pastor, Father Karl Köppel, who in that year was completing a full renovation of St. Oswald's. The Ratzinger's third child was the first to receive the freshly blessed waters for the coming year. They named him Joseph Aloisius. Just two years later they moved, so his father could take up a position in another nearby town. Marktl was not to be young Joseph's *Heimat*.

If you want to understand Pope Benedict XVI, you must understand the concept of *Heimat*. There is no direct English equivalent for this important German word, but it can be loosely translated as "homeland." *Heimat* is the place where German-speakers put down their roots: the town, the neighborhood, or village, where one is born, grows up, makes friends for life, and is generally known. Not tied to any specific political entity or party, *Heimat* is a safe haven for bad times, no matter how far and wide one travels in life. Usually people living there have a special way of speaking, a dialect or an accent, that firmly identifies them as a group and sets them apart from neighboring regions. When welcoming the Pope on his first apostolic visit to Bavaria in September 2006, Horst Köhler, the president of the Federal Republic of Germany, said, "Origin and homeland form us all. Homeland: that is more than a certain landscape. It is a way of life, a set of customs. It is music and literature. It involves convictions. It is a certain way to be in the world."[4] In Germany, *Heimat* shapes the individual.

In the United States, we rarely use the name of the city to identify the persons living in it, with the possible exception of New Yorkers and perhaps Bostonians. In Germany, the name of potentially every town, no matter how small, is regularly turned into the word to identify its denizens. A man from Vilsbiburg proudly calls himself a *Vilsbiburger*. A woman who grew up in Munich, married, and moved to another region refers to herself as a *Münchnerin* for the rest of her life. Landshut is filled with *Landshuter*. The tradition points to the fact that, generally speaking, Germans let their roots grow deeper than Americans.

Joseph Ratzinger breaks from this venerable norm; he would never call himself a *Marktler*. When he visited the community in 1986 to preach on Pentecost Monday, he said that although he has almost no memories from his first two years, the fact that he was born, baptized, and took his first steps there allows him "to feel like a *Marktler*," but this is not the same as identifying himself as such. In fact, he cannot really use a city name at all. He opens his autobiography, *Milestones: Memoirs, 1927-1977*, with the words, "It is not at all easy to say what my hometown really is."[5] The first ten years of his life he describes as *Wanderschaft*, or "being on the road." Be that as it may, by becoming Pope Benedict XVI, he changed Marktl forever, even if the place means little to him in the end.

The Pope's birthplace has become a significant tourist destination. On average, three to four buses come every day. The annual number of visitors now surpasses 200,000. A local Bavarian newspaper proclaimed, *Es päpstelt!* or "It's poping!" After the election, land was cleared for a new parking lot to keep the procession of tour buses from clogging the narrow, meandering streets. In the shops you can buy Pope cross buns, baked miters, Pope crucifix cakes, Ratzinger sausages, and, the top seller, Pope beer. Prices are inflated, but people are not dissuaded to pay them, and the suppliers in Marktl ship across the world. The local history museum has extended its hours from six days per *year* to six days per *week*, and the number of visitors has skyrocketed. The owner of the house where the Pope was born hit a jackpot. Having bought the building in the 1990s for under 200,000 Euros, she sold it to a consortium of Catholic foundations after a round of bidding that sent the price into the millions. The faithful gave a sigh of relief that it did not go to the interested Arab sheik or the prospective buyer who wanted to turn it into a restaurant. It has been turned into a museum honoring the town's most famous child and as a meeting place for those engaged in religious dialogue.

Papal tourists can view the Pope's birthplace from the outside, then walk to St. Oswald's Church where inside is the six-sided, white limestone baptismal font, decorated with angels, where Joseph Ratzinger was christened. Behind it rises a lovely altarpiece, carved in wood in the neo-Gothic style, its pointed arches and delicate tracery painted in bright colors and radiant gold, showing the risen Christ, flanked by holy women, with figures of angels and saints underneath. These works of religious art mark the beginning of the Christian life of the current successor of Saint Peter. Nearly every day groups of tourists pose before the altar and around the font for photographs.

When Benedict made his apostolic visit to Bavaria in September 2006, he made a brief stop in Marktl where he visited St. Oswald's and admired the new, twelve-foot-high bronze sculpture, in the form of a sealed scroll, that now stands in front of the town hall, just a stone's throw from his birthplace. The massive scroll is marked as the "Rule" of St. Benedict, the father of western monasticism and the patron saint of Europe. In the town's official, golden bound book, the Pope wrote, "God bless this dear place."

Suffice it to say that Marktl am Inn has become a pilgrimage site in its own right. People are drawn to the Holy Father's first home and church in order to bring themselves a little closer to him, driven by a sentiment that is entirely understandable. But apart from those two structures, Marktl is not a place of pilgrimage in the usual sense, not as much a destination as a meaningful point of *departure*.

The pilgrimage, a religiously motivated journey to a holy place and back again, is largely unknown in a predominantly Protestant country like the United States, but it has been an integral part of the Roman Catholic experience for well over a thousand years. Today pilgrims—men and women, girls and boys of all ages—come to Marktl by bus, car, motorcycle, and bicycle. They gather in the market square or sometimes on the outskirts of the town. Some hoist wooden crosses on their shoulders, hold them in their arms, or tuck them into their backpacks. Others carry the flags of their towns, parishes, and religious clubs or associations. When they leave town, the police close the road for them so they can cross the bridge over the River Inn safely. They pray as they go, silently and out loud, sometimes led by a priest using a megaphone. From Marktl they walk nine or ten miles to the southwest to the very heart of Catholic Bavaria and its most famous and holiest shrine in Altötting.

While Marktl am Inn is the site of Pope Benedict's birth, Altötting is the town where he learned how to be a pilgrim, his whole life long.

2

⟨A PILGRIM *in* ALTÖTTING⟩

"I was lucky to be born right near Altötting."

Altötting is the heart of Bavaria and one of the hearts of Europe."

—*Pope Benedict XVI*

Every year, throngs of American families, regardless of their religious orientation, make their pilgrimage to the land or world of Disney, driving or flying hundreds or even thousands of miles to get to the coastal Magic Kingdoms. There they spend large amounts of money (this kingdom makes no provisions for the poor), but it is doubtful whether they leave better off than when they arrived. By the end of their stay, the family's SUV is loaded with oversized, useless souvenirs, the kids are still wired from sugar, caffeine, and adrenaline, the parents' nerves are shot, and the effects of the amusement park rides' G-forces have severely jarred everyone's brains. Just as the commercials promise, it's a vacation you won't forget. Today most Bavarians would probably do exactly the same thing, if such a temptation were close enough at hand.

EuroDisney near Paris, the closest of Mickey's kingdoms to Bavaria, isn't a particular draw for most Bavarians. If they want to see Cinderella's castle, or its inspiration—the world-famous Neuschwanstein, built by Bavaria's Mad King Ludwig II—it is an easy day trip from Munich. The castle is very impressive, no matter how gaudy and tasteless some may find it. This testimony to a deranged monarch seemingly bent on bankrupting his royal estate in order to live out his fantasies has become the epitome of the Bavarian tourist trap: overcrowded and expensive, where the lines can take nearly as long as the trip there. But still, the overall effect of Neuschwanstein is jaw dropping, especially the views from the mountain outlooks above and from the valley below. What Disney's castles in Anaheim and Orlando lack are the actual backdrops of soaring Alpine peaks, sheer rock faces, and dark green forests. Beholding the natural beauty surrounding the mad king's castle makes the trip worthwhile, even if one never goes in.

Many Bavarians, especially the devout Catholics—whether they are rich or poor—forego Neuschwanstein and head instead to Altötting. This decidedly atypical Bavarian town has a population of nearly 13,000 and hosts at least a million visitors per year. The main attraction is one of the holiest Marian shrines of Europe, a shrine on the same level as Lourdes, Fatima, and Loreto.

In the center of the town is an open square surrounded by leafy green trees, with a simple, small chapel standing in the middle, covered by a weathered, green copper roof, topped with pointed spires. The primary purpose of the space is not for commerce or to provide the town's inhabitants with civic services—it is for religious devotion. It is believed that the Chapel of Mercy was first built around the year 700, making it one of the oldest buildings in all of Germany. Its octagonal apse remains unique in the landscape of Bavarian church architecture.

Inside the chapel is the Black Madonna, an image of Our Lady of Altötting. Carved from linden wood around 1300, the little statue was brought to Altötting in 1358 from Burgundy, an area now in eastern France. A momentous, miraculous healing occurred before this statue in 1489, in answer to the prayers of a mother whose little boy had been presumed dead; he came back to life. Ever since then, people have been coming to the shrine in hopes of receiving similar graces.

Dressed in beautifully brocaded vestments and wearing shining crowns studded with precious stones, the dark statue of the Virgin holding baby Jesus has been the focal point of petitions for several centuries. The wooden figures occupy a niche set into one side of the apse of the Chapel of Mercy, and surrounding them is an ornate, silver relief of the crowning of the Virgin. On the four adjacent sides are large glass cases filled with rich gifts from popes, holy Roman emperors, Bavarian dukes, electors, and kings, and other German princes. Visitors can see many more in the treasury museum nearby in the square.

On the remaining three sides of the apse, opposite the Black Madonna, on shelves high up the black walls, is a collection of highly decorated silver urns that contain the hearts of the princes of Bavaria, the Wittelsbach dukes and kings since the seventeenth century. These great aristocrats requested that their most vital organ remain in the company of the Black Madonna until the end of time.

What do pilgrims make of all this? They regard the artistic beauty of the priceless objects just like anyone else, but they also wonder at the mystery behind them, and, above all, they pray, as they have done for centuries. Joseph Ratzinger did the same. As a child he was deeply impressed by the chapel's "mysterious darkness, the richly dressed Black Madonna, surrounded by consecrated gifts, the silent prayer of so many people…, the presence of a holy and healing goodness, the goodness of the Mother, in whom the goodness of God himself opened up to us."[1] It is fair to say that Altötting is closer to the heart of Joseph Ratzinger than Marktl.

Today people take up wooden crosses and carry them around the outside of the chapel, just as Joseph Ratzinger did in his childhood, and throughout the rest of his life. They tread along a covered walkway that surrounds the chapel on all sides, some shuffling and scraping on their knees. They recall the Passion of Our Lord and ask for relief of their burdens, much as theirs pale in comparison to his. As they go, they pass by more than 2,000 painted wooden votive tablets that completely cover the walkway's inner walls and ceiling. Each tells a story, in word and image, of the people who have benefited from the Virgin's help, her intercession in a time of terrible crisis. Most date from the sixteenth to the nineteenth centuries, but there is a growing number from the 1980s, '90s, and the new millennium. People pace slowly, saying the rosary, silently or out loud. These are Catholics who are unembarrassed by their public devotions, and in Altötting they often find themselves to be in good company. Over a million people come to Altötting each year, a number that has recently been on the increase.

We do not know how many times Joseph Ratzinger made this pilgrimage, and he probably could not give you a number himself. He spent much of his childhood not more than fifteen miles from the city, and he has said that its proximity had special meaning for him while growing up. Together the

Ratzinger family visited Altötting on numerous occasions, from wherever the family was living in Bavaria at the time.

At the age of seven, Joseph went with his family to attend the canonization of Brother Conrad of Parzham, a simple farmer who left his village to go to Altötting to join the Capuchin friars, and serve as the gatekeeper for the next four decades. It has been said that such visits helped young Joseph Ratzinger make his final decision to become a priest, although it is difficult to find explicit support for this claim in the Pope's own writings and statements.

During his decades as Cardinal, Ratzinger visited Altötting repeatedly, without retinue or fanfare, and made his devotions there like everyone else. In 1980 he officially welcomed Pope John Paul II at the shrine on behalf of all the German bishops. The last time he came to Altötting before becoming Pope himself was four months before the election, in January 2005. For Benedict XVI's apostolic journey to Bavaria in 2006, Altötting was at the top of the itinerary.

With its connection to the Virgin Mary and St. Conrad, the place has important significance in the Pope's thought and teaching. In his homily in the square before the Chapel of Mercy, Benedict explained how Mary's example shows us all how to live and pray today:

> ...not by seeking to assert before God our own will and our own desires, however important they may be, however reasonable they might appear to us, but rather to bring them before him and to let him decide what he intends to do. From Mary we learn graciousness and readiness to help, but we also learn humility and generosity in accepting God's will, in the confident conviction that, whatever it may be, it will be our, and my own, true good. [2]

The idea that we should say "No" to self-absorption and "Yes" to God is one that suffuses the Pope's writings, his decisions, and the actions throughout his life.

From St. Conrad of Parzham, we learn about the value, and superiority, perhaps, of pure, honest simplicity. Reflecting on this humble man's unassailably holy life (1818-1894), spent in a time when more and more people were putting their unfailing trust in scientific advancement and the idea of universal progress, Cardinal Ratzinger asks one of his famously daring questions:

> *Is this a sign that the Church has lost her power to shape culture and can take root only outside the real current of history? Or is it a sign that the clear view of the essential, which is so often lacking in the 'wise and prudent,' is given in our days, too, to little ones?[3]*

Read the quotation again, and bear in mind that St. Conrad was one of the "little ones." This preference for simplicity, which entails a skeptical attitude toward abstruse intellectualism, the Pope carries with him to this day. He acquired this value during his childhood, from his small town, Bavarian, Catholic milieu, and bolstered by the teachings of Christ Jesus, he has found no reason to abandon it.

In Altötting today, one can experience a traditional, living, devoutly Catholic religiosity that is part and parcel of Pope Benedict XVI. On holy days, large groups of pilgrims come in from Marktl and other directions. Throughout the month of May, they come from all over Bavaria, going on foot from one Marian church to the next, in a pilgrimage that can last for days at a time. Hundreds of men, women, and young people follow country roads rain or shine, escorted by police to prevent traffic accidents, carrying their few belongings on their backs, intoning the Hail Mary prayer as they go.

When they reach the town, they sometimes process into St. Anne's, the glorious baroque basilica, to partake in Holy Mass and receive Communion. Others go to the late Gothic parish church, the Jesuit church, the monastery church containing St. Conrad's tomb and relics, not to mention other churches built by women's orders of the Holy Cross and English Ladies. Despite the diversity of architectural styles and interior decorations, all of these buildings have one thing in common. First and foremost, they are special, *sacred* spaces conducive to prayer and solemn devotion. No one would confuse them with a community center or concert hall.

The way people behave matches the architecture and decoration. Inside, quiet solemnity is the norm. Tourists sometimes get loud and obnoxious, but not the pilgrims. In general one does not clap, chatter, or laugh out loud either before, after, or during Mass. Catholic churches in Bavaria have floors of stone, tile, or worn wooden parquet. As far as the Bavarians are concerned, carpet belongs in the living room of one's house, not in the nave of a church.

Let us contrast this religious culture with the Catholic scene in the United States. People usually prepare themselves for Mass with reverence, but at the end, after the celebrant departs, it is normal for the church to erupt into a loud din—people greeting friends, making plans about where to go for brunch, and catching up on the latest happenings. In Bavaria, people usually do that after they leave the building; to them it is just as much a house of God after Mass as before.

The Pope teaches that the divine liturgy of the Eucharist is the very life of the Church, which is first and foremost a community of prayer. Celebration of Holy Mass should be *prayerful*, and really everything about the Catholic liturgy should be different from what we see and hear every day. The experience of meeting God should be otherworldly. Is the *tone* of the words of the Catholic liturgy consistent with a pop recording, a Broadway musical, or a rock concert? One finds such influences these days in the Catholic regions of Bavaria, but they are weak or belong to the realm of the eccentric. While Benedict XVI was growing up, they were nonexistent. During his many visits to Altötting, he drank in the air of living Catholic tradition. The Pope will never depart from it, as he learned to revere and love it in Altötting. If he authorizes adjustments in the liturgy, it will be in the interest of preserving and enhancing its holiness, simply because it is something sacred and beautiful on its own. It does not need to make any concessions to suit the tastes of shopping malls.

Cardinal Ratzinger's masterpiece, *The Spirit of the Liturgy*, renders the central issue perfectly clear: The Roman Catholic liturgy is not an occasion for the congregation to celebrate *itself* according to the values and fashions of the day.[4] It rather presents and represents what is permanent, eternal, what is true, what was revealed by God himself for all humanity for all time. If that alone does not deserve respect and awe, then nothing does really.

In this and other matters Joseph Ratzinger has been consistent throughout his life. In *The Ratzinger Report*, a book-length interview first published in 1985, he reminds us all that the Church is not *ours*—a run-of-the-mill organization to be adjusted as the local community sees fit—but *his*, Jesus', the Church's founder and sustainer, the man who rose from the dead, showing his followers, and all of us, that he was, somehow, in a mysterious way, almost unfathomably God.[5]

The Church is far bigger than the group of individuals who consider themselves Catholic in this day and age. It is a community of prayer, not a government, and it must include *all* of the faithful, living and departed, whose souls, a devout Catholic believes, do not die. *Their* values, attitudes, beliefs, and practices must stand next to our own when decisions are to be made. When Catholics say in the Nicean Creed, "We believe in the communion of saints," they refer not merely to the company of those saints canonized by the Church. *Communio sanctorum*, in the original Latin, first denotes holy *things*: "the faith, the sacraments, especially the Eucharist, the charisms, and the other spiritual gifts."[6] In addition, the same phrase refers to "all the faithful of Christ," living *and* dead, "all together forming one Church."[7] We, the living, must remember that we worship Christ *with* and *for* the departed.

Therefore the Church, Ratzinger has argued, can never be a democracy in the sense of a body of individuals invested with the unlimited power to make decisions based on the prevailing will of the majority. The Church always was and must be a hierarchy, with all power resting in Christ, who selected the apostles and set them to the work of building his Church and spreading his good news. Divine truth is not obtained through a majority vote. It is already there, it *exists*, it is given, and it must be uncovered. Democracy certainly has real strengths as a method of governing a state, but for running an institution dedicated to unchanging, revealed truth, it would be a recipe for disaster.

It is therefore reasonable to conclude that the Roman Catholic Church is the last place where the popular preference of the day should find an enduring expression. Taking the shrine at Altötting as a prime example, the Church must be a monument to the unbroken continuum that extends across the centuries,

back to Christ and at the same time forward, with consistent, hopeful confidence, to the future when he comes again. We should never try to form God
according to *our* preferred image of convenience; that would be more akin to
idolatry than worship. Above all, a community of faith must shun the temptation of giving in to *self*-affirmation. In church we should never celebrate
ourselves. It is not the place for self-gratification, which underlies most worldly
values and bad behaviors.

Inevitably some will cry out, "But we are the church!" and thereby ignore all
the others in the communion of saints: Catholics in pursuit of selfless sanctity, the "pilgrims on earth," those living in other lands, the hierarchy, and
the whole world of the dead.[8] The guiding lights of Catholic parishes should
not be utility and comfort, but beauty and truth, not banal, consumerist
"beauty" and "private truths," but those upheld by two thousand years of
prayerful devotion.

In his writings, the Pope has said that he would like to see the focus of
the liturgy return to Christ and the Eucharist, first and foremost. The
celebrant should not be the center of a liturgical show in which various
community contingents vie for attention as they do their given parts. Instead, says the Pope, we must "turn toward the Lord!"[9] In the Mass, the
people revere God, not the celebrant, and still less themselves. The altar
cross should be brought forward, front and center, so that it forms the
center of worship, whether it slightly obstructs the view of the presiding
priest.

Liturgical music must develop from prayer, not the pop charts. It must
always try to capture and convey the mystery of the presence of God.
Pop music, the Pope warns us, is "certainly no longer supported by the
people in the ancient sense (pop*ulus)*. It is aimed at the phenomenon
of the masses, is industrially produced, and ultimately has to be described as a cult of the banal."[10] Hymns should have simple rhythms and
clear, uplifting melodies. No one should be afraid of a little Gregorian
chant, which is ancient, solemn, pure, and usually *simple*. In it there
are no bizarre, bouncy, difficult rhythms, and there are plenty of spaces
to breathe. When led by the organ or piano, all but the tone-deaf can
handle it.

A smattering of Latin in the liturgy would likewise do no one any harm. The Catholic Mass was multilingual for many centuries prior to the 1960s, incorporating words from Greek and Aramaic in addition to the Latin. Saying or singing one of the shorter prayers such as the *Sanctus* (Holy, Holy) in Latin, and saying "Lord have mercy" in Greek *(Kyrie eleison)* would show the universality of the Church across cultural, linguistic, national, and temporal boundaries. It would allow the increasing number of world travelers in our highly mobile, globalizing era to participate more fully in the Holy Mass, irrespective of where they may find themselves.

The churches and shrine at Altötting are in full unity with the Holy Father and the Catholic Church. With its saints, pilgrimages, images, miracles, manifold devotions, rich traditions, and solemn celebrations, the town is a testimony to the fact that the Church is alive and well in the twenty-first century. We can all stand to learn something from it.

THE LAND BETWEEN TWO RIVERS

"[We lived] in the triangle formed on two sides by the Inn and the Salzach rivers, whose landscape and history marked my youth."

—*Joseph Ratzinger,* Milestones

The land between the Rivers Inn and Salzach, in the region known as Upper Bavaria, is where the Pope spent the years of his childhood and youth. The Inn originates in the Alps and winds its way through the Austrian city of Innsbruck, across Germany's southern border, through the eastern part of Upper Bavaria, eventually draining into the Danube. The Salzach flows from the Alps, through Austria and the beautiful city of Salzburg, making its way north to where it meets the Inn. Together the two rivers form the border between Bavaria and Austria up to the city of Passau.

The land between the two rivers is the heartland of what is known as "Old Bavaria," the historical core of the Free State where Bavarian dialects are spoken today. The region is mostly rural, marked by a lightly undulating landscape in the north that becomes hillier as one heads south toward the Bavarian Alps. Roughly in the middle is the Chiemsee, a broad lake in full view of the majestic peaks, famous for its two islands. Herrenchiemsee is the larger of the two, a wooded piece of land where a miniature version of Versailles is located—another castle built by the eccentric King Ludwig II. The smaller and lovelier island is the Frauenchiemsee, or Fraueninsel, home to a twelve-hundred-year-old convent. You can walk the circumference of the island in twenty pleasant minutes. A little more than two hundred people, residing in a total of fifty houses, call this home; you won't find a car of any kind on the island. Despite the ebb and flow of visitors, the serenity is simply delightful.

On the western bank of the Chiemsee is the village of Rimsting, the birth-place of Pope Benedict's mother, Maria Rieger, the firstborn daughter of a baker. She lived and labored with her parents and seven siblings, learning a trade as a professional cook. When she was not working in the bakery or looking after the younger children, she was employed in domestic service for the benefit of her family. From her upbringing she was used to early morn-ings, long days, hard work, and little money. She did not marry until she was thirty-six years old. The Pope has described her as a practical, talented, "very warmhearted" woman, with "great inner strength" and "a very warm and heartfelt piety."[1] His brother, Georg, said that she was usually happy and cheerful; she used to sing songs about the Virgin Mary while doing the dishes. Her warm personality complemented her husband, who was, according to Georg, "perhaps too strict." "It was a happy marriage," he continued. "The motto was: we have to live and be frugal."[2]

Coincidentally, just behind Rimsting is a rough semicircle of partially for-ested hills called the "Ratzinger Heights" (the name has nothing to do with the Pope and his family) that offer splendid views of the lake, the Alpine range, and the surrounding countryside. Benedict's father, Josef, actually came from a village called Rickering located in Lower Bavaria further north, at the foot of the Bavarian forest near the banks of the Danube River. One of nine children, he served for two years in the Bavarian military before he resolved not to return to the farmer's life, and instead became a policeman, the official guarantor of law and order in the Bavarian cities where he was stationed.[3] The Pope described him as "a very upright and also a very strict man," "markedly rationalistic and deliberate," and yet a "very religious man." These qualities ran in the Ratzinger line. His uncle Georg, a doctor of theology and a priest, had served as a representative in local political assemblies, and history remembers him for his advocacy of laws against child labor. It had been an unpopular position at first, among farmers and industrialists alike, but "he was obviously a tough man."[4]

Returning to the land between the two rivers, scores of tidy little villages are strewn across the landscape, divided by stretches of fields and tufts and patches of forest. Multiple shades of green are the predominant colors of sum-mer, emanating from irregularly shaped fields of corn, wheat, barely, oats, and other grains, or spattered in places with the bright red of poppies. Cows and sheep saunter in meadows of thick and tall grasses, speckled with soft touches of wildflowers. There are no large cities in this region, nor any significant centers of industry or commerce; Salzburg lies just beyond the southeast corner and Munich further west of the Inn.

It has not changed very much since Joseph Ratzinger lived there. It was poor then, and it is certainly not rich now, in the context of Germany's tremendous wealth accumulated since the end of World War II. Today the Free State of Bavaria is the most prosperous in Germany, but there are a number of initiatives underway today to bring more economic activity to the southeast. Perhaps its lack of money has served to protect its simple beauty. I doubt it will be transformed in the future.

The Ratzinger family did not live in abject poverty, but they occupied a rung not far above it. As a small-town police constable, the Pope's father could always afford an apartment (usually in the same building as the police bureau), food, and clothing for his wife and three children, Maria, Georg, and Joseph, but there was little money for anything beyond that. Benedict XVI's upbringing was thoroughly humble; he was certainly not born a member of any elite class. The frugality of his early years made him learn to appreciate the little things in life, the importance of helping when help was needed, and the promise to stick together through thick and thin. "This climate of great simplicity," he said in an interview, "was a source of much joy as well as love for one another."[5]

TITTMONING (1929-1932)

When Joseph was two years old, the Ratzinger family moved from Marktl am Inn about twenty miles up the Salzach River to Tittmoning, a lovely town next to a border crossing into Austria. They lived there about three years, a time of the Pope's earliest reliable memories. This place, he wrote in his autobiography, "remains my childhood's land of dreams."[6]

The hallmark of the town is a grand, rectangular, cobblestone square, maybe 300 yards long, lined with trees on both sides and down a strip in the middle. The building façades are painted in the bright, cheerful pastel colors that are seen in most Bavarian towns: light yellow and green, pink and baby blue, with ochre and an occasional olive color. The stucco façades and white window frames are squarish in shape, giving Tittmoning a more Austrian, almost Italianate, appearance. A towering fountain graces the middle of the square, and narrow little canals, built and covered with stone slabs, crosscut the public space.

The Ratzingers lived in the police bureau, which was housed in a grand old building right in the square itself. Despite the fact that in Joseph's estimation it was "the most beautiful house on the town square," the rooms of his family's apartment were small, cramped, and crooked. The concrete floors were cracked, and the stairway narrow and precarious—on the whole it was certainly less than comfortable.[7] He and his siblings did not care; the old place just made for "mystery and excitement." But for his mother, who had to run the household, it meant a great deal more work and worry. Dragging wood and coal up two flights of stairs probably was not the worst of it.[8]

Behind the square are compact little residential blocks where most of the town's populace live and work. Houses are nestled against a hillside that rises steeply above the town, up to the bulky, decrepit old castle that looms over all the other buildings. From its walls, you can see the fields stretching to the south and east, to the banks of the Salzach, and the hills of Austria across the river. At one time, the castle was a formidable fortress, but now it houses the local museum and the temporary exhibits that come through town. Its dilapidated state is half the charm.

A forest covers the hills behind the town and when the weather permitted Maria Ratzinger often brought her children there. They would make "a little pilgrimage" to Ponlach Chapel, a baroque shrine hidden away in the woods, and listen to fresh stream waters emanate and tumble down the hillside. There they would "allow the peace of the place to have its effect on us."[9] Although Joseph spent his early years in towns, he spent more time in his youth in the outdoors, I would argue, than most American suburbanites. His mother would also take him and his siblings on walks across the fields and meadows where they would gather wild lettuce and other herbs for the day's meals; sometimes they spent the entire day hiking across the Inn to Austria. Being in the midst of and playing in nature was normal for Joseph. Near Christmastime, he scavenged for the family's nativity scene, perhaps finding moss, sticks, bark, and stones for decoration. He probably never had a plaything made out of rubber or plastic. He possessed only three toys, in addition to his worn teddy bear.[10]

Tittmoning's beautiful churches are the other places Pope Benedict will never forget. Most impressive is the Church of All Souls, once part of an Augustinian monastery long since dissolved. Its pure white walls render the high altar of gold and black all the more stunning. An expansive painting of the Last Judgment just above the high altar is meant to remind every visitor just what it's all about in the end. This is the church Benedict loved "most of all."[11] He will never forget the flowers and lights that decorated this church at Easter, "that before any rational comprehension, brought home the mystery of death and resurrection to both my exterior and interior senses."[12]

Then there is the Church of St. Laurentius. More spacious inside than All Souls, the building is a late Gothic construction with baroque decoration dating from the seventeenth century. Like the Church of All Souls, here white walls encircle the space, displaying dramatic, colorful, gilded statues of Jesus, Mary, the apostles and saints, and several large paintings of biblical scenes and of the Stations of the Cross. The point of focus is the high altar, decorated in the neoclassical style of the early nineteenth century. Outside the church, on the western end, is a carved, life-sized crucifixion scene, set in a kind of grotto, and beneath it the figures of eight men and women writhe in hell's eternal fire. Another reminder.

Both churches are excellent examples of small-town Bavarian baroque. This style of art and architecture is exuberant and dramatic, at once earthly and heavenly, joyous, uplifting, and yet violent, usually preferring the fulsome over the sparse. The baroque belongs in Bavaria. The color scheme is drawn from the wildflowers found in the mountains, valleys, and fertile flood plains: pale yellow from the primrose, clover, and marigold; the thistle's soft purple; pink from the alpine rose; liverwort's pale blue; white and yellow of the aster; and the soft orange of the *Bocksbart* and *Klappertopf,* names that sound too good to be translated. The azure blue of the *Enzian* is too strong of a color for a house's façade, but you find it sometimes in the Virgin's cloak, painted on a carved figurine. The stucco covered walls of the houses and churches seem to take their white, cream, yellow, pink, purple, and blue straight from the uncut fields.

Representations of the human figure are usually baroque as well, in their fleshy bodily contours, flowing robes and drapery, and dramatic postures and gestures. And they are everywhere—in town squares, the gardens of palaces and villas, churches and monasteries, museums, art galleries, craft shops, and in private homes, usually in the family's nativity scene. Often the figurines' clothing is the same traditional garb that you can still see to this day, worn by partakers in *Fronleichnam* (Corpus Christi) processions. For the young Joseph Ratzinger these were always joyous occasions. In his book, *The Feast of Faith*, he invites his reader to share his living memory:

> *I still sense the fragrances rising from the carpets of flowers and the fresh cut birches; the decorations on all the houses are there too, the banners, the songs; I still hear the village brass, which on this day sometimes took on music beyond its ability, and I hear the bangs of the gun salutes, through which the younger men showed their baroque love of life, and while doing so also greeted Christ as well, like a head of state, yes, as the head, as the lord of the world, in their streets and in their village. The eternal presence of Christ was celebrated on this day exactly as if it had been a state visit, one that did not leave out the smallest village.*[13]

"I breathed the Baroque atmosphere ever since I was a child," Cardinal Ratzinger once said. "The Catholicism of my native Bavaria knew how to provide room for all that was human, both prayer and festivities, penance and joy. A joyful, colorful, human Christianity."[14] In turn, the baroque embrace of earthly and heavenly joy has influenced Ratzinger's psychology as much as his theology.

> *Faith gives joy. When God is not there, the world becomes desolate, and everything becomes boring, and everything is completely unsatisfactory. It's easy to see today how a world empty of God is also increasingly consuming itself, how it has become a wholly joyless world.*[15]

Returning to Tittmoning's baroque churches, one must first understand them as human attempts to create beauty for the sake of faith. Cardinal Ratzinger wrote,

I have often said that I am convinced that the true apologetics for the Christian message, the most persuasive proof of its truth, offsetting everything that may appear negative, are the saints, on the one hand, and the beauty that the faith has generated, on the other.[16]

These holy spaces are full of both at once, the many statues and paintings of the saints, beautifully portrayed. "Beauty is truth and truth beauty."[17] We should not be put off by the graphic reminders about the Last Judgment and eternal punishment. These are part of the Christian faith, much as they disturb our postmodern sensitivities. Jesus talked about them repeatedly in no uncertain terms, although most homilists these days do their best to avoid the subject altogether. If you believe in Christ Jesus, you must accept these realities. In 1997 an interviewer asked Cardinal Ratzinger what he was afraid of. After admitting that the dentist, medical procedures, and getting his thoughts and words mixed up in an important conversation were on his list, the Cardinal said, "Naturally I also have to think about the Last Judgment."[18] Anyone who takes the words of Jesus seriously should as well.

But of course there is much more to the Christian life than fear of what is to come. Benedict XVI looks back on his three years in Tittmoning with great fondness. He will never forget the wonder and marvel of puppet shows, put on in a friend's attic. Christmastime was especially magical. "Above all, the shop windows illuminated at night during the Christmas season have remained in my memory like a wonderful promise."[19] He also warmly recalls the nativity scene belonging to an older woman his family would visit; it filled the whole living room, giving the children a world in miniature, with endless food for the imagination.

Politics shortened the stay in Tittmoning. A worldwide depression had set in, inflicting the United States and Germany with staggering unemployment. Bavaria had been slowly recovering from the hyperinflation and economic collapse in the years after the First World War, and this second disaster hit just as hard. The Weimar Republic appeared feckless and quarrelsome, rendered incompetent due to political fighting between a plenitude of parties. Although Joseph understood none of it at the time, he remembers "shrill campaign posters and the incessant rounds of elections they announced."[20] He must have heard his father fulminate in the private of his apartment against the extremist Nazi party and its odious leader, Adolf Hitler.

This little Austrian hoodlum had staged a failed coup against the postwar government of Bavaria in 1923, and ought to have been shot for treason under Bavarian state law, but the constitution of the Weimar Republic did not allow it. Sentenced to a mere five years, he was turned loose after a few months of good behavior, having spent much of it dictating a long, turgid, angry work called *Mein Kampf.* During the time when the Ratzingers lived in Tittmoning, the Nazis had become the single largest party in the *Reichstag,* the national parliament, but still did not command anything near a majority. Ranks of the brown-shirted storm troopers, basically a bunch of paranoid, aggressive Nazi thugs determined to undermine the institutions of law and order, rose from 100,000 members to nearly a million.

In 1932 Hitler ran for the presidency of the Republic and lost against the incumbent, Paul von Hindenburg, a former general whose own track record against authoritarian rule was less than stellar. Joseph's parents "breathed a sigh of relief" at Hitler's defeat, but were less than convinced that the eighty-three-year-old Hindenburg would be much of a constitutional bulwark against the Nazis. "Time and again, in public meetings, Father had to take a position against the violence of the Nazis. We could very clearly sense the immense anxiety weighing him down."[21] As the local chief of police, it was his duty to uphold the law and to stop any infractions against it. Local Nazi enthusiasts wanted to suspend it while they dealt with their political opponents as they chose, claiming it was all for the safety and salvation of the nation. Hitler's rapid approach toward the pinnacle of power in Germany was "the chief reason why" Mr. Ratzinger decided to move his family yet again.[22] "In Tittmoning he had simply said too much against the brownshirts."

Also in 1932, not quite yet five years old, young Joseph had his first encounter with a leader of the Roman Catholic Church. Cardinal Michael Faulhaber, the Archbishop of Munich, came to Tittmoning for a confirmation ceremony, and while he was there he visited a *Kindergarten.* Joseph was one of several children chosen to greet him. "His imposing purple" so impressed the little lad that he resolved then and there to change his life plans; he no longer wanted to be a painter when he grew up, but a cardinal, or "something like that."[24] The anecdote is more amusing than significant. It is hardly the case that a real ambition formed at this moment, one that Ratzinger doggedly pursued until he reached his goal. The *New York Times* intimated as much, and it is a lampoon of the Pope's life history.[25]

⚓ ASCHAU AM INN (1932-1937)

Just before Christmas, the Ratzingers returned to the valley of the Inn, this time much further to the west than Marktl. Aschau am Inn is about Marktl's size, maybe even smaller, tucked against wooded hills to the north and west, with cultivated fields extending south to the riverbank. In the center there is a large, aging brewery, a smattering of residences, a little pension, a restaurant and butcher shop, all set at odd angles, with a pond and little creek wandering through. This must have been a quieter community.

In the middle of this village is a small, late Gothic church constructed from plain stone with a square tower and a needlepoint spire rising about forty yards into the air, high enough to be seen from the whole surrounding area. Four tall slender windows, topped with pointed arches, light the inside on each side of the nave. The intricately carved high altarpiece is brightly painted, its spire reaching nearly to the top of the ceiling of the apse. Statues of the Virgin and Child stand just above the tabernacle. The side altar to the left shows the Holy Family, and the one on the right the adoration of the Magi, one of whom is painted black. Here, on March 15, 1936, Joseph was to have his first Communion.

Living conditions were better here than in Tittmoning, much as the children missed the delights of town life. The family residence was, once again, upstairs from the police bureau in a newly constructed building, but it was roomy and comfortable. Although there was no bath, it did have running water. In front of the building were a pretty garden and a large meadow where the children spent many hours playing. In the middle was a fishpond that nearly took little Joseph's life when he fell in one day, but his watchful siblings got to him in time.

The move, however, did not free his father from the political storm that swept over Germany in the 1930s. To break the political deadlock, President

Hindenburg made Hitler Chancellor in January 1933. At the end of February, the *Reichstag* in Berlin went up, actually down, in flames, and by March Hitler was voted emergency powers, essentially giving him the authority to rule by decree. The Weimar Republic was dead, and a Nazi regime was rising ominously from the ashes.

According to Joseph's older siblings, all schoolchildren were sent on a miserable march through the center of the village on a cold, rainy day to celebrate Hitler's accession to supreme power. Nazi members of the village began to wear their brown uniforms with pride, and Hitler Youth and the League of German Girls sprang up soon afterward. Georg and Maria were given no choice but to take part, but Joseph was still too young. His father was "mortified"; he was now working "for a government whose representatives he considered to be criminals."[26] Mr. Ratzinger never joined any Nazi organization, despite being employed by the state.[27] And the party was anything but a distant entity; his assistant constable was a committed Nazi who dutifully took note of anything potentially subversive written, spoken, or read by the village priests.

But things were not as bad as they could have been. In this community of relatively prosperous farmers, what enthusiasm there was for the new regime did not automatically translate into a destruction of Christian, Catholic life and values. As far as he can remember, Joseph Ratzinger believes that only the local clergy were subject to being spied upon, and whenever possible his father "would warn and aid priests he knew were in danger."[28] German bishops had declared Nazism incompatible with the Catholic faith in 1932, but after Hitler came to power and signed a concordat with the Vatican that guaranteed the freedoms of the Catholic Church and the continuance of parochial schooling, the bishops revoked their condemnation and told their flocks to obey the new civil authority. Soon enough, however, Hitler broke his promises as was his wont and began to prevent priests from serving as educators.

The Führer's aim was to replace Christianity with newfangled Nazi myth. In Aschau, only one of Joseph's teachers, an otherwise bright, talented young man, subscribed wholeheartedly to the project. He erected a maypole, organized festivals for fertility, the midsummer sun, and such things, and wrote silly prayers to the power of nature, basically trying to revive ancient

Germanic religious practices, in the hope that they would displace the Judeo-Christian corruption of the pure-blooded Aryan peoples. "But in those days, such rhetorical formulas hardly impressed the sober mentality of Bavarian farmers."[29] Again we see the roots of the Pope's deep trust in the basic faith of simple people.

During his years in elementary school, the boy began to discern, with the benefit of hindsight, the beginning of his life's calling. At home he and his brother would play the Mass, using a child-sized altar given them by an uncle, wearing vestments made by their mother and aunts. One would play the priest while the other would be the altar boy; the celebrant of the day would write down and deliver little homilies to his server and the people, embodied by their sister Maria. The game was not without its dangerous side, however. Once in a procession about the apartment, whoever was holding the candle carelessly set Maria's pigtails on fire.[30]

Joseph, even in elementary school, was a dutiful, dedicated little student. He was good on the whole, but sometimes, according to his own report, he annoyed his teachers with impudent remarks. Nonetheless, he either does not remember or has not bothered to recount any specific instances. "I was not endowed with great creativity in these things."[31] As his basic education progressed, he began to compose verse and set ideas down on paper. For some unknown reason, he was moved to reflect on what he was learning, and he wanted to commit his thoughts to paper so that he could pass on his newly acquired knowledge.[32]

Something else besides his teachers was the source of his inspiration. It came in the church in Aschau where he served as an altar boy. There he began to learn the intricacies of the Roman Catholic liturgy. He came to love the candlelit Advent Masses, the Lenten devotions, and above all the Easter celebrations when the dark curtains were torn down from the tall windows, letting the light of day pour in, just as the pastor announced in song, "Christ is risen!" "This," he wrote, "was the most impressive portrayal of the Lord's resurrection I could conceive of." He learned the liturgy in translation alongside his elementary studies of his native German language. It was in the liturgies celebrated in the little church in Aschau that he came to realize something very important, a belief that he would not abandon throughout his entire life:

*It was becoming more and more clear to me that here I was encounter-
ing a reality that no one had simply thought up, a reality that no official authority or great individual had created. This mysterious fabric
of texts and actions had grown from the faith of the Church over the
centuries.*[33]

The Roman Catholic liturgy is a mystery in itself, neither immutable nor
fabricated; it is a work of God left in human hands to uphold, enrich, and
safeguard for all time.

While the light of rational, comprehending faith was filling Joseph's life, dark
clouds of war were blackening the horizon. It is almost incomprehensible to
us today how few were able to see them, but even if they did, there was little
anyone in Hitler's Reich could have done about it. Maybe it was in Aschau am
Inn that Joseph Ratzinger heard and reflected upon the rising tide of verbal
and physical attacks against the Jews in Germany. "Even as a child," he wrote
in a book about Christianity and Judaism,

*I could not understand how some people wanted to derive a con-
demnation of Jews from the death of Jesus, because the following
thought had penetrated my soul as something profoundly consoling:
Jesus' blood raises no calls for retaliation but calls all to reconciliation.*[34]

His father saw it all coming, very clearly. When Nazism first raised its
angry head, the elder Josef knew it would lead to no good. When Hitler
seized power in 1933, Mr. Ratzinger said, "Now war is coming, we need
a house."[35] Young Joseph's parents decided to use what capital they had
acquired to purchase a retirement home in the quiet Bavarian countryside,
near Traunstein, a midsized town about five miles to the east of the Chiemsee. Mr. Ratzinger, who had been fifty years old when his younger son was
born, was rapidly approaching the mandatory age of retirement for police-
men at sixty, and it could not have been coming fast enough. Perhaps the
worst moment might have been when he had to deal with one of his own
officers, a committed Nazi, who denounced the local pastor and let the
brownshirts beat him mercilessly.[36]

The future Pope's father looked forward to his sixtieth birthday with great anticipation, regarding it as a release from a stressful, unpleasant set of duties. Before this happy day, he had repeatedly applied and received extended breaks from duty, supposedly due to bad health, during which he went on numerous long hikes with his little son and told him all about his youth and childhood. He also probably told him about what was afoot in the Fatherland. Joseph remembers the caricatures of Hitler in the anti-Nazi newspaper his father subscribed to, called the *Straight Way*, which featured headlines such as "National Socialism Is a Plague!" "Hitler the Bankrupt," "Germans, Your Human Rights Are in Danger," and "Lock Up the Führer!"[37] (Nazi thugs stormed its offices in 1933, and the editor was murdered a year later in Dachau.) Once when they returned to Tittmoning to take a day hike in Austria, they found the bridge closed. Hitler would allow no traffic in or out of Austria as long as it remained separate from Germany.

Before 1937, in the hills behind Aschau the regime had installed and deployed a battery of searchlights, although there were no enemy planes to search for. Around Mr. Ratzinger's sixtieth birthday, on March 6, 1937, construction began on a munitions factory, camouflaged against air attacks. With the elder daughter, Maria, attending a convent school and Georg enrolled at the *Gymnasium* (high school) in Traunstein, the time seemed right to make yet another move.

ℰNDURING the ℕAZIS: A FAMILY in TRAUNSTEIN

After all our wanderings, this is where we finally found our true home, and it is here that my memory always returns with gratitude."

—*Joseph Ratzinger,* Milestones

Visit Traunstein today and you'll discover much of its old charm has been maintained due to the fact that the town escaped the bombings of World War II. The middle of the town sports a handsome, automobile-free, market square, with a gorgeous church at one end and a blue-and-white-striped maypole, rising a hundred feet high, at the other. St. Oswald's, originally built in the Middle Ages and destroyed by fire in 1851, was rebuilt in the neoclassical style but has maintained its opulent, exuberant, baroque interior. This is where young Joseph regularly stopped to pray on his way to school.

On all sides of the square, façades are festively painted, mostly in pastel colors, rising above a collection of small to midsized businesses, including bakeries, butcheries, and specialty shops, more often local and private than national chains. The area is tidy and attractive, set up for people first and cars and commerce second. There is a train station with easy connections to major cities—Munich and Salzburg, in this case—and the walk from the square takes you along tree-lined streets, cheerful, splashing fountains (ranging from fifty to five hundred years old), and about half a dozen beer gardens and cafes. When it comes to choices of restaurants, there are Turkish, Italian, Greek, Chinese, Indian, and Thai, in addition to German, and the rich aromas of these cuisines flavor the air as you walk by.

In early April 1937, the Ratzingers moved to Hufschlag, a little over a mile from Traunstein's city center, in the undulating countryside. Their new home was a decrepit farmhouse, two stories high with an attic, built in the early eighteenth century. From our perspective today, we might have regarded it as a glorified barn—stalls for the animals, the hayloft, and the grain storage area were adjacent to the living quarters, under the same roof. The exterior stucco walls and broad overhanging eaves made it a typical Upper Bavarian *Landhaus*. There was no plumbing in the building; water had to be fetched from the well in front. It goes without saying that there was no central heating system or remotely modern bathroom. We can imagine how "thrilled" Mrs. Ratzinger was with this situation, but for the children "it was a paradise beyond [their] wildest dreams." Even the well water was "deliciously fresh." "After all our wanderings, this is where we finally found our true home *(Heimat)*, and it is here that my memory always returns with gratitude."[1]

In his autobiography published sixty years later, Cardinal Ratzinger recalls arriving in Hufschlag in detail. The first thing he remembers seeing was the broad meadow in front covered with delicate primroses, punctuated by plum, pear, apple, and cherry trees. Next to the house was a grove of oaks and beech trees, and nearby an expansive pine forest where he spent many hours of play, exploration, and fantasy. The back half of the house (the barn side, as it were), almost certainly devoid of electricity or lighting, offered a dimly lit warren of spooky corners. The view from Joseph's bedroom window was of the beautiful mountains.

While maintaining the house and barn gave Mr. Ratzinger no end of projects—the roof tended to leak—his wife planted and tended two vegetable and herb gardens out front, surrounded the home with bountiful flower beds, and installed window boxes for additional summer blooms. It is likely that she planted her flowers in accordance with local taste: usually in two or more colors, following a symmetrical pattern repeated across the front of the building. In Bavaria, tidiness is an aesthetic quality in itself.

The members of this family did not regard themselves as particularly exceptional or deserving of special treatment or attention. Old-fashioned German family values that still were held in that day included *Fleiß*, a diligent devotion to good work, not hard, excessive, or frenetic, but good in quality and quantity. There is little doubt that the children did their share of the chores. Then there was *Ordnung* and *Sauberkeit*, orderliness and cleanliness, in many ways still a hallmark of German thought, culture, industry, government, and identity; the two were a given standard in the home. Closely related was the expectation of punctuality, *Pünktlichkeit*, as a matter of personal discipline and basic consideration for the needs of others. Behavior, especially in public, was to be *zurückhaltend*, or self-restrained, with no shouting, wild gesticulations, or blaring laughter. Public displays of emotion were in bad taste, and the voice was to be kept soft. Some journalists today criticize the Pope for being "a bad waver," and it is true that he does not gesture nearly as much as his predecessor. But the way he carries himself is perfectly in keeping with his culture.

Everything one reads about the Ratzingers calls to mind the value of *Bescheidenheit*, which refers to modest bearing, or basic humility, in word, thought, and deed. There was no place here for the will to power, the raw pursuit of heroism in any form, which was celebrated in Nazi ideology. And today the vast majority of authors, commentators, priests, and even journalists, regardless of their feelings about the Roman Catholic Church, tend to agree on one thing: the Pope is a man of deep humility. His demeanor, his bearing, his words, his writing, his work, and his life all attest to this simple reality. We should wind up the list with *Geborgenheit*, the warm feeling of safety and security, the kind bestowed by two parents who would never tear the family in two, regardless of the difficulties they may face. And finally there is *Gemütlichkeit*, an important word with no real parallel in English, referring to a cozy feeling of domestic comfort, the simple pleasure of being at home, where one belongs.

Of course the Ratzingers had their share of quarrels and trying times; no family is entirely free of them. Speaking about his parents, Cardinal Ratzinger described his father as "a very strict man," but at the same time they "had a very close relationship."

> *We always sensed the goodness behind his strictness. And for that reason we could basically accept his strictness without trouble. From the very beginning my mother always compensated for my father's perhaps excessive strictness by her warmth and kindness. . . . Yes, I have to say that it was strict, but there was still a lot of warmth and kindness and joy.[2]*

He quickly added that all the family played together, the parents with the children, so Mr. Ratzinger's firm adherence to discipline did not translate into coldness or heartlessness. Just after his retirement, he spent lots of time with his sons, indoors and out, especially with Joseph, when Maria and Georg were at boarding school. He was a talented storyteller, and told many a tale during the long hikes with Joseph. The family also enjoyed making music, increasingly so over the years. Both boys learned to play the piano and the harmonium, and Georg also studied cello. Mozart was the perennial favorite. Mr. Ratzinger played the zither to simple Alpine songs. The family also prayed together at every meal, attended Sunday and sometimes daily Mass, and said the Rosary together. "We tried to maintain a simple, Catholic, faith."[3] Without falling into pop psychology, it is fair to say that the Pope's family provided him a happy childhood. Bitter memories, such as they were, pale in the context of the simple pleasures and rural beauty that surrounded them.

Just after their arrival at Traunstein, Joseph began his studies at the newly opened *Humanistisches Gymnasium*, an all male school for university bound children and young adults, offering training in classical and European languages and other subjects. Because Joseph was one of the smallest and probably the youngest boy in his class inevitably brought its own set of hardships, to say nothing of the fact that he was the smartest. He learned his Latin and Greek enthusiastically and helped out his classmates. His grades in conduct were not always at the top because he sometimes talked back to the instructor.[4]

As the years went by, his knowledge of Greek and Latin opened up the intellectual world of classical and late antiquity—the great writers of ancient Greece and Rome—and prepared the way for his future study of theology. Furthermore, such studies provided a kind of mental protection against "seduction by a totalitarian ideology."[5] Who could be impressed by Hitler's idiotic tirades, his stupid slogans and banal rhetoric, when one is used to speeches by Cicero, Seneca, and a host of other brilliant ancient minds? None of the Greek or Latin teachers at Joseph's school were proponents of Nazism. Even the music teacher had the boys strike out loathsome lyrics, such as "death to Judah," in their state-mandated songbooks.

At first, Joseph was as far away from the Nazi regime in Traunstein as he had been in Aschau am Inn, but the changes came soon enough. His humanistic school was folded in with the local technical school, no doubt part of a package of measures to channel money from education into the military. Greek was cut and Latin reduced. Classes in modern science increased in number, religion was sliced out, and sport was introduced in its place. In 1934, Traunstein's parish priest, Josef Stelzle, was imprisoned, and a bomb exploded outside the rectory.

In March 1938 Hitler forced through his *Anschluss*, or connection of Austria to Germany. Six months later the crisis over the Sudetenland, the borderlands of western Czechoslovakia, came to a head. On September 29, 1938, the British and the French more or less handed Hitler that territory, and he responded by declaring that his ambitions were satisfied. But as history now knows, the man had no sense of limits—or honor. On March 15, 1939, German tanks rolled into Prague, and Hitler started shouting for parts of Poland. France and Great Britain made their guarantees of Polish independence. In August, the new Nazi-Soviet nonaggression pact was made public, but obviously without mention of the secret allocations of Polish and Baltic lands. On September 1, 1939, the German army invaded Poland. Britain and France declared war soon afterward, but their armies did not attack.

Joseph's family watched all of this with a growing sense of dread. In the safety of their home, while reading the daily news, Mr. Ratzinger "almost had fits of rage." He knew enough to keep quiet in public, but "he always expressed his indignation vigorously and always spoke freely to people whom he could trust."[6] Mrs. Ratzinger, for her part, dared to tell Hitler jokes to the neighbors, which could have landed her in a concentration camp if she had been turned in.[7] The Ratzingers were not eccentrics; Bavarian Catholics in general saw little in the Nazi regime to recommend it.[8] The Pope's parents saw through the forest of mendacity surrounding the seizure of the Sudetenland, and the spinelessness of the Western Allies left them flabbergasted. The French were the most disappointing of all; like many Bavarians the Ratzingers had a higher regard for them than for the "Prussians" in northern Germany. When it came to politics, the Ratzingers "were very patriotic Bavarians already by family tradition."[9] Their orientation was basically set against pan-German nationalism; why did all German-speaking peoples need to be under the rule of one government based in Berlin? They firmly supported Bavarian independence, and Austria's too.

This may seem counterintuitive to us today, but we must recall that Bavaria has a much longer history as a self-contained realm than the nation-state called "Germany." The Celtic element of the Bavarian population differentiated her from the Germanic tribes to the north thousands of years ago, when ancient Roman writers produced the first written accounts of the region. Through the entire Middle Ages she was one of the largest counties, later a dukedom, and finally an electorate in the Holy Roman Empire. From the seventeenth century onward she sided with the French time and again when she felt threatened by her neighbors. Her ruling Bavarian dynasty, the Wittelsbachs, supported Napoleon Bonaparte in his early campaigns, and for their pains the conqueror of Europe elevated them from dukes to kings. Bavaria was one of the last principalities to join Otto von Bismarck's German Empire, and even today there is constant political friction between Berlin and Munich, although not much of it is very serious. The Ratzinger family's preference for the French, therefore, had a venerable history. In their opinion, the many different German-speaking regions of Europe should not have been forced into a single state. Most people today, looking at the course of the twentieth century, would probably agree.

That being said, Hitler's first land grabs were not without some immediate benefits for the family. The Austrian border was opened once again, and the Ratzingers could visit beautiful Salzburg with ease. The war sharply reduced the number of tourists in the region, and the price of tickets to the concerts, operas, and plays at the world famous Salzburg Festival plummeted. Joseph attended in 1941, enjoying for the first time in his life cultural delights normally reserved for wealthier people. One should never forget the modesty of the Pope's socioeconomic background. The experience of Nazism, however, and the gathering storm of World War II had another, far more important effect on Joseph's life.

After Easter 1939 he decided, after two years of study at the *Gymnasium*, to follow in his older brother's footsteps down the path to the priesthood. We do not know exactly how this decision was made, but he clearly felt a strong attraction to the vocation and to the Church as a whole. Hitler may, in fact, share in the credit. In April 2006, during a discussion with a youth group in St. Peter's Square, a twenty-year-old Canadian student asked the Pope why he became a priest. Benedict answered,

There was the Nazi regime. We were told very loudly that in the new Germany "there will not be any more priests, there will be no more consecrated life, we don't need this anymore, find another profession." But actually hearing these loud voices, I understood that in confronting the brutality of this system, this inhuman face, that there is a need for priests, precisely as a contrast to this antihuman culture.[10]

He transferred to the Minor Seminary of St. Michael at Traunstein, a boarding school. His pastor encouraged him, and the whole family was determined to make it happen. Mr. Ratzinger's pension was modest to say the least, but his sister, Maria, who had finished her degree at technical school, obtained a good office job working for a lawyer in Traunstein. Also Mrs. Ratzinger went back to work as a cook in a nearby town. The women's income effectively allowed both boys to pursue their priestly vocation.

Most of the 170 seminarians were of the same socioeconomic class as the Ratzingers, from the families of farmers, workers, craftsmen, petty bureaucrats, and small-time businessmen. Joseph made friends soon enough, and his brother was there to help him, but his many happy hours of solitary study and play were over. He had to live a regimented life with scores of squirming young boys. He slept in a large room with forty others, who all rose at 6 a.m., attended Mass, and walked to school in two long columns. Every week they confessed and prayed the Rosary together. There were sixty in his study hall, and the worst of it were the two hours of sports every day—chasing, kicking, throwing, and catching balls and the like—"a complete torture."[11] His youth and small size compounded his general lack of interest and ability in team sports. Although most of the boys were patient with him, he hated knowing that he was the weak link. One of the few welcome changes in the coming of war was that the seminary was soon turned out of its building to make room for a military hospital; their new quarters allowed no space for sports. For exercise the boys would go on long hikes through the wooded hills, go fishing, and play about in the streams, activities in which Joseph excelled. Thereafter his enjoyment of the seminary significantly improved. He came out of his shell and became a member of a real community.

In April 1940 the German army saw speedy victories in Scandinavia, rolling over Denmark and defeating Norway in a matter of weeks. One month later, the next to fall were Belgium, the Netherlands, and Luxembourg. The British, who had come to bolster Belgium, fled back across the Channel, leaving the French to stand on their own. France fell faster than anyone expected. Hitler and his regime seemed invincible. Most people in Bavaria and throughout Germany either rejoiced at these notable military achievements or at least took a measure of pride in the accomplishment. But Mr. Ratzinger was nobody's fool. "My father," the Cardinal wrote,

> *was one who with unfailing clairvoyance saw that a victory of Hitler's would not be a victory for Germany but rather a victory of the Antichrist that would surely usher in apocalyptic times for all believers, and not only for them.[12]*

In the Ratzinger household, each battle won was a cause for mourning.

Modern historians share his assessment. Steven Ozment, the McClean professor of Ancient and Modern History at Harvard University, made the same argument in his sweeping, one-volume history of Germany. Hitler, according to Ozment, regarded Christianity as another Jewish poison concocted for the Aryan people, "along with democracy, capitalism, liberalism, internationalism, and even modern art."[13] Once the Jews and the Bolsheviks had been eliminated, Hitler's next project would have been to expunge the Christian faith from Germany and as much of the rest of Nazi-dominated Europe as possible. The awesome evil he and his regime did perpetuate, that nadir of humanity called the Holocaust, was not to be the end of the story.

Hitler's march of victory continued, through the Balkan states and over Greece, but there were signs of a coming shift in the winds. No massive invasion of Britain took place in 1940-1941, despite its having been frequently announced, and the invasion of the Soviet Union on June 22, 1941, immediately appeared to be a terrifying example of military hubris. Cardinal Ratzinger remembers the beautiful summer Sunday when he and his classmates heard the news. They were on a field trip at a nearby lake, but the news "hung over us like a nightmare and spoiled our joy."[14] Among themselves the boys recalled the defeat of Napoleon's Grand Army, which marked his eventual downfall. They thought of

Russia's nearly limitless landscape and could not conceive of the quick victory their screaming leader had promised them.

Militarization spread over the country. The seminary had to move again and again into smaller spaces. The Ratzinger boys returned to their parents' home. In 1942 seventeen-year-old Georg was drafted into the army and served in logistics and combat in France, Holland, Czechoslovakia, and Italy. Wounded in Italy in 1944, he had a stay in the military hospital that occupied his beloved old seminary building; then he was sent back to the front. Joseph, who was fourteen, continued his studies at the *Gymnasium*, improving his command of ancient languages, increasing his knowledge of German literature, and trying his hand at translating Catholic liturgical texts.

Joseph's spiritual life bloomed along with his adolescence. "This was a time of interior exaltation, full of hope for the great things that were gradually opening up to me in the boundless realm of the spirit."[15] It kept him going, his source of hope, amid the rising tide of death around him. More and more names of the boys who had been taken from his school turned up in the lists of the fallen, and when he was fourteen, one of his cousins, a child with Down syndrome, was taken from his parents by Nazi social workers and murdered by medical therapists.[16] Fear for his brother's fate on the front must have been a source of constant worry.

His own time came soon enough, and it began in the Hitler Youth in 1941 on the day he turned fourteen. Since the later 1930s, all ten-year-olds were expected to join this organization each year on April 20, Hitler's birthday. By the early 1940s it had become almost impossible to avoid. Historians have found cases, mainly from devout Catholic families, where the parents refused to let their children participate. At the third failure to comply, the local police would get involved and usually procure participation through arrests or fines, and thereafter the child would be marked, banned from certain games and sporting events. Normally there were two training sessions per week and two camps per year, mainly for sports, singing, and some basic indoctrination. It was meant to be fun for the kids while developing preparatory skills for later military training.[17] Standing up and proclaiming oneself a conscientious objector was always an option, but it was potentially suicidal. Dachau was the destination for some of these brave people. Others were used to serve as an example of Nazi "justice": Hans and Sophie Scholl, who distributed antiwar fliers at the university in Munich in 1943, were quickly arrested, tried, and beheaded, in four days flat. That sent a certain message.

Joseph Ratzinger joined the Hitler Youth while he was in the minor seminary; it was a matter of finances.[18] Without it he would not have received the significant tuition discount that had made his schooling affordable for his family. When he left the seminary and returned to the *Gymnasium*, he stopped going to the meetings altogether. Then luck came into play. As before, his family still badly needed the discount which was tied to attendance, and the local administrator, "a very understanding mathematics teacher, . . . himself a Nazi but an honest man," told him, "Just go once and get the document so that we have it." Joseph must have looked down and shaken his head, saying nothing. "I understand you," the man said, "I'll take care of it."[19] The kindness of a halfway decent man got him out of it. That the British and American press could identify the Pope with or as Hitler Youth is absurdly unfair, but not entirely unfounded.

Compulsory military service was not long in coming. In 1943, at the age of sixteen, because he was still on paper a "boarding-school student," the government told him to go board in the barracks at the antiaircraft units in Munich. Naturally all time not spent in class at the *Gymnasium* in Munich was devoted to military duties. His first assignment was with a unit defending the factory of Bavarian Motor Works (the now famous BMW) that made airplane engines. He worked with the range-finding equipment, locating the bombers and conveying that information to the artillery.

Throughout 1944 the air attacks on Munich increased; no other city in Germany with the exception of Berlin endured a greater number of nighttime bombings. Joseph's nights must have been hellish, but the days revealed another evil. Right next to his barracks was a small concentration camp, Allach 1, a subsidiary of the infamous Dachau. There he saw heavily armed SS troops driving Eastern European prisoners, basically slaves, to work in the factory. The SS normally cloaked their worst abuses in secrecy, so Joseph probably never observed the beating, torture, and murder that characterized the system, but there was no doubt about the ruthless exploitation involved.

In September he was formally drafted into the military. Stationed briefly near the Ammersee, a beautiful little lake southwest of Munich, Joseph worked on the telephone system for his battery, which was supposed to bring down Allied planes, something they never managed to pull off. Instead, their installation became a new target for the Allies; one of his comrades was killed and several were wounded. Whenever he had free time, he read the few good books he could get his hands on, wrote poetry in Greek, and sometimes obtained permission to attend Holy Mass with other Catholic soldiers.

Later he was sent to work in Burgenland, near the convergence of the Czech, Hungarian, and Austrian borders, in preparation of the Soviet onslaught. There he was trained how to wield, present, march with, and meticulously clean a shovel. Treating the tool like a semisacred object struck him as particularly absurd. The commanding officers were committed Nazis, who wrenched the groggy boys out of their beds in the middle of the night, lined them up, and berated them to volunteer for the SS. Joseph and a few of his comrades replied that they were determined to join the Catholic priesthood. After receiving punishment, mainly verbal derision, they were spared future recruitment efforts. Joseph spent most of his days uprooting vineyards to dig tank ditches, or standing guard over forced workers. The weapon he carried was not loaded. On one occasion, he saw SS troops driving a long line of half-starved Jews, most ill, many without shoes, and all dressed in rags, on their way to "safety."[20] It was another colossal Nazi lie. The death march was a typical way to empty concentration camps toward the end of the war. Those who fell were shot. As there was no destination, very few, if any, made it.

The labor, the slaughter, it was all in vain; Hungary surrendered to the Red Army in October. Joseph was somehow spared the fate of so many young men who were sent to die fighting the inevitable. Almost inexplicably, on November 20, instead of being handed a pistol and sent to the front, he merely received his civilian clothing and was sent back to Germany. On the way toward Munich, the train passed through Traunstein. Joseph jumped off and walked home.

It was an idyllically beautiful fall day. There was a bit of hoarfrost on the trees, and the mountains glowed in the afternoon sun. Seldom have I ever experienced the beauty of my homeland as on this return from a world disfigured by ideology and hatred.[21]

For the next three weeks, no new orders came to his parents' house, so he had a time of rest and recovery, marked by gratitude and the renewal of spirit.

The summons to join the regular army came soon enough, but mercifully his commanding officer, who must have seen that the whole suicidal charade was going to end fairly soon, tried to lighten the burden. Instead of being sent to the front, in the winter of 1944-45 and the following spring, Joseph was stationed for duty in and around Traunstein, where he had to parade about in formation, sport a new uniform, sing Nazi songs, and show the populace just how much strength the wretched *Führer* still had in him. An injured, infected thumb kept Joseph from ever using a weapon. A doctor wanted to amputate it, but his mother's care proved more effective.[22] Unfortunately even the news of Hitler's death in early May did not free him from service; the Americans had not yet reached his part of Upper Bavaria. There the Nazis held power over the local populace.

Enough was enough. Joseph went AWOL. He knew that soldiers around Traunstein had been ordered to shoot deserters on sight, but he did not care. He snuck out of the barracks, his arm drawn up in a sling, took a back road, ducked through a small tunnel under the railroad, and ran into two soldiers. If they had been hardcore Nazis, they might well have killed him on the spot. That this happened elsewhere is well documented. They looked at him, then one said, "Comrade, you are wounded. Move on."[23] This was a moment in which basic, human reason was more compelling than military discipline.

His presence at his parents' house was no doubt welcome but potentially dangerous. As forced billeting had become a common practice, the Ratzingers had a string of military guests, all of whom were empowered or obliged to turn the lad in. His father always took the opportunity to treat them to tirades about how the delusional Hitler had ruined the country and the rest of Europe with it. In the early days of May, two SS men dropped in, took an interest in Joseph, who was clearly of military age, and started asking questions. Despite the very real dangers of this situation, Mr. Ratzinger answered with an angry lecture. Instead of shooting them both, which they might well have done, the SS men left the next day. In the Pope's words, "a special angel seemed to be guarding us."[24]

Then it was the Americans' turn to arrive in Hufschlag, bristling with weapons, understandably nervous about snipers and other guerillas, and of all places, they picked the Ratzingers' house for their local headquarters. Joseph was told, probably at gunpoint, to put on his uniform, hoist his hands, and join the crowd of prisoners standing in their beautiful meadow. His mother clearly feared that he would be killed by the men who had bombed Bavarian cities for months on end. He was allowed to pack up some things before being marched for three days to Bad Aibling, from which he was transported to a huge, open field within sight of the city of Ulm. There he stayed for weeks, with roughly fifty thousand other prisoners, enduring meager rations and almost no shelter, irrespective of the weather. There was also no way to keep track of the passage of the hours and days. He remembers the Americans shooting like mad one day, "a real fireworks show," from which the prisoners gathered that Germany had finally surrendered (May 8). But his incarceration wore on, until on June 19 he was finally handed the papers that guaranteed his freedom. Transported as far as Munich, he was told to manage the last seventy-five miles on his own. Accompanied by another fellow from near Traunstein, he set out on foot. They had not gone far before a milk truck stopped, the driver asked where they were headed. He hooted at their answer; he was going straight to Traunstein.

When Joseph set eyes on the city in the evening light, he recalls, "the heavenly Jerusalem itself could not have appeared more beautiful to me at that moment."[25] He heard the congregation singing in the parish church. It was the Feast of the Sacred Heart of Jesus, and members of his family were certainly inside. But he did not want to interrupt the service with a reunion scene, however happy it was sure to have been, so he hurried to the family home instead. His father, who was at home, greeted him with joy, astonishment, and relief, and his mother and sister soon joined them after the service was over. "In my whole life," Joseph wrote, "I have never again had so magnificent a meal as the simple one that Mother then prepared for me from the vegetables of her own garden."[26] In such statements, one can readily see Joseph's fundamental humility, sincere piety, and deep appreciation for the simple.

The final gift was the safe return of his brother, from whom they had heard nothing since April. Fear of his death had been constantly on their minds; "a quiet sorrow hung over our house."[27] In fact, Georg had been taken prisoner by the Americans and later released after the war's end. His sudden appearance in July released "an explosion of delight." After greeting everyone, Georg sat himself at the piano and filled the house with the hymn every Bavarian churchgoer knows by heart today, "Grosser Gott, Wir Loben Dich" ["Holy God, We Praise Thy Name"]. At last the family was reunified; the Nazi nightmare was over.

After the end of the war, Mr. Ratzinger made a pilgrimage to Altötting to thank God for the safe return of both his sons. This was a perfectly reasonable thing to do under the circumstances. Time and again all the members of his family had come into grave danger and yet somehow all were preserved from harm. Gratitude should rightly go to the Author of history.

These years were formative in the Pope's life. How could they not be? Few of those in the United States today can say that they have encountered overwhelming, institutionalized, unavoidable evil firsthand, and for that they should be thankful. We can scarcely conceive of our democratic republic turning into a murderous, oppressive, totalitarian dictatorship, led by a madman who is bent on destroying everything around him in the name of a perverse, racist, superhuman, suicidal heroism.

From Joseph Ratzinger's extensive writings, one can extract three fundamental lessons about the nature of evil and how it comes to take command of humanity at various periods in history. All three lessons are clearly derived from his youth in Nazi Germany. The first is that evil is at its most effective, its most seductive, when it is banal: "The greater it is, the more pitiful, the smaller the element of true greatness."[28] Hitler is the epitome. This little man was basically a lazy, common crook, a failure in all things except two, his tendency to dodge bullets and bombs—in World War I, the 1923 Putsch in Munich, and a number of assassination attempts—and his ability to whip a crowd into a frenzy by throwing temper tantrums at the podium.

Nazism was an extended exercise in glorifying the banal. The art and propaganda were tasteless, the obsession with militarism was legendary, and the predominance of the will over right and wrong is reminiscent of a toddler's version of the way the world should work. Nothing about it was truly uplifting. Nothing about it was self-denying or self-giving. It confused self-sacrifice with obedience to the whim of a petty megalomaniac. It taught that transcendence came through giving in to one's basest instincts, especially when it came to violence. It did its best to undermine and then annihilate truth, and whenever that happens, the way is open for the rule of selfish willfulness. The Nazis took over the institutions of government ruling over the German people, a civilized, disciplined, obedient population, and through those institutions it cowed more millions than it seduced. The number slaughtered all throughout Europe may well have exceeded both.

The second lesson about evil is that all attempts to destroy God are ultimately self-defeating, no matter how liberating and empowering such measures may feel at first.

> *In the course of history we have had more than enough of these experiments in doing without God, and giving man what he wants by sheer effort, through the structures of power. All these experiments have shown, in a negative sense, what it's really about. They hold up a mirror to the Church and to each individual: whenever we try to do without God, try to bypass him and to put the world right by our own systems, whenever we think that the satisfaction of material needs is the real key to the problem, then we solve nothing; we destroy things; we do the work of Satan.[29]*

The modern state cannot save people. It was never meant to. Marxism and Nazism were serious attempts to unseat God by the state, in the vain hope that such a move would solve all problems and create a new kind of humanity, but both ended up wallowing far beneath. What is true for history on a grand scale is applicable to the individual case. When people try to become their own saviors, the sole authors of their own selves, lives, and morality, they almost inevitably slide into a pointless, materialist, brutal solipsism.

We can see this at work in the modern and postmodern attitude toward the good, old-fashioned feeling of guilt. Here is what Cardinal Ratzinger had to say to the charge that Christianity fostered feelings of guilt in order to control the masses:

Well, of course, such a misuse of guilt feelings may occur. But it is worse to extinguish the capacity for recognizing guilt, because man then becomes inwardly hardened and sick. Just think a stage further, to an intensified form of the inability to recognize guilt. That was what was intended in Nazi education. They thought they were even able to commit murder, as [Heinrich] Himmler expressed it, and still remain respectable—and thereby they were deliberately trampling on human conscience and mutilating man himself.[30]

The elimination of guilt is essential for killing. Abortion is a case in point. What is it but the extinguishing of a human life? These tiny, developing persons are usually nameless, less often faceless, but basically hidden from view. But they are what they are. There is no denying it. There may be a whole set of reasons for believing it best to terminate a pregnancy, but because doing so involves the destruction of a human life that is not one's own, it can never be made respectable. The necessary laws and legal precedents are empowering and liberating, to be sure, but the deed can never be decent, humble, or good.

The third lesson has to do with the *reality* of evil, something so obvious that it bears repeating in this day and age of moral relativism. Good *exists*, most of us see evidence of it every day, and the same goes for evil. Evil need not be so spectacularly murderous in order for it to be *real*. All Americans should reflect for themselves about our popular media, entertainment industry, and culture. To what extent does it glorify the commonplace, the base, the vulgar, and the puerile? And to what extent do members of our society ape these examples? And how many of these behaviors lead to more destruction and misery than good?

This is not to call out bat-winged demons and devils prancing about in red spandex. When asked how one recognizes evil, the first thing Cardinal Ratzinger said was, "I would say that no one can demonstrate the existence of the devil."[31] But the fact that each of us can commit deeds that are malicious, perverse, disordered, destructive, and generally odious should make us stop and think. Every human being has the capacity for the demonic, and we know of examples that are spellbinding. Just look at the hypnotic power and utter depravity of Adolf Hitler. Time and again his generals would resolve to tell him off, but in his presence they failed to do so. Firsthand witnesses tell us he sometimes seemed to enter into a kind of trembling ecstasy, after which he would say, "He was there again." Once, before the war started, when listening to the arrangements for Mussolini's visit to Berlin, Hitler interrupted, saying, "No, none of that is right. I can see how it ought to go," and then spouted forth a description of his vision. This totally unexceptional little man could fascinate the masses and release their fury, almost without fail. The fact of the Holocaust alone should stand as sufficient evidence that "Hitler was a demonic figure."[32]

The evil we see every day is far less dramatic and horrific than Nazi Germany's. When discussing the stupendous economic growth experienced in the latter half of the twentieth century, the Cardinal stated that this was not necessarily and purely a good thing. In the newfound wealth and the so-called ethics of market capitalism, he saw "a sign of the Satanic in the way in which people exploit the market for pornography and drugs in the West." Again we should not think of cartoon devils at work, but rather understand "Satanic" as unequivocal evil. He continued his critique as follows:

> There is something diabolical in the cold-blooded perversity with which man is corrupted for the sake of money, and profit is drawn from his weakness, his temptability and vulnerability in the face of temptation. Western culture is hellish when it persuades men that the sole aim of life is pleasure and self-interest.[33]

This statement raises a question: Is it not a sign for us all that when we start to look at other human beings in terms of monetary utility, we are on the wrong track? Each of us must answer this for him or herself. And finally, I hope you see how Joseph Ratzinger's lifelong commitment to humility and simplicity must of necessity lead to a dimmer view of pleasure and self-interest than many people maintain today. There is nothing intrinsically evil in pleasure, but it should never be the reason for existence.

Good comes from God, while evil comes from our failure to abide by what he wants us to do and be. Evil, according to Cardinal Ratzinger, "does not originate from within God. . . . It comes from freedom."[34] This last statement may be jarring to our American sensitivities, but I think you will find in the end that the Pope is right.

Having gone over these very important matters, the last thing I mean to do is give you the impression that Pope Benedict has a morbid, paranoid concern with evil in mankind and history. If you had lived his life, if World War II had happened right before your eyes, on your doorstep, in your homeland, and you were in your teens, wouldn't it have remained with you, in some way, for the rest of your days? A summary of his thoughts on the subject seemed appropriate at this point, given the magnitude of the events. But there are far greater forces at work in his thoughts, powers that drive him to this day—one being love.

5

from BOY *to* PRIEST: FREISING *and* MUNICH

"I am a perfectly ordinary Christian."

—*Joseph Ratzinger,* Salt of the Earth

Joseph Ratzinger's priestly vocation came to him gradually, more like an incoming tide than a rogue wave. He said he never had a lightning-like experience of sudden illumination; based on his life and his writings, it is fair to say that the man is not a mystic. In his autobiography, the first appearance of a mature decision to become a Catholic priest appears in the narrative of the war years. If by that time he could tell it to an officer of the SS, then it is clear that his mind was made up, come what may. If forced to give an explanation for the decision, the only reasonable one is love.

From his early childhood he loved Christian stories and mysteries, he loved the ancient languages of the Church's most important texts, and he loved her other worldly liturgies. He loved her art and music, too, but most of all, he loved Christ Jesus. For Joseph, Catholicism provided the best way to contend with the nightmare of what his country did to itself and the rest of Europe and yet still find cause for hope, to see the meaning of it all, to take solace in the fact that it was all part of God's plan for the world.

FREISING

The next stage in his life journey was to take place in Freising, where he studied philosophy and theology at the major seminary. The archdiocese of Munich and Freising is one of the most ancient in Germany. According to tradition, the diocese of Freising was first established in the early eighth century by Saint Corbinian. One of the legends associated with him has found its way onto Benedict XVI's coat of arms. During a visit to the Holy See in Rome, a bear attacked and killed Corbinian's donkey, and the saint's severe scolding cowed the bear into submission. To make amends, the bear carried the load the rest of the way to Rome where Corbinian freed him from his burden. This bear has been part of Ratzinger's insignia for decades, as bishop, cardinal, and then Pope; it reminds him that he is a pack animal of God. "I have become your donkey, [Lord], and in just this way am I with you."[1]

Rising on a high, steep hill in the middle of Freising is the *Domberg*, or "cathedral hill," that offers a view of the land around in all directions. The higher elevation enables the double white towers and grey-green spires of Freising's largest church to be seen from many miles away on a clear day. The cathedral's interior, that stretches over eighty yards in length, under an enormous barrel-vaulted roof, is a blaze of late baroque décor. The interplay of sculpture, stucco, paint, and gold leaf is one of the most beautiful in Bavaria. And in anticipation of Pope Benedict's apostolic visit in September 2006 the cathedral in Freising received a full renovation. Today it is truly splendid to behold.

With its seat in the heart of the Isar valley, Freising was a center for religion, learning, and culture for many centuries. In 1818 it was merged with the urban diocese of Munich, and the bishop's seat was transferred to the larger of the two cities. At the beginning of the twenty-first century, the archdiocese includes about two million Catholics, which comprises more than half of the general population. In their service are about one thousand priests and deacons in 750 parishes, and around 600 monks, friars, nuns, and other religious.[2]

The town of Freising surrounds the hill and extends away from it on all sides. The public space in the tidy streets has maintained its Catholic identity. A modern mural of both the Virgin Mary, the patroness of Bavaria, and St. Corbinian looks down on the central square from the front of the city hall. In the middle of the open space is a tall marble column supporting a gilded statue of the Virgin Mary. There is clearly no debate about annihilating religion from the public sphere in this town. Today some Freisingers maintain that their town and the surrounding region has the highest fertility rate in all of Germany. Considering the constant graying of the general population, it is assuring to see families making a real investment in the future.

In 1945 Freising had sustained some damage from aerial bombing, but little in comparison to the devastation in Munich and other cities. The seminary buildings were still serving as a military hospital for POWs awaiting repatriation in other lands. It took months before the seminarians could return to their allotted rooms for study and instruction. They were a motley crowd of about 120 men, ranging in age from nineteen to forty, but they were unified by having lived through the horrors of war. For every one of them, the church had been their rock, withstanding the lashing waves of Nazi ideology. They all had hope for the future, a time of peace and reconciliation. From the *Domberg*, looking east across the fertile Isar Valley, they could watch the sun rise as it always had and always will, with the promise of yet another day in the life of the world despite men's fits of self-destruction.

From 1945 to 1947, Joseph and his brother, Georg, went to Freising to study at the seminary, where both of them rapidly made names for themselves: *Orgelratz*, or "Organ-Ratz" for the musical Georg, and *Bücherratz*, or "Books-Ratz" for Joseph.[3] "Whenever you went in the library, there sat Joseph," said one of his fellow students.[4] And Joseph did read widely, in theology and philosophy, particularly of Romano Guardini, Josef Pieper, and Martin Buber, in German, French, and Russian literature, and even in the natural sciences, the groundbreaking work of Heisenberg and Einstein, learning about the shifts in human thought over time. He found rewarding intellectual companionship in his fellow students and teachers, especially in Alfred Läpple, a doctoral candidate in philosophy, twelve years his senior, with whom he spent many hours in formative conversations. There was also time for artistic enjoyment, for music and even a bit of theater, but mostly for silent prayer in the seminary chapel. The hours of private prayer and the holy liturgies held in the cathedral comprise for Joseph his "most precious memories" of Freising.[5]

He was also able to observe Cardinal-Archbishop Michael von Faulhaber, whose personal "aura of dignity" and the "awe-inspiring grandeur of his mission" gave the young man a role model he would have the opportunity to emulate later in life.[6] Before becoming a bishop in 1917, Faulhaber had been a professor of the Old Testament, and a member of a group called

"Amici Israel" (Friends of Israel), dedicated to fighting anti-Semitism within and beyond the Church. Emblazoned on his bishop's coat of arms there was a menorah for all to see. The Cardinal had detested Nazism all along and condemned it in 1932. Shortly thereafter, however, he joined the other German bishops in telling the faithful to give Hitler's new regime a chance, in the vain hope that democracy, as enshrined in the republican constitution, would tame it, that the Nazi chancellor would uphold the terms of the Concordat he had signed with the Vatican. But they were quickly disabused.

At the end of 1933, Faulhaber delivered a series of Advent homilies in Munich, in which he defended the lasting validity of the Old Testament, emphasized the Jewish roots of Christianity, and condemned racism. Turning Nazi anti-Semitism on its head, he declared, "Either we believe in the divine inspiration of Holy Scripture or we must say to the Jewish people, 'You are the most ingenious race in the history of the world.'" These homilies were published, printed, and 200,000 copies circulated. Nazis pilloried him in the press, and thugs in the street took potshots into his office. Thereafter Faulhaber seems to have quieted down, reasonably fearful that further protests on behalf of the Jews would lead to reprisals against Christians.[7] In 1937, however, he secretly wrote much of Pope Pius XI's encyclical that condemned Nazism as a set of pernicious falsehoods and predicted its eventual downfall.[8]

At the end of the first semester in 1946, during a requiem Mass in remembrance of the priests and seminary students who fell in the war, there was nothing to stop Cardinal Faulhaber from condemning Nazi ideology and its contorted worldview as something inhuman, which came

> *either from the madhouse or out of Hell itself. These were spirits from the depths, and there were also demons at work. I mean that racial arrogance that carries within it the seed of eternal warfare. I mean the insane idea that modern warfare can bring a people prosperity and future happiness, only if they are ready to die to the very last man. I mean the satanic principle that the criminal deed of one individual implicates his whole clan. I mean the devilish hate that supports wiping out non-Aryans first and then Christendom itself.*[9]

He said that the Germans must purge themselves of these vile ideas and restore human rights to the individual, but not to the other extreme! All priests must bring God's rights to the communal life. They must dedicate themselves to caring for souls, living in accordance with the heart of God. There is no doubt that the Cardinal's words molded Joseph's mind and heart. For the next six decades, his writings and speeches condemn Nazism and its host of lies as completely and powerfully as Faulhaber ever did.

The first two years in Freising must have been a wonderful experience, to satisfy the intellectual and spiritual thirst from the war years. Ratzinger summed up the study of theology in two simple questions: "What is really true, what can we know?"[10] At one level, the field broadens understanding of the faith; at another it must address the role of God, of divine action, in the whole course of Western and world history. Joseph's hunger for knowledge only increased the further he advanced. In 1947 he and a couple of his colleagues applied for and received the bishop's permission to continue their studies at the state theological faculty at the University in Munich, where the pedagogical emphasis would not be so directed toward priestly formation but more to training the next generation of professional scholars of theology, lay and clerical. "My hope," he wrote in his autobiography, "was to become more fully familiar with the intellectual debates of our time by working at the university, so as some day to be able to dedicate myself completely to theology as a profession."[11] He had developed a wish, if not a precise goal: to be a scholar and professor.

As a student in Freising, he completed his first work of real scholarship, a joint effort with Alfred Läpple: an original, first-time translation of St. Thomas Aquinas's Latin treatise, *Quaestio disputata de caritate,* "Disquisition on love."[12] It was never published, but nearly sixty years later, as Pope Benedict XVI, his first papal encyclical, "Deus caritas est," would address the same subject, explaining, with the help of Aquinas, how God is love.

⚜ MUNICH

Munich, the capital of the state of Bavaria, was first mentioned in a twelfth-century document. In the early years, the town was a place to cross the Isar River, next to a Benedictine monastery that had been there for centuries.

The Wittelsbach dukes soon took it over for their court in Upper Bavaria, and thereafter Munich grew on a diet of ducal patronage, local agricultural expansion, and revenues from the salt trade. After 1805, the city was named the capital of the newly created Kingdom of Bavaria. It served as the seat of the royal court, of the realm's parliament, the newly established archdiocese of Freising and Munich, and the university that was removed from Landshut, a picturesque town downriver to the north. Following World War I, Munich became a hothouse for extremist politics, and there in 1923 Hitler staged his failed bid to take over the Bavarian government and topple the Weimar Republic.

In 1947 Munich and its great university was still a heap of rubble, so the theology department had to be accommodated in an eighteenth-century converted royal hunting lodge, Fürstenried, about five miles south of the city center. The situation was anything but luxurious. The castle itself, with extensive surrounding park and gardens, was still serving as a veterans' hospital, and the living situation for the students reminded Joseph of the military barracks. He slept on a dormitory bunk bed in an outlying annex that housed two professors, the administrative office, and the library. The director, Professor Josef Pascher, who also lived there, imposed a strict regimen of daily Mass, lunch in a common dining area, where he personally ladled out the soup, and evening readings from the Gospel. On Saturdays they all rode the tram into Munich, took up their shovels, and helped to clear the debris from the bombed-out university buildings.[13] Lectures in Fürstenried had to be held in an unheated greenhouse on the grounds. There were no classes scheduled from Christmas to Easter due to lack of heaters and fuel.

The Nazis had shut down the theological department before the war, because Cardinal Faulhaber had refused to accept faculty who supported Hitler, so the faculty had to be rebuilt, drawing on refugee academicians from the parts of Germany that had been handed over to Poland and subsequently cleared of their German inhabitants. We in America tend to forget that after the war twelve million Germans were expelled from their homes across eastern and central Europe and sent to remake their lives in a shattered country. Two million died en route, mainly children and the elderly. The fact that "they started the war" does not turn that instance of ethnic cleansing into a righteous deed.

One of these dispossessed was Gottlieb Söhngen, a professor of fundamental theology, who provided a formative influence on the young scholar. Ratzinger described Söhngen as a "radical and critical questioner." For him no subject was untouchable, nothing taboo, and at the same time he was a man deeply committed to his Catholic faith. His questioning was a sign not of professorial arrogance or irreverence, but of the boldness of his belief. According to him, no Catholic should fear any question, and no thought calls for violent suppression. The theologian should speak first and foremost not for himself but for the faith of the Church, something that he *receives* and does not think up himself. And through all the horrors of the Nazi era, Söhngen managed to maintain his easy, humane sense of humor.[14]

Ratzinger became a theologian of the same strain. Söhngen took the young scholar under his wing, so to speak, even treating him to performances of opera in Munich.[15] Throughout all of Ratzinger's writings, we find the same courage to ask the hard question—Why should anyone believe in any of this? —and an even greater confidence in the answers, which allows him to take on any intellectual challenge to the faith. On April 3, 2007, Pope Benedict XVI exhorted all theologians, professional and amateur, to keep on asking questions. "Only if we ask questions, and are radical with our questions, radical as theology has to be, going beyond specializations, only then can we find answers to these fundamental questions that affect all of us. Before everything else, we have to ask questions."[16]

In Fürstenried he attended lectures taught by several other superb scholars, each of them contributing to his intellectual formation in their own way. While other papal biographers describe them and their ideas in detail, suffice it to say here that Ratzinger's studies formed his thought for the rest of his life. From a host of great philosophers and Christian thinkers he learned a set of basic truths, best summed up by Alfred Läpple:

> *Life as a gift from God is more than a well-balanced story. It is quite different from a life according to Kant's categorical imperative of duty. The story of a life should become one of faith. You are not the property of the state. You are not the property of your parents, but you belong to God and to God alone. Every human being is the image of God, every, including the unbaptized. It is God who searches with you for the path*

that your steps should follow. Life is a shifting construction site, where work moves on when one job is done.[17]

By 1949 enough of the university buildings in Munich had been restored so that the theological faculty could return to the city, but the situation was still basic at best. Ratzinger's dormitory on the fourth floor of the main buildings could only be reached from the outside, by means of a rung-ladder, but his room had a little heater and there was a water source in the hall.[18] Ratzinger's intellectual growth continued as the great city of Munich slowly rose again from the miles of bombed-out, war torn ruins.

BACK TO FREISING, AND INTO THE PRIESTHOOD

In 1950 Joseph completed six semesters of theological study, passed his exams with top marks, and returned to Freising for a final two semesters of preparation for the priesthood. At the same time, Professor Söhngen urged him to take part in an academic competition, a kind of glorified essay contest, in which the winning piece of writing would be acknowledged as a dissertation toward the doctoral degree. Söhngen oversaw the competition, and the topic he selected was exactly in line with Joseph's interests: "The People and the House of God in St. Augustine's Doctrine of the Church." Joseph had studied Augustine in Söhngen's seminar and had developed a strong connection with the writings of the Church Fathers. Given that the paper had to be written in nine months, Joseph devoted all his free time to the project during summer vacation and the final two semesters of priestly study and training. His sister, Maria, typed up the final text for submission. Joseph's essay won, needless to say. He received a *summa cum laude,* and after an oral examination, the doctorate would be his.

During his six years studying theology, Joseph struggled to find reasonable answers to life's most important questions in light of the Catholic faith. For him personally, in preparation for the priesthood, he had to contend with the prospect of lifelong celibacy. Studying and living in Fürstenried, he was always at very close quarters with women as well as men. During his walks in the park and private prayer in the chapel, he must have seriously considered whether it would not be better for him to have a family. He also must have wondered whether he was best fit for parish life, with its manifold demands for religious and community leadership for young and old alike. And there was no guarantee that he could fulfill his "secret wish" to become a professor. As a priest of the church, the ultimate decision would not have been his to make. But he remained undaunted. "I always had the basic direction before me, but there was no lack of crises."[19]

He was ordained on Friday, June 29, 1951, with his brother and about forty other seminarians in the cathedral in Freising by Cardinal Faulhaber. It was a gorgeous summer day, and the pews of the cathedral were filled with friends and family members. Nonetheless, when Joseph and his forty companions lay prostrate on the floor before the altar, he felt "troubled by an awareness of the poverty of my life," but the invocation of many saints consoled him. "I knew I would not be left on my own."[20] The eighty-two-year-old Cardinal and all priests present laid their hands on the assembled deacons to give them the gift of the Holy Spirit. When Alfred Läpple stood before Joseph Ratzinger, the latter looked up and said, "Thank you." When the venerable Cardinal laid his hands on Joseph, a songbird—not a dove, but maybe a lark—flew from the high altar through the church, twittering exuberantly. "We should not be superstitious," Ratzinger advises us in his autobiography, but nonetheless he had to understand this little moment as a sign of encouragement from above: "It is good this way. You are on the right path."[21]

Little more than a week later, both Ratzinger brothers said their first Mass in their family's parish church of St. Oswald in Traunstein on July 8, in Latin, Joseph at 7 a.m. and Georg at 9 a.m., both accompanied by a choir singing the prayers set to music by Joseph Haas and Joseph Haydn. They imparted their first blessings on the many people who spontaneously and joyfully invited them into their homes. This confirmed for Joseph that his priesthood had little to do with himself, but everything with Christ and his message of love for all mankind. Afterward, the Ratzinger brothers celebrated with their mother's side of the family in the village of Rimsting on the Chiemsee. There they enjoyed the view of God's majestic, free gift to Bavaria—her mountains, fields, forest, and largest lake.

BACK TO MUNICH, AS CHAPLAIN

For ten months, from 1951 to 1952, Joseph Ratzinger served as a chaplain for the parish of Holy Blood in Bogenhausen on the eastern side of Munich. His list of duties was grueling but normal: sixteen classes of religious education per week for second to eighth-graders; three homilies every Sunday (one for the children's Mass, two for adults); hearing confessions 6-7 a.m. daily with four additional hours on Saturday afternoons; baptisms, weddings, and burials; and the youth group, including their camping outings. His pastor, Father Blumschein, struck him as a model priest, in that he gave himself totally to his flock through unrelenting service kindly and readily rendered. Blumschein often let Joseph preach the homily while he celebrated the rest of the Mass. In the limited time Joseph had to himself, he read and played the harmonium, a mini reed pump organ. After his elevation to the papacy, someone in this parish found the instrument and sold it on eBay to an avid collector. At least the money that came in went to pay for a new organ for the parish church.

Bogenhausen was a parish with vivid memories of its most recent martyrs, men who were all accused of supporting the July 20, 1944 assassination attempt against Hitler. Ludwig Freiherr von Leonrod, a member of the parish, was one of the conspirators, and a diplomat, Franz Sperr, was killed along with 200 others throughout Germany on trumped charges or mere suspicions. Two Jesuit pastors for the parish, Alfred Delp and Hermann Joseph Wehrle, met the same fate—the former for his alleged support of the planning, the latter for merely having been Leonrod's confessor. There was also a large group of families who had objected loudly to Nazi efforts to remove the crucifixes from school classrooms and suffered for it in various ways. Some were resentful that the Cardinal-Archbishop of Munich and Freising, Michael von Faulhaber, had not been more squarely on their side. Hermann Theißing, a parishioner who was a teenager at the time, remembers how the new chaplain once preached about the office of bishop, explaining it to his flock in terms of the meaning of the Latin *episcopus*—itself a derivation of the Greek επισκορος—which can be translated into English as "overseer" or "superintendent," but in the case of Greek and its German equivalent, also as "scout" or "lookout." Whether Ratzinger intended the sermon as a defense or a subtle critique of Faulhaber is unknown. Theißing thought the latter and was impressed: "The homily was an 'aha' experience for us; my father was thrilled."

Ratzinger learned much from his predecessor in Bogenhausen. The martyred Alfred Delp, a convert to the Catholic faith, boldly stated his belief in the Church's universal mission in a book called *Man and History*, a work that

made him a target for Nazi persecution. Catholicism, Hitler and his hench-
men decried, as well as Judaism, had only contributed to the enslavement of
German peoples. Both needed to be wiped out in order to attain freedom for
the master race. On the other hand, Delp, writing in the 1930s, saw man in
modern times as a figure in a tragedy, one surrounded by a dense forest of lies
and life-threatening threats. He argued that the lack of belief in his own day
and age ran deeper than mere atheism; it shriveled the human soul and cor-
rupted the conscience and the faculty for discerning right from wrong.[22] Only
Christ Jesus, he said, was the true man (as opposed to the Nazi "new" man,
who is merely his own will), and through him each of us can become most fully
human. "Man, created in the image and likeness of God, is at the center of history," Delp wrote, while the Nazi idea of truth being contingent on nationalism,
race, and the individual will was simply false.[23] Views similar to these appeared
repeatedly in Joseph Ratzinger's writings over the next half century.

Also from Delp, Ratzinger took special note of a certain saying: "Bread is
important, freedom is more important, but most important is unfailing worship."[24] The Church is, first and foremost, neither a charitable institution, nor
a proponent for social and political justice around the world, but a community of prayer. Given this fact, whenever and wherever she neglects her worship,
even for the sake of concentrating on other, socially relevant activities, she
will eventually falter in all. As to human history, by which Ratzinger means
the proper way for each of us to live a human life, then, now, and always, the
lesson is about temptation, or "setting God aside, so that he seems to be a secondary concern when compared with all the urgent priorities of our lives."[25]

Father Joseph struck people as capable and dedicated, "one who listened, gave
answers, and behaved unpretentiously." There were some difficult moments
for him. Once during the carnival season before Lent, a group of boys knelt
before him and begged him to come to their party and Ratzinger reluctantly
agreed, but he showed up without a costume or mask. When he walked in, in
the usual black suit and white collar, someone called out in disgust, "Whoa,
look at that! He's come as a chaplain!" Joseph turned around and left. Hermann Theißing remembers burning with embarrassment.

While in parish service at Bogenhausen, especially through working with
the young people and their parents, Ratzinger learned "how far removed the

world of the life and thinking of many children was from the realities of faith and how little our religious instruction coincided with the actual lives and thinking of our families."[26] Parish life showed him how distant and rarified the world of academic theology could become. He did his best to convey what he had learned to those whom he was supposed to guide. On May 24, 1952, Ratzinger wrote a short poem to a little girl, a student in one of his religion classes, who was maybe eight years old at the time. The two stanzas are set apart, probably showing that the first is a quotation, the second being his own composition:

Wie auch die Winde wehen:	However the winds blow
Sollst ihnen zum Trotze stehen;	You should stand against them
Wenn auch die Welt zerbricht–	When the world falls apart
Dein tapfres Herz verzaget nicht.	Your brave heart won't despair.
Ohne die Tapferkeit des Herzens,	Without the heart's bravery,
die den Mut	which
hat, unerschütterlich den Geistern	has the courage to withstand
der Zeit und	unshakably
der Masse zu trotzen, können wir	the spirits of the time and the
den Weg	masses,
zu Gott und den wahren Weg	we cannot find the way to God
unsers Herren nicht finden.	and the true way of our Lord.

He signed it, "In remembrance of your catechist, Joseph Ratzinger." It is not unusual for Bavarian elementary school students to keep a small album of verses from their classmates and teachers. Ratzinger's gesture was not one of favoritism; we know of at least two other children who received similar poems from their chaplain.[27]

BACK TO FREISING, 1952-1959

Cardinal Faulhaber had other plans for Joseph Ratzinger besides parish work. The chaplain in Bogenhausen was called to return to Freising, this time as a *Dozent*, a lecturer or teaching assistant, making him the youngest faculty member at the seminary in Freising, as of October 1, 1952. Joseph's reaction was mixed. The academic life is what he had really wanted for some time, but during his months in Bogenhausen, he had come to love parish life, especially its intimate connections with so many people. But the decision was not his to make. In addition to his teaching duties, he had to complete his doctoral qualifications: an hour-long oral and a written exam in each of eight fields, and a public debate on theses from all branches of theology. In addition to giving three lectures per week on the theology and administration of the sacraments, he had to prepare a series of homilies to be read in the cathedral and more for the seminary's own chapel. This was a real challenge, but once again he pulled through. In July 1953 he became Dr. Joseph Ratzinger, to the great delight of his parents, as they watched him cross the stage in full regalia, at the age of twenty-six, one of the youngest in all Germany.[28]

In 1953 he learned that there was an opening at the College of Theology and Philosophy in Freising (an institution separate from the seminary), and that the other professors in that faculty were hoping he would become their colleague. But he had yet to write his *Habilitation*, basically a second dissertation, if he wanted to become a full professor in the German academic system. An interim instructor was hired for a year to cover the chair's duties while Joseph wrote his *Habilitation*, once again under Professor Söhngen's guidance, this time about the theology of thirteenth-century Franciscan scholar, St. Bonaventure. Before it was completed, he assumed the duties of the professorial chair at the college, and moved into a comfortable apartment on the *Domberg*. From November 1955 he brought his parents to live with him there. The farmhouse in Hufschlag near Traunstein and the long walk to the town had simply become too burdensome for the aging couple who had reached the ages of seventy-eight and seventy-one respectfully. His sister started to make plans to join them.

Joseph finished the *Habilitation* by the end of 1955, and Professor Söhngen loved it. But the second reader, a professor named Michael Schmaus, flat out rejected it, saying that it was not up to the standard of the theological profession, which would have put an end to Ratzinger's professorial career then and there. "I was thunderstruck. A whole world was threatening to collapse around me."[29] Joseph's first consideration was his dear parents. Where would they go after he was sent away from Freising? He thought of applying for a parish position with housing in Freising, but then again, maybe the *Habilitation* could be salvaged. It was true that the typist who prepared the submitted version had made a lot of errors, but it was equally true that Joseph had attacked a number of Schmaus's own interpretations of the Middle Ages, something that academics tend to take very personally, at times to an extreme.

Schmaus totally disagreed with one of Joseph's central arguments, namely that "revelation" for St. Bonaventure does not refer merely to a set of truths communicated from God to mankind, to be comprehended almost exclusively by the human intellect. Revelation is more than that, Joseph argued, a process inextricably tied up with history itself. It is God's revealing, or uncovering of himself to humanity, over time, through Jesus Christ and the Holy Spirit, who speak anew to every age. God's Word cannot be confined to mere words in a text, namely Holy Scripture, a finite, historical document, cobbled together in the first centuries of Christianity and interpreted thereafter by the Church. Revelation, Ratzinger said, was bigger than the Bible, but this was only part of the condemned *Habilitation*. Thanks to Söhngen's energetic intercession, Joseph was not failed outright but granted permission to submit a revision. He decided to expand the third part of the work, which had to do with St. Bonaventure's theology of history and his debate with another Franciscan scholar of his age, Joachim of Fiore. On this part of the text Schmaus had not bled red ink. But Joseph had only two weeks in the summer of 1956 to write it! Schmaus had declared it would take him years.

Joseph Ratzinger proved him wrong. The text was on the short side at two hundred pages, but it was completed and typed competently this time. This time the text was accepted, but Joseph still had to pass an oral exam, which took place in February 1957. Held in a packed auditorium at the University of Munich, the exam rapidly turned into an all-out debate between Schmaus and Söhngen. After presenting the results of his research, Joseph just stood there, letting the professors hold forth their differences. At the end, he had to wait in a hall while the battle continued among the rest of the faculty behind closed doors. After a long time, he was curtly informed that he had passed. The trial was over! Without passing, his academic career could not have progressed as it did, and history would have been different.

As of January 1, 1958, he was serving as the professor of fundamental theology and dogma, living with his parents in Freising as before. At the College of Philosophy and Theology, he rapidly became very highly regarded among the students, male and female, for his exceptional brilliance and modest character. Georg Lohmeier, a student of his at the time, said, "Women took a liking to Ratzinger, who was boyishly good-looking—we students understood that. Already then he showed how learned he was, much smarter than all the other professors together. You could tell as much, although his manner was humble and almost childlike. He was always available for questions about theology, even when no lecture was being held. He debated in Latin; we noticed he could do that better than anyone else."[30]

Joseph Ratzinger's professorial career took off like a rocket. Only a few months after receiving his professorship in Freising, the University in Bonn, the capital city of Western Germany, invited him to accept a professorship in fundamental theology. For Ratzinger, this was "a dream come true," but caring for his parents was his first priority.[31] By that time, however, his brother had completed his professional studies in music and become the choral director of St. Oswald's, their former parish in Traunstein. There Georg was granted the use of a modest house in the center of town, with adequate space for the elder Josef and Maria Ratzinger. Though both were horrified at the idea of yet another move, the opportunity for young Joseph was too golden, as was the thought of returning to "their unforgettable and still beloved Traunstein."[32]

In 1959, Joseph left Bavaria for the Rhineland, accompanied by his sister, and his brother and parents returned to the small city they had come to regard as their home. Traunstein, like Marktl am Inn, Tittmoning, and Aschau, would like to claim Joseph as one of its own, but as in the other cases, his time there was too limited to put down a taproot of his own. He was always glad to return to see his family, school, and old friends, but opportunity kept him on the move, further and wider than his Bavarian *Heimat*.

NORTH, SOUTH, and BACK AGAIN

"While Bavaria is a land of farmers and owes its special beauty, permanence, and inner peace precisely to this characteristic, I now found myself in a landscape with a wholly different quality about it."

—Joseph Ratzinger, Milestones

BONN

The city of Bonn lies in the northwest of Germany on the River Rhine, near the border with Belgium, France, Luxembourg, and the Netherlands. As the seat of government for the postwar Federal Republic of Germany, this quaint little city had become a cosmopolitan center for politics, ideas, and culture in the Cold War era. The pulsating life of the city and the ceaseless traffic along the Rhine gave Joseph "the feeling of openness and breadth, of the meetings of cultures and nations that for centuries had occurred here and made one another fruitful."[1] This was nothing against his beautiful Bavarian homeland, but at any rate it made for a stark contrast with his homeland's agrarian culture, with its settled, simple, constant quality.

Beginning in April 1959, Joseph lectured on dogmatic theology in the largest auditorium at the University of Bonn, filling it day after day. This was his first position at a university where he naturally met and mingled with scholars and students of diverse academic fields and disciplines. He also rapidly befriended some of the leading intellectuals of the day, including Hubert Jedin, the great historian of the Catholic Church, and Paul Hacker, a passionate scholar of Sanskrit, Hindi, and the religions of India, to say nothing of his mastery of Greek, Latin, Slavic languages, and the history of the Reformation era in Europe.

Although this kind of contact was certainly rewarding, Joseph suffered from occasional bouts of homesickness for his native Bavaria, but he was not alone. His sister, Maria, who had never married, had come to live with him in Bonn and manage their simple apartment, which was across the street from a Ford auto repair station.[2] Fortunately, an elderly Bavarian countess named Almeida, who had heard about the young theologian, looked him up in the telephone book, and called him. Soon afterward he and his sister were included in a select little community of so-called Bavarian exiles, who joined the countess for afternoon coffee and cake, and good company. According to one of Ratzinger's former students, the friendship lasted till the countess's death twenty years later.[3]

During the first summer vacation in August 1959, Joseph and his sister returned to Bavaria to see their parents and brother in Traunstein. After a day trip to their old haunt in Tittmoning, they returned to find that their father had suffered a serious stroke after a six-mile walk with his wife. Josef Ratzinger died two days later, his loving family standing at his bedside. The old man was able to indicate his gratitude although he was unable to talk. Joseph and Maria returned to Bonn greatly saddened by the suddenness and gravity of the loss.

⚓ VATICAN II

It was around that time that Joseph came into contact with the Cardinal Archbishop of Cologne, Joseph Frings, a redoubtable figure despite his advanced age and near blindness. When Pope John XXIII announced the convocation of the Second Vatican Council in 1962, Cardinal Frings asked the thirty-five-year-old Professor Ratzinger to serve as a *peritus*, or official theological adviser. How could the young priest-professor have refused? A Church Council was a rare event of global significance, for him the opportunity of a lifetime. Cardinal Frings soon began to send him drafts of the documents that would be presented to the bishops of the world who were to gather in Rome. Ratzinger found their content solidly and faithfully Catholic, but the language, style, and tone struck him as more scholarly than pastoral and missionary.

When the Council convened, Ratzinger followed Frings to Rome, where he was able to exchange ideas with the greatest theologians of his age, including Henri de Lubac and Karl Rahner among many others. With Ratzinger at his side, Frings rejected the documents submitted by the Vatican for summary approval and insisted on altering the lists of committee memberships. Later Frings used a speech written by Ratzinger to call for a reform of the Vatican Curia, attacking in particular the workings of the Holy Office, the institution once known as the Inquisition, and later renamed the Congregation for the Doctrine of the Faith. The Cardinal supported the decision to allow the use of vernacular languages in the celebration of the liturgy, but there was not a whiff of liturgical or theological revolution in the air that Joseph could detect. When the Council came to discuss divine revelation, Frings fought against the notion that God's self-revelation to mankind in history was tantamount to and contained in the Bible. The text he relied on most was Ratzinger's. For three years, the young professor traveled back and forth between Rome and the Lower Rhineland, managing to fulfill his academic and conciliar commitments at the same time.

The Second Vatican Council has a history of its own, too broad and complicated to be covered in this work. For Joseph Ratzinger, suffice it to say, it solidified his understanding of the faith, the Church, and Catholic theology.

> *My basic impulse, precisely during the Council, was always to free up the authentic kernel of the faith from encrustations and to give this kernel strength and dynamism. This impulse is the constant of my life. ... What's important to me is that I have never deviated from this constant, which from my childhood has molded my life, and that I have remained true to it as the basic direction of my life.*[4]

This sentiment puts him firmly in line with John XXIII, known to posterity as the "Laughing" or the "Beloved" Pope, who called the Council for the sake of *aggiornamento*, or "updating" the Church's message, so that she could communicate more effectively in a rapidly changing modern world. Pope John never intended the Council to turn Catholicism into something she was not or to cut away the moorings to tradition. Ratzinger dedicated the rest of his life to upholding, defending, and implementing the Council's resolutions as correctly as possible.

⚜ MÜNSTER

In the middle of the Council proceedings, Ratzinger moved again. During the summer of 1962, he learned that the chair in dogmatic theology at the

University of Münster was open, and that he was the desired replacement. After nearly a year of deliberation, he accepted, taking with him the doctoral students whom he had been training at Bonn. The growing jealousy of some of his colleagues and the widening divisions with the department of Catholic theology made him fear that his students might suffer the same torments he had experienced during the storm over his *Habilitation* in Munich. Cardinal Frings made no objection.

Münster is a lovely little city built mainly of red brick, known to this day for its Catholic identity, an exception to the northern German norm. The three years Joseph spent there were pleasant and productive. Although the flat landscape of the city and its environs was hardly as impressive as the Bavarian Alps, it was perfect for riding a bicycle, which Joseph used to get about, just like his students. He never owned a car, and always wore his priestly black with the white collar. As in Bonn, he filled the lecture hall to capacity week after week, as early as 8:15 a.m., although roughly half the students who attended were actually enrolled in his courses.

What was his secret? It was not a matter of delivery. Although his light tenor voice was easily heard throughout the auditorium, he rarely made eye contact with his students, preferring instead to lecture from a point high up in the back corner of the room. He never developed a repertoire of dramatic gesticulations.[5] The answer to his popularity lay in his lectures and speeches, in the clarity of the writing and quality of mind that underlay them. In order to discipline his thought, which at times could become abstruse, he would read his lectures beforehand to his sister, who was well endowed with Ratzinger intelligence even if she had never undergone a university education. If Maria said that something was too dense or unclear or otherwise incomprehensible, he would rework it. It was a great pleasure for him if, while reading to her in the kitchen, she slowed the pace of her labor and let the cooking spoon slip from her hand. Then he knew his message had touched her heart.[6]

But raw intellectual power is not enough to make a great teacher. Siegfried Wiedenhofer, an Austrian who studied with him in Bonn and Münster, described his manner with students as "uncomplicated, without a trace of vanity, generous, and helpful." Ratzinger was open to discussing with them much more than the subject matter of the given course: techniques of theological scholarship, ways to serve the Church and humanity, the right way through various personal difficulties.[7] While in Münster he regularly invited small groups of students to his home to treat them to a Bavarian evening, presumably consisting of delectable dishes, cheerful music, and lively bantering conversation using the dialect of his *Heimat*.[8]

But as in Bonn, happy new circumstances were quickly clouded by the sadness of familial loss. Once he and Maria were established in Münster, in the latter half of 1963, they heard that their beloved mother had contracted stomach cancer. To the end Mrs. Ratzinger kept her son, Georg's, house in Traunstein in order, despite her emaciated body and increasing weakness. One day she collapsed while shopping and was confined to her bed. Once again the Ratzinger siblings gathered at their parent's bedside. She died nine days before Christmas. Joseph's first role models in life and faith were gone from this world. Of them he wrote, "I know of no more convincing proof for the faith than precisely the pure and unalloyed humanity that the faith allowed to mature in my parents and in so many other persons I have had the privilege to encounter."[9]

During the next years in Münster, Ratzinger continued his work for the Second Vatican Council, and became more and more concerned by its development and representation in the media to the population at large. He issued his first warning in 1965, in a presentation at the university about Church reform. He delivered a similar message the year after at a conference in Bamberg, in northern Bavaria. The gist of it was this: It was wrong to view the Council from a modern democratic point of view. More and more people were coming to view the assembly of bishops merely as a parliament of the privileged. Didn't they vote to accept and reject documents? Didn't they revise them in committees? Didn't they take the advice of theological experts, recognizing that most of the bishops, being pastors and administrators, were not? The bishops certainly seemed to be acting like a parliament. But who elected them as representatives of the faithful? Why should they occupy positions of authority over Catholic theologians when the same appeared to be telling them what to say? The whole structure of the Church seemed to be upside down and turned inside out, a medieval relic that badly needed a popular overhaul.

The problem with these views is that they lead to the understanding of the faith as something manmade and not given; something fabricated and not *revealed.* The Creed cannot be revised, Ratzinger stated boldly. The Holy Scriptures were complete, and Catholic tradition cannot be simply swept from the table to be replaced with something more in keeping with the times.

Take, for example, the reform of the liturgy, which was initiated by the Council and completed under Pope Paul VI in the years that followed. It was a move to restore clarity, to expose the liturgy's architecture and enhance its meaning, involving the active participation by the people with the priest in the celebration of the sacrament. One could describe it as at once moderniz-ing and yet profoundly conservative, a return to the ancient Roman liturgy as purely as possible. Ratzinger was mostly supportive but certainly not instru-mental in any way. He had nothing against the old Latin rite, the so-called Tridentine Mass, the liturgical revision completed by the Council of Trent in the sixteenth century, known for its extensive use of Latin, the general silence in the congregation, and the priest celebrating facing the altar. But he thought the old rite was in danger of collapsing in on itself. The liturgy of the Mass, he said later, "is not just a privilege of the clergy, and not to be enclosed in a glass shrine as though it were a priceless heirloom, but is, by its very nature, the worship of God by all in common."[10]

Ratzinger readily accepted the liturgical reforms that came in the wake of the Council, which allowed for greater use of the vernacular, more prayers to be spoken by the congregation, and the celebrant to face the faithful over the altar. He was appalled, however, at the almost immediate prohibition of the old Latin rite, the basic replacement of one missal by another. That above all, he argued, gave the impression that the liturgy is merely something thought up by a group of people at a given time, to be reshaped and replaced by others as they happened to desire it.

In its form and content, the Catholic Mass is something organic, "a living de-velopment," a gift to human history, which must be preserved in its continu-ity.[11] Hip-hop masses for teenagers and teddy-bear liturgies for little kids are just not appropriate. And no parish or community is to regard the liturgy as the property of its constituent members. When the Council embraced a new openness to the world, it did not mean that liturgy is merely a celebration of the useful social work that each parish performs. The openness to the world reinforces the fact that the Church is a missionary institution, and her primary means of evangelization are prayer and the sacraments. It is against her mission to close in upon herself, or to throw her sacraments up for grabs.

The Council would officially end on December 8, 1965, and then the real fighting began, and in some circles still goes on to this day. For over four decades, Ratzinger has held firmly to his interpretation of the great event, which is based on the Council's four central documents: the Constitutions on the Liturgy, Revelation, the Church, and the Church in the Modern World. These are to be *read* first in their entirety, and taken at face value, before one starts extrapolating general principles that are actually stated nowhere. Indeed, Cardinal Avery Dulles, SJ, a famous American theologian, has been able to find only one area in which Ratzinger has apparently changed his tune: bishops' regional conferences. In the 1960s he spoke of the Synod of Bishops as a vital institution, "a permanent Council in miniature," an intermediating body between the bishops and the Pope, founded with theological justification.[12] Perhaps he saw them as a means to help liberate the pope from Roman Curia's rigid bureaucracy. Nearly twenty years later, however, Ratzinger declared bishops' conferences to be without a theological basis, merely useful, coordinating bodies for practical purposes. But this is at most a minor matter.

·⸬⸺ TÜBINGEN

Tübingen, located in Baden-Württemberg, Bavaria's sister state in Germany's south, is a small city whose tightly packed houses and old-world charm were thankfully preserved from Allied bombing during the World War II. This riverside town sustains one of Germany's most venerable universities, an institution with a long history of excellence in theology, especially in Lutheranism. The university had tried to get Ratzinger to join its faculty as early as 1959, but it was not until 1966, when it established a second chair in dogmatic theology that he took the job.

Why did he go? There was nothing wrong with Münster. "I began to love this beautiful and noble city more and more. And yet there was one negative aspect: the great distance from my native Bavaria, a land with which I have deep inner bonds. I was being drawn to the south."[13] Plainly and simply, after several years in Germany's north, he wanted to be closer to his *Heimat*. His sister was apparently of the same mind. She had never gotten used to the rainy flatlands of the northwest and the sometimes not so subtle derision with which northerners react to the Bavarian accent—the dialect they usually find inscrutable.

In Tübingen Ratzinger cut a memorable figure. He was often seen pedaling through the narrow streets on his old bicycle, dressed in black, sometimes sporting a thick sweater, with a beret on his head. A student of his described him as "not yet forty, already had white hair, but a smooth, young face, with strikingly alert eyes, that looked good. At times he smiled dreamily." His high voice "sounded soft, dignified, and somehow informal."[14] He frequently celebrated Mass in the chapel of a nearby Catholic girls' dormitory and sometimes would take the ceremonial role of tapping the beer keg at university festivals.[15] Living together, as before, with his sister, in a small rented house, the two were much happier in Tübingen than they had been up north.

Another appeal of Tübingen was the presence of another star among German theologians, Professor Hans Küng, who had also been at *peritus* at the Second Vatican Council. Ratzinger had reviewed his doctoral work, knew him, and liked him personally, and Küng had strongly supported bringing Ratzinger to the faculty. They had dinner every Thursday, edited a journal together, and frequently shared comments on each other's lectures.[16] But the two of them differed sharply as to their theological appraisals of the Council, something that they accepted as natural and to be expected in academic circles, and not a serious hindrance to their collegiality. Küng was a much more enthusiastic supporter of structural Church reform, and he was particularly critical of the concept of papal infallibility. In the years to come, he would be cited by the Vatican and suspended from teaching at a Catholic institution for espousing views that are, frankly, not Catholic. Ratzinger had nothing to do with this decision.

While at Tübingen, Ratzinger completed one of his greatest contributions to theology. His masterpiece, *Introduction to Christianity*, quickly became a best seller when it first appeared, selling at least 88,000 copies over three decades, in twenty languages (most recently Russian), which is a promising sign for the gradual improvement in Catholic-Orthodox relations. But its author remains modest in his appraisal of the book, which is basically a transcription of a series of tape-recorded lectures he delivered at Tübingen: "I was and am conscious of its many flaws, but through it I was able to open the door for many, and this brings me satisfaction. . . ."[17] The work is an extended explanation of the Apostle's Creed, which is recited at Sunday Mass all across the world. (In the United States, the Nicean Creed is used more often.) If you are a Catholic who has a shadow of doubt about what you are actually saying when you speak this part of the liturgy, you should read the relevant portion of Ratzinger's book. (The Table of Contents will tell you right where to go.) If you would not describe yourself as a believer but are interested in Christianity, this book will explain what the religion is all about.

It is organized exactly according to the phrases of the Creed. As usual the author's thought is crystal clear and based on solid learning, evidence, and argument. Ratzinger gives space for counterarguments and lays them before the reader in brief, fair terms. When at times the discussion becomes somewhat abstruse, the author gently guides the reader back to the basic question at hand, summarizing what he has to say at the end of most sections. As usual, Ratzinger's books do not make for light reading, but the prose is always clear, and he never tries to disguise confusion behind a screen of jargon.

Introduction to Christianity is shaped around a single question: But what if it is true? In other words, what if Jesus really was born of a virgin? What if he really was a divine man, the Son of God, God himself? What if he really rose from the dead? Ratzinger acknowledges most modern arguments to the contrary, but he argues that the simple acceptance of these wondrous occurrences cuts through the Gordian knot of doubt, skepticism, and cynicism. When you look at what has happened in the world, at what happens this very day for so very many people, it just might be the simplest and most reasonable explanation.

In this book, we find the same message that the Pope is working to spread today, something he has believed and taught throughout his life: the Christian faith, like that being called God, does not come from within but without. The Lord is not a creation of our subjective thought; he is not subject to the whims of our individual conscience. "The point at issue here is whether man in his relations to God is only dealing with the reflection of his own consciousness or whether it is given to him to reach out beyond himself and to encounter God himself."[18]

Ask yourself, *What is reality for me?* Are you the central being in your life, basically an island unto yourself? Are you merely a thing, a biological mechanism, however wonderfully complicated, that can only think in and of itself, in response to exterior stimuli? Or are you not a thing but a person, a one and only "I," a unique and mysterious creation never to be replicated before or since? And if you believe this, is there another being that made you, freely, as you are and can be, a being that basically gave you as a gift to yourself and others? And did this being create the universe *as it truly is* (which is far greater, more complicated, and mysterious than how we claim to know it through the various fields of science)? And can you, limited and imperfect as you are, enter into a relationship with this creator, ineffable and limitless as he is? The Christian answer to this last question is a definite "Yes." How? Through faith, because the faith that we experience, like our very lives, is *given* to us, and therefore we are in no position to alter it without dishonoring the giver, whether in the name of reform or progress or rationalization or whatever. Try as we might, we cannot think better than God. This simple idea, one might say, lies at the heart of Ratzinger's so-called conservatism. The gift of revelation is to be preserved, protected, and not subject to constant revision lest we mutilate it beyond all recognition.

This does not mean, by any stretch of the imagination, that he thinks the Church has been perfect over the centuries. The chronicles of scandals are as well-known to him as to any reader of history. But these do not distress him. Rather, he takes heart in them, only in the sense that such sad occurrences remind us that the Catholic Church is not holy because of the people who bear various titles, say the ceremonies, and wear a variety of costumes. Her message is what makes her holy. Her ability to bestow hope, and to show people the right way home, is proof of her special nature.

In the same year that *Introduction to Christianity* appeared (1968), Europe and the United States had to accept that they were in "the sixties." While U.S. college campuses were in an uproar, mostly about the Vietnam War, the military-industrial complex, and the Cold War against Communism in general, university students in Germany protested against everything their parents' generation stood for and promoted Marxism as the truth, the right way out of the dismal past into a bright, promising future. Revolution was in the air again, glorious and romantic, but much sexier and hedonistic than it had been in the previous two centuries. Young people were besotted with sex, drugs, rock 'n' roll, Lenin, Che Guevara, communes, hippies, and a rendition of Jesus who thought it was all just great.

The young revolutionaries aimed to divest the universities of their burdensome adherence to tradition in all its forms and to replace it with a new ideology, positive and utopian, in order to achieve a Paradise on earth. Forget about the other side of eternity. What counted for them was the here and now. For many, their Christian faith was strong, but it had shifted from God to man. The Church was to be the means to a glorious end, at once unrealistic and unassailable.

As dean of the faculty, Joseph Ratzinger had to deal with this at a number of levels. At home in academe, he had no problem debating the most serious issues, answering the most challenging and fundamental questions the human mind can conceive, but the late sixties saw the dialogue of reason turned into one of violence and intimidation. In his lecture hall, people distributed Marxist fliers, whistled, heckled, and behaved like a bunch of borderline adults, or overly developed four-year-olds. But things never turned violent; no one jostled him or took away the microphone. "I myself had no problem with the students," he said.[19] Most of the demonstrations were led, he claimed, by members of the "nonprofessorial staff," which included university bureaucrats, instructors, and professors' assistants—basically untenured faculty members and administrators.

Ratzinger responded by standing his ground. His brother says of him, "He is not aggressive at all, but when it's necessary to fight, he does his part, as a matter of conscience."[20] When the members of the Catholic student union demanded to elect their own chaplain, Ratzinger refused, saying that was, is, and shall be the right of the bishop. When the union of Protestant theology students circulated fliers declaring the crucified Christ a symbol of sadomasochism and the New Testament "a document of inhumanity," Ratzinger and a Protestant colleague appealed to the members to tone down the rhetoric, but to no avail. The chants of "Jesus be damned!" went on unabated. In an interview years later, Cardinal Ratzinger told what he learned from the uproar at Tübingen:

I understood that it is impossible to argue with terror . . . and that a discussion with terror signifies collaboration. . . . In these years I also learned where a discussion must be broken off, so that it does not turn into lies, and where resistance to the preservation of freedom must begin.[21]

A few who knew him or witnessed the events of 1968 say that he generally grew quieter as the antics became more hysterical.[22]

Some have written that this was the most distressing period in Ratzinger's life.[23] I do not see how such a theory could be true, unless Ratzinger had somehow forgotten everything he had lived through in World War II. Admittedly the threat of nuclear war was very real to these young people, and they were disgusted with the silence of their elders in regard to German crimes against humanity in World War II. Many had just cause for complaint, but the protests, sit-ins, concerts, and orgies were more reminiscent of an extended adolescent fit than a world-altering revolution. The revolutionary wave of the late 1960s was just as atheistic and nihilistic but more hedonist than its Nazi ancestor.

Ratzinger had seen all of this before in Bavaria during his youth under the Nazis, and it must have been thoroughly depressing. The difference this time around was that the student protesters did not have the institutions of government in their control, try as they might. It kept things from getting completely out of hand. Yet this was more than adolescent venting of pent up frustration. A real left-wing terrorist organization did grow out of the student movement, the so-called "Red Army," a group of kidnappers and assassins that later claimed dozens of lives across Germany. Through it all, according to Wolfgang Beinert, a fellow priest, Ratzinger kept up his discipline of prayer, liturgy, scholarship, and teaching. When he, his siblings, and friends took little outings to various shrines and churches in the surrounding Swabian countryside, Ratzinger would light a candle before an image of the Virgin and pray "with the simplicity of a peasant."[24]

He was generous with his left-leaning hippie students. One long-haired, shaggy-bearded fellow who chose the theme of "Redemption as Liberation" for his final exam in dogma, argued, in perfect keeping with the fashion of the day, in favor of Marxist-leaning liberation theology, that salvation must entail liberation not just for the soul, but for the whole person, especially in his social and

MARKTL AM INN

The Ratzinger family lived in the upstairs apartment of this house in Marktl am Inn for two years after Joseph was born. The new bronze "Benedict column," commemorating the Pope's visit in September 2006, is in the foreground.

MARKTL AM INN

The neo-Gothic altarpiece in St. Oswald's Church in Marktl am Inn. In front is the font where Joseph Ratzinger was baptized on April 16, 1927. (Photo by Christine Vinçon)

ALTÖTTING
The Chapel of Mercy is the most sacred shrine of Bavaria.
(Photo by Christine Vinçon)

ALTÖTTING
A front-row snapshot of Pope Benedict
XVI greeting the faithful in Altötting,
September 2006. Behind him is Cardinal
Friedrich Wetter of Freising and Munich.
(Photo by Michaela Spranger)

TITTMONING
A lateral view of the colorful façades
in Tittmoning's main square.

THE CHIEMSEE

A view across the Chiemsee toward the Alps beyond.

(Photo by André Schneider, www.rabbarien.de)

TRAUNSTEIN
The Ratzinger family farmhouse in Hufschlag, near Traunstein, with winter snow.

FREISING
The spectacular baroque interior of the
cathedral in Freising, decorated for Christmas.

REGENSBURG
From the banks of the River Danube, a timeless view of the city of Regensburg.

REGENSBURG
St. Peter's Cathedral in Regensburg, from the gate on the eastern side of the square.

REGENSBURG
The famous twelfth-century stone bridge over the Danube at Regensburg.

MÜNCHEN

The center of Munich, the *Frauenkirche* (Lady Church) on the left
and the neo-Gothic *Neues Rathaus* (New City Hall) on the right.

political dimensions. "Ratzinger was less than pleased," the man recalls. "I saw that in him. But he only smiled mildly and gave the theme a somewhat different nuance: 'Redemption as Liberation'—with a question mark, eh?"[25] The student passed without tribulation.

Still other commentators claim that the events in Tübingen transformed him from a liberal, reforming Catholic theologian into the stodgy, conservative, defensive Ratzinger caricatured in the media in the last four decades. But to make such a claim implies that there was a fundamental shift in his thought about a whole array of matters essential to the Church. Personally, I have not been able to find such a thing. In 1968 he did sign a declaration calling for more freedom for theologians teaching at Catholic institutions, and in the following year he signed another in favor of a wider elective process for choosing bishops, but shortly afterward he withdrew his support from the latter, saying in effect that he had been pressured into doing the wrong thing.[26]

One thing is for sure. The upheaval at Tübingen showed him, yet again, how theology can throw itself at the cloven feet of politics. Growing up in Nazi Germany, Ratzinger knows that a revolutionary political movement that promises future utopia is a lie—and usually lethal. He has noted on more than one occasion how many Christian theologians bought into the whole Nazification of the faith; i.e., the attempt to turn Jesus into an Aryan who had a real will to power and martyred himself in a struggle against the Jewish power structure. The fact that so many readily accepted this revolting, racist recasting of the Christian story shows how subject the human mind can be to deception. At the end of the 1960s Ratzinger watched a group of theologians leap into bed with Marxist messianism. "The worst books," he has said, "destroying the figure of Jesus have been woven from the apparent results of scientific exegesis."[27]

Joseph Ratzinger may be a professional scholar by training, but his Catholic faith is simple, from a humble Bavarian background. For much of his career, he has explicitly warned people against listening to professors of theology when it comes to basic matters of faith. Although he is not alone in this point of view, among theologians he is definitely the member of a minority.

A recent study by a scholar at Notre Dame points to just how distorted the theological landscape has become. The results of a nationwide survey show that the majority of undergraduates take introductory courses in religion primarily in order to mature their belief and hone their command of ethics (70 percent at religious colleges and universities and 50 percent at secular), but only a minority of professors and instructors share the same goal (42 percent at religious institutions and only 8 percent at secular).[28] What accounts for the divide? What other goals could the instructors have in mind? Why the discrepancy?

Most theologians teaching at American Catholic institutions of higher learning are hostile to a traditional, unadulterated faith. If you do not believe it, then note what is presented at theological conferences. Many feel that the Gospels have always been and always will be misread and misapplied by the coterie of elderly men who comprise the uppermost echelons of the Catholic hierarchy. The magisterium is to be mocked, dismissed, ignored, attacked, and denigrated almost as a sign of good manners among those who are really in the know. Many theologians in this day and age tend to argue that Jesus was a liberator and a rebel. His message was about improving the world while we are in it rather than waiting for it to pass along in its messy way as it does. Jesus was merely a pleasant teacher from the Levant, fabricated by his borderline followers into a figure that makes a mockery of reason. His message was one of individual liberty, freeing the Jews from the strictures of Old Testament law. The essence of Christianity is the wholesale relief from burdens of all kinds.

To the Gospels and patristic literature they apply the scholarly tools of linguistic deconstruction, historical criticism, and analytic philosophy (if you have never heard of any of these you are not missing much) and the results are, well, self-fulfilling postmodern prophecies. Above all, Jesus wasn't really God in the flesh (an inexplicable proposition in terms of material science) but a liberator and rebel, whose struggle was against Imperial Rome rather than the local Jewish priestly hierarchy, the Pharisees, and others. The Gospels are little more than bigoted, anti-Semitic tracts, by writers who were attempting to make good with Rome for the sake of their fledging church venture. Catholic tradition, doctrine, and orthodoxy is all about power and domination, devoted for many centuries to homophobia and sexism, obsessed with sin and damnation, and generally oppressive to humankind. Such theologians make elaborate arguments in favor of same-sex relations and relationships of all forms, easy divorce, abortion and contraception, female priests, and the like, all in the name of increasing human freedom.

To Pope Benedict, all these theological arguments, however ingenious, are merely examples of *Beliebigkeit*, one of those wonderful German words that defies direct translation. It refers basically to the business of living life the way you want to, according to your individual taste and pleasure. I would associate it with pride. For centuries scholars, like almost everyone else, have tended to suffer from this sin—history abounds with glowing examples. Theologians these days are shaping the Gospels to fit their own desires, will, pleasures, etc., however perverse they may seem in the context of nearly twenty centuries of Christian thought.

Indeed, the Gospels anticipated the problem with the theological profession. You can find it in the temptation scene in Matthew (4:5-7), when the devil challenges Jesus to hurl himself down from the Temple parapet. Evil wields a perfect quotation and misapplication of Psalm 91: "Will not the angels bear you up, lest you dash your foot against a stone?" Cannot I, or anyone, use sacred writings to undermine what others have said, and continue to say, in faith? According to Ratzinger, "When theology becomes mere knowledge about biblical texts and about the history of the Christian faith, but is not associated with other existential decisions, then it does not serve faith but destroys it."[29] Jesus Christ is and was as he is and was on his own terms, best explained by those closest to him, then and now. All attempts to redefine him according to the prevailing cultural or political norms of the day are, when you think about it, actually ahistorical.

Think about a few of the renditions from the last century or so: Christ as an enlightened man of reason, a scientist, a Marxist, a revolutionary, a mere moralist, a hippy, a New Age relativist, a gay liberator—and then there is Dan Brown's depiction in *The Da Vinci Code*. The fact that all of these contrast glaringly with one another, and that none lasted for long, is the best testimony to the falsehood they hold in common. The challenge for us is to take Jesus on his own terms, and if we cannot, then we should just be decent about it and leave him alone.

One last word from Ratzinger about this matter: "This is *His* Church, and not a laboratory for theologians."[30]

ᴛHE PLACE HE CALLED ᴴOME: ᴿEGENSBURᏩ

"His bond to the city and diocese of Regensburg, where he used to be a theology professor, comes through his family. His brother lives there. His parents and sister are buried there."
—*Friedrich Cardinal Wetter, former Archbishop of Munich and Freising*

"Here I really am at home."
—*Joseph Cardinal Ratzinger*

After a year of turbulence in Tübingen, Joseph Ratzinger took a step down, so to speak, to leave a less than optimal situation. In October 1969 he began teaching at the new university at Regensburg, an institution lacking Tübingen's prestige, but he did not care. It does not take much experience in academe to learn how hollow that concept truly is. What use is fame and reputation when it has become infected with violence and irrationality? The move to Regensburg took Joseph back to his Bavarian homeland, to a small city beautifully situated on the Danube where the three Ratzinger siblings could be together again. His brother, Georg, had moved from Traunstein to Regensburg in 1964 to serve as the music director of the Regensburg cathedral and the famous *Domspatzen*, boys' choir. Since that time, Joseph and Maria visited him in Regensburg three times per year. The two knew the city well when they made their move.

THE NEW HOME

Pope Benedict has said he values Regensburg for its "intertwining of preservation and renewal in the city, of dynamism and youthfulness." Regensburg began as an ancient Roman camp built at the best place to ford the Danube, and you can still see Roman stonework in the city's old walls and gates. While the Roman Empire collapsed and vanished into history, this city never died out. It was the center of a large, important diocese during the Middle Ages, and it became the preferred site for Imperial Diets, or congresses, of the Holy Roman Empire for several centuries. Its array of church architecture is unparalleled. Within one square mile you can walk into a Romanesque church (now a museum), the soaring gothic Cathedral of St. Peter, the baroque Carmelite Church, and the exuberantly rococo "Old Chapel," where Pope Benedict recently blessed the newly restored organ that was named after him. Regensburg is also a university town with a young population and more pubs per square mile than anywhere else in Europe (or so the claim is made). On the city's outskirts are several cutting-edge firms in biotechnology, to say nothing of giants like BMW, Siemens, and Infineon, and Internet-based companies like Amazon.com. Regensburg is a thrilling combination of the old and the new.

Ratzinger's arrival in Regensburg appeared less than auspicious at first. During the move, a policeman making his rounds stopped the brothers in their borrowed car because it fit the description of a thief's. The officer checked the Ratzinger brothers IDs and let them go with the words, "Then drive on, in God's name!"[1] At the university there was no space for the theology department, which was housed in the city's former Dominican cloister, until the new buildings south of the city could be completed. When they were, they turned out to be about as ugly as one can imagine. When I first saw it, I really thought it was a prison complex. Dull and grey as a prison complex, the concrete structures cast in massive, clumsy shapes stand as icons to the tastelessness and inhumanity of the postmodern age. But bad architecture was unable to scare off raw talent. While Ratzinger was there, once again as dean of the faculty and later as vice president of the university, the institution built top quality departments in the humanities, sciences, and law.

Joseph's professorial salary allowed him to purchase a lot and build a house in the neighboring suburb of Pentling just south of the city, where other university professors, instructors, and scholars resided. From 1970 he lived there with his sister, with a spare room set up for their brother, who usually stayed in an apartment belonging to the choir school in the heart of Regensburg. The house in Pentling (Bergstrasse, 6) is really nothing special: a two-story, squarish concrete building, covered with a layer of white stucco, which until recently was somewhat soiled, cracked, and flaking. A fence surrounds the modest and unadorned yard. For many years there were only two simple bronze statues, one of a cat and one of the Virgin Mary, but they were removed for safety's sake after 2005. "Otherwise," the gardener said, "they would have been long gone." In preparation for the Pope's visit in 2006, his friends and neighbors had the house painted, a new fence built, and rosebushes planted. In a televised interview, the Pope said all the trouble people were taking was "a little embarrassing."

In Pentling, Joseph Ratzinger made himself at home in a Bavarian way. He got to know the mail carrier by name as well as the leader of the local volunteer fire department, whom he gently scolded for swearing on at least one occasion. He frequently took guests to the neighborhood inn, called "The Old Gate" *(Altes Tor)*. He kept a cat during the first few years in Regensburg, and after it died, he befriended the neighbor's, a feline called Chico.[2] For years the three Ratzingers would meet on Sunday afternoons, regularly at the house in Pentling, but also in Regensburg. On those occasions, Joseph and Maria would attend Sunday Mass or a concert featuring the boys' choir conducted by Georg, then the three would go to the Bishop's Court, a well-known restaurant right near the cathedral of St. Peter, to enjoy white sausages. They usually relied on buses or taxis to get to town, although sometimes Joseph's assistant in the theology department would drive them to places when necessary.[3] For the quarter-hour commute to the university Joseph rode his bicycle. Neither he nor Maria ever bothered to get a driver's license.

It was part of Joseph's rhythm to stay up till ten at night and rise at six the next morning. He would walk to Ziegetsdorf to celebrate daily morning Mass in the parish church, then head to the university for a day of work. For years Maria worked as the head secretary of a large firm, in addition to keeping the house clean and the kitchen well stocked. Georg would usually come to visit, and the three siblings would go to pray before their parents' grave. In 1974 they transferred the remains of their parents from Traunstein to the cemetery nearest to their home, plain evidence for their common desire to keep the family together. It is typical among devout Bavarians that someone in the family maintains the grave of the departed parents, and that all family members visit it regularly, after weekly Mass if possible, and always on All Soul's Day. The fact that Joseph had his parents' remains moved to the graveyard near his house in Pentling shows that he was planning to make that one of the duties in his retirement. As Pope, when he got his half day of private time with his brother, the two of them visited the grave site, where the Pope knelt and prayed for their souls.

At the university there was some of the Marxist revolutionary furor that had been prevalent at Tübingen, but not to the same extent. During one of his lectures, demonstrators carried into the auditorium a coffin decorated with the slogan, "Here science will be brought to its grave."[4] But recorded memories such as these are few and far between. A doctoral student who came with Ratzinger from Tübingen said that during the 1970s many theology students were deeply concerned about the "democratization of the Church," but the discussions were "not at all comparable to the brutal power struggles that we experienced in Tübingen."[5]

In Regensburg it did not take Ratzinger long to establish his usual reputation for excellence in teaching, based on his enthralling lectures, and his talent for encouraging discussion, fully analyzing his students' thoughts, and showing them the way to improve.[6] Former students say that his soft voice and brilliant thinking made him seem younger than his prematurely white hair indicated. A former student of his, Dr. Wilhelm Gegenfurtner, recalls that Ratzinger often joined the students on day trips; he was always open, friendly, and patient, wearing a simple smile on his lips. His lecture hall was packed, and he was accessible to students, especially to the least experienced of them. His exams, it was said, were not known for being terribly difficult. He soon established a circle of first-rate doctoral students from all parts of the globe—the United States, Canada, Benin, China, and Korea, among others. A professor recalls: "It was a newly founded university, and if an African was seen on campus, we said, 'That's a student of Ratzinger's.'"[7] It is said that he frequently helped cover the expenses of his poorer students, especially those from Third World countries.[8]

Beginning in 1970, in addition to his normal university duties, Ratzinger offered a weeklong theology course during the university's vacation time. The idea was most likely not his own but that of the well-known theologian and philosopher, Romano Guardini, who had contributed so much to scholarship and the liturgical reform movement in the early part of the twentieth century. Participants in Ratzinger's course would live and pray together, sharing a relaxed daily rhythm of activity, and engage in theological discussions. This was likely Ratzinger's preferred way to educate and develop his own thought. There is much less to gain from an academic culture of endless, embittered, and aggressive debate.

Ratzinger established a special friendship with one of his university colleagues, Reinhard Richardi, a legal scholar and practitioner. Richardi would drive Ratzinger home after meetings of the faculty senate, the two of them reflecting on what had been discussed. During the years of 1973–75, both men became deans of their respective faculties, so they had even more matters to discuss on a regular basis. Soon the Ratzinger siblings and the Richardi family celebrated various birthdays and anniversaries together. Georg Ratzinger would sit at the piano and accompany the Christmas songs, with everyone singing together. The friendship developed quickly, but when Joseph was named Archbishop of Munich and Freising in 1977, the Richardis thought it would go by the wayside. But Joseph did not let that happen. The whole family was invited to Munich for the banquet following Joseph's consecration, including the three little ones, who were the only children present.

When Joseph and Maria took breaks from Munich to return to Pentling, they visited the Richardis as before. "One must uphold tradition," said the Richardis. "I am of the same opinion," Joseph replied. The menu for the evening meal was almost always the same: a simple Bavarian noodle soup, slices of cooked meat or filet of chicken breast, followed by vanilla ice cream covered with warm, unsweetened cherry sauce.[9] When Joseph went to serve in Rome in 1982, the Richardis made it a tradition to spend a week in that splendid city. The Cardinal always made time for them, usually a dinner, and sometimes even arranged to join them for a day trip.

After Maria Ratzinger died of a stroke in 1991, the Richardi family played the surrogate role of family for Joseph and Georg. Joseph celebrated masses for the Richardi's twenty-fifth, thirtieth, and fortieth wedding anniversaries, in addition to weddings for the children and baptisms for the grandchildren. Joseph got to know them all. In fact, Reinhard Richardi says that the Cardinal's serious discussions with his teenage son, who went through the normal phase of questioning and challenging everything, were what kept him Catholic. When Joseph came from Rome at the end of December, the Richardis made sure that all the children and grandchildren were there to celebrate the Christmas season. The Cardinal would inspect the nativity scene with the children, and when he pointed out to granddaughter Anna that the plastic Playmobil® figurine of a nurse really did not belong there, the little girl retorted, "I put it in for when Maria and Joseph get sick."

On another occasion, Cardinal Ratzinger was sitting outside on the Richardis' terrace, sipping coffee on the terrace, when the two-year-old grandchild, Sebastian, came up to him and said, "Hey, Cardinal, come inside. I want to show you something." The Cardinal rose and followed the little fellow inside, to find an array of colorful dominos, spread out on the living room floor. Ratzinger knelt beside him on the floor—they have a cute snapshot of this—and listened to Sebastian's exposition about how the game was played. Margarete Richardi says that he always listened as well to children as to other adults. According to Magarete and her husband, Joseph always remained true to himself—a born listener, with a deep, authentic humility.

To this day, Richardi's wife, Margarete, the chairperson of a Bavarian association for Catholic women, frequently visits the nearly blind Georg Ratzinger, reading books and newspapers to him. It is mainly through him that the Richardis and the Pope exchange personal news and messages. Only occasionally does the Holy Father contact the Richardis by telephone. Meetings as in the past are no longer possible with one or two notable exceptions. On the Monday after his consecration as Pope, he invited a group of Regensburgers (including the Richardis) to lunch. When Margarete, who was wearing a long skirt and a bright red jacket, entered the room, Benedict said, "Look there! Mrs. Richardi in Cardinal-red, and still pure Bavarian!"[10] When Pope Benedict came to Regensburg in 2006, he was able to spend a few minutes with his friends of old. The new distance imposed by the reality of the papal office will most likely not destroy the personal bond, an obvious clue to the character of Joseph Ratzinger.

The Richardis were not the only close friendships established during the Regensburg years. There was the philosopher Ulrich Hommes, who engaged in stimulating conversation with Ratzinger for over three decades—at first when they were university colleagues, and then for a twenty-year annual get-together, whenever Joseph had the chance to come to Regensburg. After Hommes' wife died, Ratzinger made a point of inviting him to his house and accompanying him to his wife's grave. According to Hommes, "Everyone says" that Ratzinger is

> *a wonderful person. Personally very humble, thoroughly compas-*
> *sionate and very affable. He has a pronounced feeling for beauty in*
> *our world, beauty in art and in nature. He is not at all pedantic and*
> *certainly not interested in power. On the contrary, he loves humanity.*
> *And he is very devout, convincingly and contagiously devout.[11]*

Another of his university colleagues, Wolfgang Beinert, says that Ratzinger's humility went so far as to make him seem shy. He was extremely reluctant to show his own feelings about a subject or situation, but he was always friendly and understanding toward others, especially his students, listening to their concerns about their studies and careers. Beinert described Maria Ratzinger as "extremely intelligent and gifted," as much as her brothers, he added with emphasis. Never married, Maria kept close to them, as she had promised her parents she would. She invariably accompanied her brothers on day trips. This woman, says Beinert, deserves respect and praise, although her brothers earned more attention in their careers.

While there are those who call him shy, we must remember that Ratzinger was well known and usually in contact with many people. Once, on the way home from a retreat, he and a friend stopped along the road to buy some asparagus, and the woman selling them invited them to dinner. Ratzinger accepted and, according to Hubert Schoner, "soon found himself in a chaotic family tableau, with children scampering around the table. But he enjoyed it immensely."[12] Some guests at his house in Pentling like to tell of his affinity for cats. Frequently the neighbor's feline, Chico, would come over for attention. One day, shortly before Maria had finished making dinner, the cat came and laid a dead mouse respect- fully at Joseph's feet on the porch. He picked it up by the tail and carried it inside. When he returned, he made some joke about the selection of meat for dinner.

One thing all his Regensburg acquaintances agree upon: the Pope is as humble a person now as he has been his entire life. He was never known to flaunt his successes or trumpet his victories. During the 1980s and '90s, when Cardinal Ratzinger was based in Rome, he was offered a chauffeur service whenever he visited Regensburg, but he never took advantage of it. He and his brother preferred to use the public bus line to and from their home in Pentling. And the word from the diocese is that Cardinal Ratzinger never interfered in its business, as he would have had every right to do.

Returning to the university, it did not take long before Joseph was made dean of the faculty and later vice president. He never sought these administrative positions, and only took them out of a sense of duty. In the faculty senate, his colleagues say he never lost his cool. He was normally quiet during the debates, and after some time, he would volunteer to speak, quickly and fairly summing up the main views expressed and adding his own perspective on the issue. The president at the time, Dieter Henrich, said, "When he did raise his hand and say something, then the whole heated discussion was over. That shows what authority he already had even then."

In Regensburg, Ratzinger's corpus of scholarly, theological writings continued to grow. "The feeling of acquiring a theological vision that was ever more clearly my own was the most wonderful experience of the Regensburg years."[14] He published more than seventy articles and ten books on a staggering variety of topics: the fundamental principles of Catholic theology, liturgy and the sacraments, ecclesiology, Christology and Mariology (theological studies about the nature of the Church, Christ, and Mary), biblical exegesis (explanations of Holy Scripture), the history of Christianity in Europe, Church politics, social ethics, and music, Catholic-Orthodox dialogue, relations with branches of Protestantism, Catholic liberation theology, and the legacy of Vatican II. If there is one theme that unifies his writings on these subjects, it is his firm dedication to explain the Catholic faith to the common man—a faith that stands in its fullness, firmly rooted in Scripture and tradition.

His writing continued to attract a wider audience than Germany's academy. After his arrival at Regensburg, Pope Paul VI invited him to join the International Papal Theological Commission, a body of scholars working to keep the papacy up-to-date about the latest developments in theological scholarship. It was in that body that he became acquainted with the great Swiss theologian, Hans Urs von Balthasar, and in 1972 the two founded an international, scholarly journal for Catholic thought, *Communio: International Catholic Review*, started to meet the rising tide of relativism, the latest false promise of salvation, both within the Church and without. *Communio* thrives to this day, with fourteen different branches (as opposed to mere translations) in Europe and Latin America. It rigorously maintains a high standard of theological scholarship while staying close to the magisterium and Catholic tradition. It does not argue in favor of transforming the Church into something she is not and cannot become. Since its founding, Ratzinger has contributed over forty articles to *Communio* alone.

How can one write so much in only eight years? How does he do it? Actually, in an old-fashioned way—by hand, using a fountain pen—but there is much more to it than that. With good reason he has been called a "Mozart of theology."[15] Ratzinger writes his works the way Wolfgang Amadeus Mozart composed: straight from the head and heart, in finished form from beginning to end. If you look at the first draft of a Mozart piece on display at one of the great libraries of the world, or even at an Internet image, you will see what looks like a finished copy, ready to be placed on the conductor's music stand. From time to time, you will see a single chord with a line drawn neatly through it, the corrected version standing right next to it.

Compare Mozart's scores to those of Beethoven or Brahms, or most any other great composer, and the difference is startling. The other composers' works are sometimes scarcely legible. Many things are scribbled out, redone, crammed in the margin, looking like a much worked initial draft.

Ratzinger generates volumes in his head as he writes them out by hand or simply speaks. While he was archbishop of Munich and Freising, a bishop recalled that Ratzinger "would dictate while pacing up and down in the room, and you could then print twenty pages without a single mistake. The way he talked was fit to print."[16] "Ratzinger is a Mozart-type in theology, uncomplicated and charming," says an old village priest in the Chiemgau who has known him for half a century. "He is not problematic. He never scolds. He never complains. He's always kind, always cheerful, a Mozart-type. He too knew heaven and hell, but he never loaded down his music with his private problems."[17]

The Pope's secretaries and assistants say he writes lengthy quotations from other sources verbatim, *without looking them up*, some of them from works he has not read in many years. When the work is done, he or an assistant writes up the footnote references and checks the quotations and citations. The dimensions of his memory are gigantic.[18] He also remembers in great detail important moments in the lives of scores or even hundreds of people. When he sends congratulatory letters to priests on the thirtieth, fortieth, or even fiftieth anniversary of their consecration and first Mass, he often includes a vivid recollection of what happened at that occasion.[19] Returning to his books, in Regensburg his sister, Maria, would type up the pages filled with his lean, angular script, and as always, she would let him know whenever the writing and the thought behind it became impenetrable.[20]

Life for Joseph Ratzinger in Regensburg in the 1970s was good. He was back in his homeland; he had his siblings, a good job, an international reputation, and a pleasant, comfortable life. I am certain that if he had had his own way, he would have resigned his post in Rome in 2005 and returned to Bavaria to live out his days in his house in Pentling, in the company of his brother, writing and lecturing as he pleased. It would have been a well-earned situation, but the author of history handed him another duty, and it would have broken the code by which Ratzinger lives to have done anything but accept it. For decades he has taught that a hallmark of Christian belief is the forsaking of one's own will, desires, and goals in preference for those of God.

In June 2006 the mayor of Regensburg and a delegation of thirty-five others journeyed to Rome to give the Pope its highest honor. After the general audience, they handed him the document that declared him an *Ehrenbürger*, an honorary citizen of the city with a special set of legal privileges. The city has given out this honor only forty times in its history, and Pope Benedict XVI is the only living recipient of it. In a way, it is a pity that he will never be able to take full advantage of it.

Thus the title of this chapter must be set in the past tense. He can no longer call Regensburg his home. As Bishop of Rome and Vicar of Jesus Christ, he now belongs to the world community of Catholic Christians, and when he dies, his remains will most likely be interred forever in St. Peter's Cathedral in Rome, not Regensburg. During his apostolic visit to Bavaria in 2006, Benedict visited his brother in Pentling and prayed at his parents' grave, quite possibly for the last time. Popes do not retire.

ARCHBISHOP and CARDINAL

*"['Bishop' is a] form of the Greek term episcopos. This word means
one who has a vision from on high, who looks with the heart."*

—*Pope Benedict XVI,*
Wednesday audience, May 10, 2006

When Joseph Ratzinger came to Regensburg, he swore to himself that it
would be his last move.[1] But destiny had other plans. In the summer of 1976,
immediately after the death of Julius Döpfner, the Cardinal-Archbishop of
Munich and Freising, the word was that the theologian at Regensburg was on
the short list of candidates for the successor. Ratzinger was inclined to dismiss the idea; he was perfectly content where he was and had never imagined
himself in such a position of leadership. He had also less than one year's worth
of service in a pastoral capacity. He had plenty of administrative experience, as
dean and vice president at the universities in Tübingen and Regensburg, but
the differences between a state-run academic institution and a major Catholic
diocese are enormous. The appointment would have been a daring oddity,
given the fact that the candidate had spent less than a year in parish service.

It was not long before a representative of the Pope, the diminuitive Archbishop Guido del Mestri, paid Ratzinger a visit in Regensburg, chatted in fluent
German about various matters, and then as he was about to go, handed him
a letter, telling him not to read it now, but at home, and then to think it over.
The letter was from Pope Paul VI, whom Ratzinger had never met in person,
but the Pope knew him through his *Introduction to Christianity* and through
vivid memories of his work at Vatican II. To Ratzinger, the appointment was
"a surprise, in fact, a shock."[2] He consulted his confessor, and the reply was
immediate: "You must accept."[3] He went to Mestri at his hotel and unloaded

all his worries, especially those concerning his sometimes delicate health and general aptitude. Mestri smiled, nodded, and asked if he would comply with the Pope's wishes.[4] Without fanfare or celebration, Ratzinger penned a note to the Pope on a sheet of the hotel's stationery.

BACK TO MUNICH AND FREISING

In March 1977, Ratzinger had to swear fidelity to the constitution of the state of Bavaria before the Minister-President, the Minister of Culture, and other officials. Only then could the consecration, scheduled for late May, take place. It was held in the cathedral in Munich on the eve of Pentecost in 1977, a joyous occasion graced with gorgeous weather, the first consecration of a Catholic archbishop to be televised live in Germany. Brother Georg conducted the Regensburg cathedral boys choir, which performed music by the German-Jewish composer Felix Mendelssohn-Bartholdy.[5] The occasion reminded Ratzinger "what a sacrament is—that what occurs in a sacrament is reality."[6] During his first homily, he said, "A bishop does not act in his own name. He is not there to spread his private ideas, but to be an emissary who has a message to deliver, one that is greater than he is. . . . He is not the boss but a coworker."[7]

After the ceremony, he went to pray before the gilded statue of Our Lady, atop a high column that had been erected in 1638 in the *Marienplatz* at the heart of the city, in thanks for its deliverance from total destruction by Swedish invaders during the Thirty Years' War. For many years the column was the destination of processions and no one could ever say how many liturgies, litanies, and rosaries have been said at its base. The welcoming cheers of the faithful reminded Archbishop Ratzinger that their excitement had nothing to do with his person, except for the fact that he was to be their next "bearer of the Mystery of Christ. . . . It was joy over the fact that this office, this service, was again present in a person who does not act and live for himself but for Him and therefore for all."[8]

Thus ended Joseph Ratzinger's career in the ivory tower of academe. There is a reason why he ended his autobiography in 1977 even though he wrote it in the mid 1990s: After becoming an archbishop, he could no longer pretend to be an individual pursuing his own self-fulfilling career. The story of his own life was over. No matter where he would be—whether in Freising, Munich, or

Rome—or what he would do—as an archbishop, cardinal, or pope—after his consecration, the whole purpose of his existence was to serve the Church and uphold Catholic truth, to perform holy deeds (the sacraments) and spread the Gospel of Christ, just as the first apostles had done.

For his motto, he chose "Co-Worker of the Truth," a phrase stemming from John's third letter in the New Testament, showing in a concise way how he conceived his new identity. He would merely be one of many, in the great, ongoing epic in human history that is Christianity in the world. He would support truth, based on Holy Scripture and Catholic tradition, more as something to be tended for its fruits than as a prize to be won in battle. In his coat of arms, in keeping with the bishops of Freising from the last thousand years, appear two images of the head of a crowned Moor, although no one really knows what the symbol stands for. Left with two free spaces, he chose a shell and a bear. The shell is reminiscent of St. Augustine who, when he saw a little boy on the beach spooning the sea waters into a sandy hole, was struck by the parallel with his own knowledge of God. The mind of man can no more understand the mystery that is God than the hole can hold the waters of the world's oceans: a humble statement by one of the world's great theologians. The bear refers to an old story about St. Corbinian (see chapter 5). Once again inspired by St. Augustine's teachings, Ratzinger chose the bear to depict himself a pack animal for God, to go wherever God wills and take on whatever burdens it pleases God to load on his back.

His new archdiocese was traditionally associated with the red hat, which came soon enough, a mere three months after his consecration; in fact, on June 27, 1977 a consistory in Rome made Joseph Ratzinger a Cardinal of the Church. It is fair to say that he was chosen due to his solid scholarship, brilliant writing, and faithful teaching. The elevation meant that Ratzinger never had to scrape and clamber through the ranks of an administrative hierarchy. He stepped out of academe into the foremost ranks of Catholic leadership. There was no chance for him to pursue a careerist path in Vatican circles.

Much of what a bishop does, in a predominantly Catholic country like Bavaria, is extremely pleasant. Joseph Ratzinger had been a well-known professor and had been much appreciated as a teacher, but now he was cheered wherever he went. He was the central focus for numerous ceremonies and processions, dressed in the rich vestments reserved for members of the episcopate. People looked to him as an authority and inspiration far beyond the range of a university professor. He crisscrossed his large, wealthy diocese, preaching in gorgeous churches and being feted in dozens of parishes. He had the privilege of confirming children and ordaining new priests. He blessed babies and posed for photographs with proud parents and untold numbers of other people. He occupied a beautiful little palace in the heart of the city of Munich and was automatically inducted into the upper echelons of the Bavarian state and society. But that is only part of the job.

The rest is a bit like a nightmare. Once an auxiliary bishop in Boston related to me what his predecessor told him on his elevation. "Congratulations," he had said, "Now you will never have a bad dinner as long as you live, nor will you hear the truth either." Ratzinger, in accordance with his motto, dedicated himself to speaking truth to his flock. "What would Jesus find," he asked in his first public letter, "if he came to a parish today?" The answer cut to the chase: stubborn, selfish mediocrity of heart, "the coldness of those who regard themselves alone as true Christians." He said there was nothing wrong with the mantra "be nice to each other," but "it does not quite reach the height of the Gospel." He warned against "clogging the heart with possessions and pleasures" and against the "spiritual pollution" so prevalent in modern, moneyed Western culture.[9] You can imagine how well this went over.

A bishop is a target. Everyone expects him to solve all problems and satisfy all demands, and everyone he has to talk to has never done anything wrong. In the administration everyone is overworked, and no one is paid properly. Many parish members, especially the more privileged sort, are under the impression that, as the local religious authority, the bishop can change the administration of Catholic sacraments and the content of religious truths to suit local preferences. If he fails to agree, then he is to bear the blame for not seeing things their way.

A bishop is an overseer. He must make sure the Church is functioning as she should, and if this involves disciplining and defending, then so be it. Ratzinger did not shy away from conflict where it was necessary, and in his day there was enough of it. He had to deal with the mutually loathing groups of Catholics, one of whom claimed that the Second Vatican Council had ruined

Roman Catholicism, set against those who argued that the Council was merely the beginning of a perpetually frustrated process of radical reform. In 1977 there were only four candidates for the priesthood in Munich's seminary, and ordained priests were leaving the Church at a scandalous rate. Most written accounts of Ratzinger's years as archbishop dwell on the areas of difficulty while totally ignoring the positive moments and achievements. There are four events or topics that made the news but probably did not take up more than a small minority of his time.

The first had to do with a sacramental "experiment" that began under Ratzinger's predecessor, Julius Döpfner, which basically stopped requiring the schoolchildren who were to receive their First Communion to go to confession beforehand, leaving that sacrament for a year or two later, if at all. Presumably, the idea behind it was that the happiness of receiving God should not be dampened by the burdensome and scary business of fessing up childish wrongs. Perhaps in the spirit of the 1970s prominent people believed that confessing would make them feel bad or have less fun or harm their self-esteem. These individuals, lay and clerical, most likely reflected the attitudes of the opulent, indulgent middle classes. It is difficult to imagine Bavarian farmers making such demands and arguments on behalf of their children. Ratzinger was adamant. "No, the child has to confess."[10]

Confession is a relief, not a burden; it unburdens the encumbered soul. Almost everyone dreads going at some level, but that tells more about the human condition than about the nature of the sacrament. My friend who is a priest told me that after sixteen years of weekly confession, he still feels a little tightness in the chest, a sense of resistance, before he goes. But the unburdening before God brings relief every time. Children need to learn that the chance to tell the truth, to clear the air, to ask for God's forgiveness, is an opportunity, not a mere nuisance. Archbishop Ratzinger promptly stopped the experiment, but it took some doing to get all pastors to comply. He showed himself open to debate and discussion, and where possible, compromise and accommodation.

The next big media event involved a spirited, politically involved, thirty-three-year-old Jesuit, Hans Bischlager, who organized a "march of penance" in observance of the fortieth anniversary of Nazi Germany's invasion of Russia in 1941, and to admonish NATO in its nuclear weapons policy with regard to the same Communist state. To mark the occasion, he celebrated Holy Mass in the Marienplatz at the center of Munich dressed in a penitential robe made of jute, before leading the forty-odd, similarly clad participants on a fifteen-mile march to the former concentration camp at Dachau. The police got to them first and seized the robes, upholding a ban on politically charged uniforms and clothes. When Archbishop Ratzinger was informed, he demanded an explanation within ten days, not out of defense for Nazi military strategy, but in protection of the liturgy that had been politicized to a grotesque extreme. The costume made a mockery of priestly vestments. Ratzinger had nothing against a penance service per se, but to combine it with a popular gesture of public protest was to mix oil and water, or saltpeter, sulfur, and charcoal. Bischlager was told to celebrate Holy Mass according to established norms, precisely, and if he persisted in his creative approach to the liturgy he would be suspended.

The Jesuit responded with an explanation of his motives but struck back with a civil suit in the local district court. Taking the matter to the secular authorities was unnecessary and probably embarrassing for everyone involved. Ratzinger forbade Bischlager from celebrating any more services in the archdiocese, and his Jesuit provincial persuaded him to drop the court case. Later, Bischlager lost his license to teach at Jesuit schools and subsequently left the order. Ratzinger repeatedly warned all his priests, younger as well as older, never to be seduced into reconstructing the Catholic faith as an instrument of politics.[11]

The third topic was rather different on the surface of it, but similar at the roots. It had to do with the appointment of a professor of theology at the University of Munich, Johann Baptist Metz, the so-called "father of political theology." Metz, like Ratzinger, came from small-town Bavaria and made a soaring career as a proponent of liberation theology, the fusion of Marxist and Christian ideas that was born of the spirit of 1968. For years, Metz had assailed the Roman Catholic Church for being an instrument of bourgeois society, i.e., for supporting personal autonomy, private property, societal stability, and economic success, and making a mockery of her stated "messianic" virtues, repentance, love, and the readiness to suffer.[12] The department was unanimous in their support of him, and students collected signatures on petitions in added support.

The appointment was not Archbishop Ratzinger's to make, but there was nothing stopping him from registering a serious protest with Hans Maier, the presiding Minister of Culture who has the final word in most matters relating to education in Bavaria. We do not know what was said, but Ratzinger's favored candidate, the less famous theologian, Heinrich Döring from the University of Passau, was chosen for the position. Ratzinger probably argued that a professor of fundamental Catholic theology should support the Catholic faith and not try to turn it into an ideology of worldly revolution, which it is not and never was. A storm of complaints ensued, and a host of bad jokes. Among disgruntled pastors it was said, "I am the Lord, your professor. You shall have no other foreign professors besides me."[13]

The high point of Ratzinger's tenure as Archbishop of Munich and Freising was reached when Pope John Paul II came on his first visit to Bavaria in November 1980, which was the joyous background for the fourth big fuss that wasn't. At the final Mass held on the sprawling *Theresienwiese* (the fairgrounds where the famous Oktoberfest is held), Barbara Engl, the twenty-nine-year-old diocesan chair of the German Catholic Youth association, addressed the Pope on behalf of German young people as planned, but she departed from the text approved by the German Bishops' Conference. The Church, she said, seems "afraid" when it comes to reform, and it responds to issues of sexuality with restrictions and condemnations. Many young people cannot understand why the Church insists on celibacy for the clergy when the priest shortage is getting worse day by day, or why increased female occupancy of Church offices is not allowed. Engl spoke clearly and calmly. The Pope understood every word but gave no immediate response to the questions because time was limited, no dialogue was scheduled, and the winds were icy cold.

People were outraged. That same evening, the diocese's press spokesman claimed Engl had deceived them. Numerous members of the clergy were furious with her words, and in the days that followed she received a pile of angry letters from people all over Germany, decrying the shame she had brought upon them all. Other priests and lay people (young and old) thanked her for asking the critical questions that were on so many people's minds. Ratzinger was hard to read. The press claimed he seemed annoyed and embarrassed. He was quoted as describing the incident as "tactless and inappropriate."[14] It must have been an awkward moment, but was he as angry and scandalized as the media portrayed him?

Ratzinger made neither condemnation nor response. Why should he have? We should not forget that the decades of his academic career were spent in dialogue with other scholars and students, grappling with all kinds of difficult questions about matters great and small. His books are filled with them. They challenge every aspect of the Christian faith. He routinely asks why anyone should believe any of this. By 1980, questions about the Church's teaching about sex and celibacy were old hat. In June 2007, when Pope Benedict talked to a group of 10,000 young people gathered in Assisi, Italy, one young man asked whether truth really existed, it being more tempting to believe that each person has his or her own truth. This question obviously implies a much greater attack against Catholicism than anything Barbara Engl mentioned.

Furthermore, Engl claimed that the text she read was not something she thought up on the spur of the moment but the result of collaborative work with the youth leaders of the diocese, and she claimed that Ratzinger had seen it beforehand! He had told them to reformulate the points of critique into questions. The revised seventeen lines were sent to the secretariat of the German Bishops' Conference, but no response was forthcoming. Did they get lost in the shuffle of plans for the Pope's visit? The members of the media had only received the first, officially approved version; they were the ones most taken aback and, as usual, on the lookout for a juicy controversy to write about.

If all this is true, then Ratzinger could not have been very surprised by her words. If he had, in fact, said that her words were tactless and inappropriate, it was probably because she had decided to read her critical statements anyway, not posing them as questions, and without the approval of the German bishops. At any rate, he did not take time to speak to Engl afterward and help her through the media storm. But was it really his responsibility? She made her decision and the popular response was what was expected. When a Pope comes to a Catholic region, it is usually a time of general rejoicing. In the weeks that followed, word came from Rome that John Paul II had thought about Ms. Engl's questions and was not angered by any of them. Any other response would have been out of the ordinary. The Pope had survived Nazism and weathered decades of Communist atheism; the standard Western questions about sex and women do not bear the same set of teeth. She had made no personal attack. I would not doubt that John Paul II felt a measure of respect for her honesty and boldness, but this is pure speculation. On the whole, however, the episode seems to have been much ado about nothing.[15]

Such was the nature of the position, and Ratzinger led his archdiocese to the best of his ability from 1977 to 1981. Assessments will vary as is to be expected. Some in the clergy drew favorable comparisons with his predecessor, Julius Döpfner, saying that where he had been the fatherly figure, Ratzinger had tried to be more brotherly. Fr. Klaus Günter Stahlschmidt, who had been a chaplain at the time, sent him critical letters about this and that, all of which were answered almost immediately. Others said the archbishop spent too much time writing at his desk than engaging in personal discussions, but anecdotes tell another story. Once a priest in Munich wrote him a short note saying, "I do not always agree with your theology, but I'm working on it. And I like you personally." The letter writer expected either cold silence or a real scolding, but instead he received a warm, lengthy letter saying that it is not necessary to agree with the bishop about everything, "and a bishop really needs to hear it if you like him." Ratzinger's closest coworkers remember his even temper, his attention to their private worries, his lack of authoritarianism, his friendliness, affability, and love of life.[16] One said he was easy to care for: "He ate what was put on the table."[17]

Among the people, many loved his humble presence and the uplifting, uncompromising content of his homilies, addresses, and letters. He preached against *Beliebigkeit*, that tendency to want to live life merely and totally according to one's personal tastes, and he warned against the falsehood of relativism, in protection of simple faith against the elite presumption of intellectuals. Others, however, found him distant, unpopular, and arrogant. There was one occasion when protesters interrupted a speech he was giving at the University of Munich with a loud chorus of misappropriated Marian lyrics. Eyewitnesses said that he kept his composure, but after a few minutes he walked out, followed by 1,200 members of the audience to the Ludwig Church a short distance down the street, then picked up where he had left off. These things happen to bishops who do not mince the message of Christ.[18]

The truth is that he did not try to please everybody in every matter. He thought it better to speak the truth and get people to sit up and listen to it, however negative their reactions. He had his work cut out for him: in his words, "exhaustion of the faith, decline in vocations, lowering of moral standards even among men of the Church, an increasing tendency toward violence, and much else." He was in no position to smile blandly and welcome all these changes in the name of postmodernism. According to Ratzinger, "A bishop whose only concern is not to have any problems and to gloss over as many conflicts as possible is an image I find repulsive."[19] And yet he always sought to discuss the issues with the opposing parties, for the sake of clarity and mutual understanding. Even Munich's largest newspaper, the *Süddeutsche Zeitung*, said, "Of all the conservatives in the Church, [Ratzinger was] the one with the greatest capacity for dialogue."[20]

He communicated constantly through the written and spoken word; his pen rarely lay still on the desk. He enthusiastically took up the cause of the "new evangelization," as called for by John Paul II, a forceful, energetic proclamation of Catholicism, its truth and its values, in the rapidly secularizing world. He published over two dozen books, none I can recommend more to you than *Co-Workers of the Truth: Meditations for Every Day of the Year* (English translation, Ignatius Press, 1992), because it presents an assortment of compelling passages from Ratzinger's writings, one for each day of the year, as a set of meditations.

This brilliant, exalted Cardinal-Archbishop neither forgot nor neglected his humble past. He maintained contact with the people and institutions that were instrumental in his vocation. He made frequent trips to see his siblings and friends in Regensburg, where he remained on the university faculty as an honorary professor. He also took the time to visit a hospitalized woman who had served as his secretary. He usually brought her a little present, chatted a while, then blessed her before leaving for his next appointment.[21] One of his last acts as Archbishop was to establish a foundation for the boarding school at St. Michael's Seminary in Traunstein, which would guarantee its survival during times of financial difficulty. But, as in almost all other stages of Ratzinger's career, his stay in Munich did not last as long as he expected.

9

CALLED to ROME

"From the very beginning it was clear to me that during my time in Rome I would have to carry out a lot of unpleasant tasks. But I think I may say that I have always sought dialogue and that it has also been very fruitful."

—*Joseph Ratzinger,* Salt of the Earth

*I*n November 1981, after little more than four years of service, Pope John Paul II called Joseph Cardinal Ratzinger from Bavaria to Rome, to lead the Congregation for the Doctrine of the Faith (CDF) as its Prefect. The Pope had asked him before, but the Archbishop had said it was just too early to leave his diocese. Even the second time, it took a while for the Pope to talk him into it. What finally persuaded him was John Paul's agreement that he could keep on writing works of theology in the capacity of a private scholar, independent from his capacity as Prefect. It turned out that there had been an adequate set of precedents, and the Pope saw no hindrance in the present case. To a certain extent Ratzinger did not really know what he was getting into. He was well enough acquainted with the office as it functioned, but as he said later, "The world of the Roman Curia was basically completely foreign to me; I had no connections with it."[1] In this position Ratzinger would stay longer than anywhere else, serving for twenty-four years as Prefect, although even this was not due to his choice. He tried to resign twice in the 1990s—once after a small stroke sent him to the hospital, and then again a few years later—but each time the Pope denied his request. In 2001, after he turned seventy-five, John Paul II still would not let him go.[2]

The Cardinal-Prefect and the Pope worked well together. The two men had first met at a synod in 1977, and their friendship began at the conclave of 1978 after the death of Paul VI, the one that selected the ephemeral John Paul

I. Ratzinger had an immediate, high regard for the Polish cardinal's honesty, intelligence, authenticity, and holiness, and especially his humor, despite all the struggles and suffering he had observed and undergone throughout his life. "Here was a person who had nothing artificial about him, who was really a man of God and, what is more, a completely original person who had a long intellectual and personal history behind him."[3] Two months later, Cardinal Wojtyła was named the successor to St. Peter. It is pointless to speculate on Ratzinger's role in that decision.

The two shared much in common: a past overshadowed by Nazi terror, a common loathing for the atheist tyrannies of Marxism, a similar approach to the documents of Vatican II, and a common commitment to the philosophy of dialogical personalism. It can be summed up very simply in the fact that each and every human being is not a mere thing, not an *it*, but a person, who lives his life as an *I*. Everyone experiences other people, one's neighbor, through language, speech, and dialogue, as a *you*, and the same applies to God, who made all people in his image. This includes those who cannot speak: the unborn and the severely handicapped. Philosophical personalism, in the words of Pope John Paul II, "consists in the priority of ethics over technology; in the primacy of the person over things; and in the superiority of spirit over matter."[4] In his work for the Holy See (i.e., the Pope and the institutions helping him to govern the Church), Cardinal Ratzinger was to enjoy the Pope's full support.

PREFECT OF THE CDF

Ratzinger's new job was awful, the opposite of occupying a cushy academic chair, bolstered by a plush tenure cushion, at a prestigious research university where he could write what he wanted and when he wanted, speak only to the people who shared his interests, engage in rarified controversies as they appealed to him, and keep teaching to a minimum. As Prefect, he could not pick his work to suit his fancy, and he basically had to deal with everything gone wrong in the world of Catholicism.

It has been pointed out all too often that the CDF's ancestor is the Roman Inquisition, which was instituted during the Middle Ages to combat heresy, or errors in religious teaching, using a methodical procedure of inquiry and adjudication. It was originally conceived to be a step up from the traditional, Germanic barbarian way to handle such accusations, which often involved trial by ordeal, by dueling, or by lynching and mob violence. As everyone knows, the Roman Inquisition had a death toll and plenty of instances of corruption, but relatively speaking it was mild compared to adjudicating institutions in its day. The Inquisition became more murderous when the state co-opted its powers to further its own interests, nowhere more so than in Spain, where inquisitors sought out signs of disloyalty to the Crown. This historical truth is not an excuse by any means. The current form of the CDF derives from 1965, and it is now known as the "Holy Office." The Prefect and his staff of forty colleagues are meant to defend the purity of the faith as cases are brought to it; they do not smoke out any hidden enemies. The cases deal with people and publications (mainly in the Church's institutions) that may be seriously departing from Catholic faith, teaching, dogma, and doctrine in some way, willingly, willfully, or unwittingly. And there is no lack of them.

The various decisions made by the CDF from 1981 to 2005 tell us much about the institution, its collegial atmosphere, its passive nature, its careful proceedings, its commitment to dialogue, and its gentle approach to discipline, but rather little about Joseph Ratzinger. In the words of the current Prefect, Cardinal William Levada, the CDF produces documents that are "magisterial interventions that, responding to objections or deformations of the faith, or proposing with authority further reflections on revealed doctrine, support and help theological research."[5] It does not simply condemn free thinking theologians, but points out the areas of Catholic thought they need to consider— established truths passed down through the generations—that they might have neglected or diminished. The goal is to keep Catholic theology consistent with the faith of the apostles and the tradition that extends from them. If necessary, the CDF can demand that the persons in question take time from their duties to reconsider their individual positions, or, if they prove intransigent, the CDF can prevent them from teaching at Catholic institutions of learning. That is all it can do. It can only really state what is in line with the faith and what is not. The magisterium in Rome is so important because it keeps the faith on a single, broad highway where there are many lanes, and at times some rather daring and precarious movements between them. But those who go off the road are just headed for the tumbleweeds.

Most biographies of Pope Benedict dwell on the more celebrated cases that the CDF had to take on, usually without saying why. A number of biographies cover Hans Küng, Ratzinger's former colleague at the University of Tübingen, although he was handled before Ratzinger joined the CDF. Nonetheless it bears mentioning because it is a case in point. Küng's repeated attacks on various aspects of the papal office naturally raised the question of his adherence to Catholic teaching. Dialogue proved fruitless, and Pope Paul VI told him to take a year off teaching to reconsider his position on papal infallibility. Küng did not alter his stance, so he was deprived of the charge to instruct in the name of the Church and immediately became a living martyr for free thought, tolerance, liberalism, democracy, empowerment, and so on. Thereafter he followed his own path, professionally and intellectually, and he told Ratzinger in 1982 that he much preferred the new arrangement over the old. Küng continued to develop his thought about a "world ethos," world peace, and unity among religions. He is the classic example of the Catholic thinker who thought his way out of Catholicism.

Far too much ink has been spilled about liberation theology, a movement within the Church mainly in Latin America that is now essentially a spent force. To make a long story short, theologians of that ilk reenvisioned the Church as an instrument of political activism, of social revolution, to establish a kind of utopia on earth, admittedly for the benefit of the poor. The problem is that all too often it condoned violence and inhumanity as a weapon against the rich, powerful, and wrong-thinking, much in the way of Marxism. The CDF led by Ratzinger and supported by a Polish Pope who knew Marxism all too well, did its best to direct the movement into a proper, completely Christian channel.

In the case of Gustavo Gutiérrez, one of the originators of liberation theology, the dialogue with the CDF led him to reshape his thought and bring it back into line with that of the apostles, the Church Fathers, and Catholic tradition.[6] Other instances were not so successful. A Franciscan Marxist from Brazil, Leonardo Boff, condemned the hierarchical structure of bishops and priests and recommended dismantling it. Ratzinger had actually been one of Boff's dissertation advisors in the 1960s, apparently to no avail. The CDF asked him to take a year to rethink the issue, but it did no good. Boff eventually left the Church.

In addition, there was a flock of dissidents, each with his own, mostly regional, following. Fr. Charles Curran, a voice for American liberal Catholicism, assaulted Catholic teaching about sexual morality in a number of ways. While he did not leave the Church, the Catholic University of America fired him when he refused to come to an agreement with the CDF on the content of his teaching at a school chartered by the Pope. Curran sued, lost, and moved to a Methodist university. The Vatican made no move to defrock him or restrict his writing. In South Asia, there was Tissa Balasuriya, a senior theologian from Sri Lanka, who denied salvation through Jesus Christ, the need for baptism, and Mary's virginity. During the process he refused to sign a statement of Catholic faith, one that included the ban on the ordination of women. He was finally excommunicated in 1997. As a last example, there is Anthony de Mello, an Indian Jesuit, who, in seeking to reconcile eastern and western religion, turned Jesus into a guru, calling God a "pure emptiness." He died in 1987, and the CDF condemned his work in 1998.[7]

In 2000, the Western media zeroed in on Ratzinger when the CDF published a document entitled *Dominus Jesus*, mainly in response to such confusions from the Indian branch of the Church. This text reaffirms what the Catholic Church has said since her formation many centuries ago and restated during Vatican II: that Jesus is the Lord, the truth, the way to salvation and eternal life, and that his Church has to have an episcopacy deriving from the apostles and a worthy ceremony of the Eucharist. It does not say that no one outside the Church can be saved. It does not say that the will of God is identical to, totally defined by, and limited to the Catholic Church, but it does say that she is the best, the fullest of those that follow Christ's will. Media coverage featured expressions of annoyed regret from university theologians and members of Catholic religious orders better known for their reformist tendencies than their adherence to continuity with tradition. While perhaps *sounding* impolitic, it *said* nothing that has not been said plenty of times before.

No one should be under the impression that the CDF was solely concerned with the so-called "liberal" side of Catholicism; it had to address all instances of serious *error*. One of the more serious controversies involved a French archbishop, Marcel Lefebvre and his followers, who since 1970 has not only refused to say the *novus ordo*, the vernacular liturgy instituted after Vatican II, but has also refused to accept the Council's document on religious freedom.

In 1988, when Lefebvre ordained four bishops without the Pope's consent, he basically started a schism and thereby incurred a sentence of excommunication. All along, Lefebvre and his Society of St. Pius X acted on their own initiative; the Catholic Church reacted as the situation demanded.

The CDF under Ratzinger also made a major contribution to Catholic-Protestant reconciliation. In 1999, in the interest of establishing a theological basis for further advances in ecumenism, Ratzinger helped to author the "Joint Declaration on the Doctrine of Justification," which was then accepted by the Catholic Church and the Lutheran World Federation. During the Reformation in the sixteenth century, one of Martin Luther's many slogans was "salvation by faith *alone,*" which put him squarely at odds with Catholic tradition's insistence on the efficacy of faith *and* good works. Catholics and Lutherans had been quarreling about it ever since, until the two sides agreed on the text in the Declaration.

> *Together we confess: By grace alone, in faith in Christ's saving work and not because of any merit on our part, we are accepted by God and receive the Holy Spirit, who renews our hearts while equipping and calling us to good works.*[8]

Although a number of Lutheran groups rejected it, the World Methodist Council signed on as well in 2006. The document shows how major religious Christian communities can overcome a turbulent past and come to agreement about something as mysterious as salvation. It bodes well for the future.

Under Cardinal Ratzinger, the CDF opened its doors, at least partway. It allowed professional scholars to work in its archives, dating back to the infamous days of the Inquisition, for the purposes of research. In an interview Ratzinger said it took so long to arrange because the rooms in the archives were not at all set up to support such activity (retrieving materials, reading, writing on computers, photocopying and microfilm services, etc.) and funds were generally lacking. For years the CDF had one word processor at its disposal for the forty member staff. In the 1990s Ratzinger held frequent press conferences in Italy about the work of the CDF. Fr. John Rock, a former staff member, said, "He met often with the Italian press and truly won them over. They respected him because of his candor, which was not at all typical of a curial bishop."[9] The *Süddeutsche Zeitung*, Munich's main newspaper which has had many a critical thing to print about the Prefect of the CDF, stated, "In the Vatican it is said that without Joseph Ratzinger, the Congregation's number of condemnations and punishments would have been much higher."[10] Bishop Vincenzo Paglia von Terni said more or less the same: "He was still the most open man there."[11]

Nonetheless, the disciplinary cases above beg the question: Why were he and his team so militant against these creative, independent thinkers? Ratzinger's answer: "We feel our duty is above all that of protecting the faith of little ones."[12] "Little" refers to size of mind as well as body. Christ's message belongs to the simple as much as to ingenious intellectuals, and the former are not known for trying to change it. He remembers very clearly from his childhood in Bavaria the "inconspicuous saints, simple people, . . . kind old farmers, kind dutiful mothers who have given up their lives for their children, for their family, for the Church, and always for the other people in the village as well."[13] History supports him; on the whole, the simple have a better track record for humility, goodness, and sanity. Furthermore, on a number of occasions Ratzinger has cited the Gospel where Jesus articulates the special punishment awaiting those who corrupt the little ones. This is something he wants all people, including himself, to avoid.

In addition to this important work, Ratzinger had to deal with reams of petitions, inquiries, various investigations, and the business of what to do with wayward priests, including all those prosecuted in the American sex abuse crisis that broke in 2002. Perhaps much of the time it was a deeply unpleasant occupation, trying and depressing, in which the Prefect became the target of abuse more often than the recipient of gracious thanks. But the issues were wide-ranging and interesting. The CDF had to issue official statements about artificial insemination, women ordained as priests, Catholic politicians who support abortion and contraception, ministry to the needs of homosexuals, ecumenism, and the universality of Christ and the Church's mission in his service. The Prefect brought all these matters before the Pope during their regular Friday meetings, adding an additional meeting on Tuesdays when extra time was needed.

More noteworthy are the monumental, extra tasks that John Paul II handed the staff of the CDF, not to complete all by themselves, but to coordinate, oversee, edit, and get ready for publication. First, in 1982, there was the revision of the Code of Canon Law, the body of law that runs the Church, followed by something not successfully accomplished in over four centuries: a new catechism. This massive reference work, if you will, consists of definitive, concise explanations of all points of Catholic faith, and is fully in line with the documents of the Second Vatican Council. After this task was completed in 1992, there came the *Compendium*, an abridged version of the Catechism, in 200 pages as opposed to 800, that was finished in 2005 just after John Paul's passing. For the latter two projects in particular, Cardinal Ratzinger presided over the drafting, revision, and final preparation of the writing. His thought and phraseology are traceable in both. The Catechism and the *Compendium* will be the basic texts that explain the Catholic faith for decades to come.

In terms of procedure, the forty members of the CDF work as a team, using the most basic technical equipment for writing and communication, in conjunction with the bishops of the world. Many who came on their regular visits would stop in to see the Prefect who, using his half-dozen spoken languages, conversed with them directly about whatever pressing issue they wanted to address. Supporters and critics alike acknowledge Ratzinger for having listened to all sides of the argument, being open to discussion, and even welcoming public debate. In doing the research for this book, I am under the impression that just about everyone who ever met and wrote about him has noted his natural ability and desire to listen intently. This does not mean that he behaved with perfect equanimity; Ratzinger is the first to admit that he is less than saintly when conflicts become personal. "That in a personal controversy I occasionally react too harshly, I concede without further ado."[14] One of the constant challenges of being the Prefect is to prevent the work from becoming personal. The stakes are the truth, not his personal opinion.

For all these duties, the Holy See compensated Cardinal Ratzinger with the princely sum of 3000 euros per month, which had to cover the expenses for his household, lodged in an apartment in Rome (Piazza della Città Leonina, #1, apartment 8), just beyond the walls of Vatican City. As Archbishop of Freising and Munich, his monthly income from the state of Bavaria had been twice as large. Every day he walked to work, a few hundred yards to his office in the Vatican, his worn briefcase in his left hand, his silver hair visible under his black beret. His sister, Maria, had come with him from Munich to take care of the cooking, cleaning, and maintenance, which was made more difficult by the fact that she knew no Italian. She never took to Rome the way he did, but she accepted her situation because she wanted to help her brother in his vocation. Ratzinger is and was a priest, a coworker in the Lord's vineyard, before he became a professional scholar, and whenever the opportunity arose to serve the Church and the faith, he really could not say no. That was as true in April 2005 as it was throughout his entire life.

To see what was really on his mind, when he was done with the labor for the day, we must look at his private publications. These show more about what matters to him, more about his thought on many issues, than his work as a functionary in the CDF. How he found time for articles and book projects is a worthy question in itself. Friends of mine told me that the priest who married them, Monsignor Nevin Klinger, worked for a while as one of the Cardinal's undersecretaries in the CDF, and he said the man's work capacity was unbelievable. Ratzinger could keep many complicated arguments, documents, and projects in his head at one time, and often at the end of a day, when his secretary's brains were shot, Ratzinger would go work on his latest book project.[15]

⟡ BEST SELLERS AND MASTERPIECES

As said previously, Ratzinger's one condition to Pope John Paul II when he accepted the position was that he be allowed to continue to write and publish privately, as a theologian and cardinal, who could think out loud and in print about the Church and the world at large without always making binding statements in the name of the magisterium. We will begin with three book-length interviews with professional journalists that became best sellers and made Ratzinger perhaps the best-known figure in the Catholic world after Pope John Paul II. These popular works are engaging, demanding conversations that range over a wide field of challenging topics; they are arguably Ratzinger's most accessible works.

The first to appear was *The Ratzinger Report: An Exclusive Interview on the State of the Church,* translated in English in 1985, after great success in the Italian and German markets. While the text is as wide-ranging as its title indicates, I want to relay Ratzinger's perspective on two things of fundamental, almost obsessive interest to Americans today: money and sex. Money, he points out, is *not* the measure of all things, even if it seems that almost nothing can be done without it, and no matter how rich one may be, wealth does not entitle its possessor to all things. In a capitalist society such as our own, we need to remember that we are neither our own creator nor our own master, no matter how much we may will it to be. There is a similar situation with regards to sex. Our natural sexuality, that which is a structural part of our bodies, is not ours to make, discard, or exchange, although people can certainly alter their inclinations to fit shifting tastes as a matter of will. The human appetite for money and sex cannot afford to lose a healthy respect for nature. "To respect biology is to respect God himself, hence to safeguard his creatures."[16] Accepting this truth will bring peace to the appetites.

If you happen to disagree with him, ask yourself the question he poses: do those who reject the bonds of nature find in their postmodern, self-designed reality "an increase of happiness, a greater balance, a vital synthesis, richer than the one discarded because it was deemed to be obsolete?"[17] While answers can only be found on an individual basis, there is a host of data that indicates that the general response lies deeply in the negative. And as usual, it is the women who suffer more than men due to the contemporary loathing of the limits of human nature. Women, Ratzinger claims, give up the most in the current crusade to masculinize them, to discard their modesty, however natural and automatic it may feel, to tame their fertility in order to maximize their ability to provide immediate sexual gratification, and to denigrate any natural, personal inclination toward virginity.

The next book-length interview, *Salt of the Earth: The Church at the End of the Millennium,* which first appeared in 1996 and in English a year later, was an international best seller, and the best choice if you are going to read a single book by Joseph Cardinal Ratzinger. The interviewer is Peter Seewald, a German journalist and lapsed Catholic who had panned Ratzinger in print in 1993, but Ratzinger agreed to spend a day or two with him anyway. The experience returned Seewald to the Church. Although the book shows a heightened interest in the Church in Germany, the range of intelligent, probing questions reveals the Cardinal's perspective on matters far greater. Divided into three parts, the interview entails a brief dialogue about Ratzinger's life and upbringing, then turns to the problems facing the Catholic Church throughout the world, and ends with a section about the future of Catholicism, humanity, and the world as they enter the third millennium. Ratzinger had no preparation for the interview and saw none of the questions beforehand. At one point he broke off the exchange to have a little time for private prayer, but that was the only interruption. He never asked Seewald about his past or made any comment about his prior attacks. Ratzinger's answers are correspondingly fresh, immediate, compelling, and insightful. After it became an international best seller, Ratzinger said he was thoroughly surprised by the response.

An even more astounding volume is the next chapter, so to speak: *God and the World: A Conversation with Peter Seewald* (2002), a weekend discussion at the Benedictine monastery of Monte Cassino, the order's motherhouse founded by St. Benedict himself. This accessible book wonderfully reflects the astounding range of Ratzinger's knowledge and understanding. I simply cannot sum up its contents here, but the original German subtitle, "Believing and Living in Our Time," should give you an idea of the conversation's breadth of topics. After 460 pages, you have to remind yourself that all this was *said* in a single weekend, and Ratzinger never had the opportunity to look anything up. Seewald studiously prepared the questions beforehand, while the Cardinal "had to rely on the inspiration of the moment."[18] The result is as uplifting as it is impressive.

In addition to these interviews is a whole row of books that reflect the extent of their author's learning and his masterful ability to synthesize. I will only refer you to a handful.

For all those with questions or doubts as to what the Catholic Church is, *Called to Communion,* a little volume of 165 pages, is the most concise and authoritative explanation I have ever encountered. She is, first and foremost, a community of prayer, devoted to making God's love real in the world, offering forgiveness for those who turn away from sin. She is neither a social club, nor a political party, nor a welfare organization, although she cannot avoid the activities of all three. The book defines the pope, the bishop, and the priest, and shows the way toward real reform without cutting off and throwing away the past for the sake of the ephemeral present.

The Spirit of the Liturgy, as you might well guess, explains what happens in the Catholic Mass and all that it is meant to be and mean. Ratzinger shows a dazzling ability to interpret word, gesture, sight, sound, and scent. I must confess that in places the work can be extremely difficult to understand, but overall it leaves no doubt as to how the liturgy is best performed. What should we do if there are disagreements, new ideas, or rival interpretations? "Turn toward the Lord!"[19] At the center of everything should be the Cross, the God who comes to us even as we come to him, in the Eucharist. If the Mass is primarily the celebrant doing his own show for the pleasure of the congregation, that would turn a divine gift into a genuine farce.

Of course the greatest challenge to Christianity, and indeed to all religions, in our day is relativism, and its normal companion, nihilism. For many people, to state that something religious is true automatically implies that all other views are then false. So for the sake of equity, it is easiest to conclude that nothing can really be true and that we ought to regard all views equally, only in so far as they make no claim to absolute truth. The result is that no one should really believe in anything. A recent nationwide survey of American housewives asked them what virtue was most important for their children to learn. By far and away the first choice was tolerance. This speaks volumes about the state of America today. Tolerance only became a virtue rather recently.

Ratzinger's *Truth and Tolerance: Christian Belief and World Religions* addresses this thorny issue and makes the case for the existence of truth in a context of religious pluralism. He argues that the best way to proceed with interreligious dialogue is to grant the reality of God. "It is the dynamic of the conscience and of the silent presence of God in it that is leading religions toward one another and guiding people onto the path of God. . . ."[20] Missionary Christianity in the world, he maintains, is not a form of ideological imperialism over cultures such as those in sub-Saharan Africa, but "the history of the spread of liberating truth and love."[21] The idea of a totally tolerant, valueless culture is a lie. If relativism reigns supreme, then man can be nothing but a mere living object, a consumer of product and energy, a laboring device, valued in no other way apart from an amount of currency. The universal commonality of human experience everywhere in the world points more to the existence of absolute truth than to relativism and nihilism. Christianity, a synthesis of faith and reason, seeks to bring man to true knowledge of himself, and the reality of God, of reason and truth, cannot be replaced by good intentions. The book is densely written, a powerfully argued cross between intellectual history and Christian apologetics. It will be read and cited for decades to come.

With regard to Judaism specifically, his *Many Religions, One Covenant: Israel, the Church, and the World* describes the Jewish identity of Christ and explains the statements from the Second Vatican Council about the same. Ratzinger's basic argument is that Christianity does not counteract or replace Jewish law, but rather opens it to the entire world. In this issue as in all things, we should not endeavor to be like the God that creates, destroys, and lords over all, but the God who shows by example that we should be meek, humble, simple, and good, on a daily basis.

Finally, we come to Cardinal Ratzinger's contributions to history, cultural criticism, and political philosophy in two particular books: *Values in a Time of Upheaval* and *Christianity and the Crisis of Cultures*.[22] The first title is a collection of essays on the state, freedom, progress, democracy, majority rule, conscience versus authority, terrorism and the war against it, the future of Europe or the lack thereof. The book contains many of the ideas from *Truth and Tolerance,* but delivers them in plainer terms. In *Values,* Ratzinger issues a clear warning to European secularists: "A culture and a nation that cuts itself off from the great ethical and religious forces of its own history commits suicide." "Reason capable only of recognizing its own self and that which is empirically certain paralyzes and destroys itself."[24] The future for postmodern Europe is looking grim. If the brave new world of the twenty-first century West totally rids itself of the Christian values on which it was built, it will send itself headlong into history's next great struggle against evil.

In *Christianity and the Crisis of Cultures,* Ratzinger indicates he expects that evil to come out of the growing chasm between man's technological ability, particularly in the field of biotechnology (we might throw in nuclear weaponry as well), and his diminishing sense of moral restraint in using it. If we live as if God did not exist, then everything in life is open for change as we see fit. "Where nothing can be taken for granted, everything becomes possible, and nothing is impossible any longer."[25] Time will tell whether Ratzinger's message will prove to be prophetic. In this case, I hope to God he's wrong.

His publications have won him recognition as a world-class intellectual. The most prestigious honor society in France, the *Académie française,* elected him into its exclusive ranks, the first bishop since Cardinal Richelieu in the seventeenth century, and the first German bishop ever. He assumed the position—there are only forty—occupied by the great Russian physicist, humanitarian, and Nobel Laureate, Andrei Sakharov, joining the timeless company of Albert Einstein, Winston Churchill, Konrad Adenauer, and Vaclav Havel.[26] He debated with Jürgen Habermas, perhaps Europe's best regarded secularist philosopher, about reason, faith, and secularization, particularly with reference to liberal democracy.[27] Ratzinger's reputation as an academic has even risen into the heavens themselves; in 1990 astronomers named a newly discovered asteroid after him, (8661) RATZINGER.

·⛾THE BAVARIAN HUMORIST

Throughout the two dozen years in Rome, Ratzinger maintained his Bavarian connections. In his apartment in Rome he subscribed to the main newspaper in Regensburg and the Catholic periodical from Altötting. Early every Thursday morning he celebrated Mass in German in the church at the German cemetery in the Vatican. He came back to his homeland three to four times per year, visited his brother, old friends, and former students and colleagues in Regensburg, attended the Passion play at Oberammergau and concerts and conferences in Salzburg, prayed at a number of Bavaria's beautiful Benedictine monasteries, and hiked in the Alps. Often these were working vacations. It was in Regensburg that he met with the Bavarian leader of the German Protestant church and other theologians to put into final form the joint Catholic-Protestant declaration on a common theology of justification. As a final example, there is the popular Bavarian television personality Petra Schürmann, who lost the ability to speak after the sudden and tragic death of her daughter. Ratzinger invited her to Rome and spent lots of his time consoling her.[28]

And Bavarians never forgot him. After he became the Archbishop of Munich in 1977, the order of Bavarian Mountain Marksmen made him an honorable member, and when he left for Rome in 1982, he told them and the gathered crowd of onlookers, "I will always remain a Bavarian, even when I am in Rome." From then on they came marching, dressed in their traditional garb, to celebrate his sixtieth and seventy-fifth birthdays and the twenty-fifth anniversary of his becoming a bishop, with rounds of loud rifle fire. They came to celebrate his elevation to the papacy in Rome, and they greeted him noisily when he came on his apostolic visit to Bavaria in 2006. Many note with pride that it is the first time in the history of the Church that a Pope is counted among their members. In this Benedict sees no cause of embarrassment: "Your firearms have nothing to do with violence, hate, revenge, or destruction; they serve for joy, that it will be heard, splendidly, and will grow louder, in this world." In April 2007, the Marksmen attended the celebration of the Pope's eightieth birthday with their usual noisy pomp. Addressing the crowds, he said in German that the sight of all the Bavarian flags and *Trachten*, or traditional costumes, lifted his heart and made him happy.

While the world press has excoriated Ratzinger for decades for being the dour, killjoy Panzer Cardinal, in Bavaria he was decorated for his sense of humor. In January 1989, at Munich's "Narrhalla" carnival ball, he received the Karl Valentin Orden Award, in honor of the famous folk singer, humorist, and cabaret artist who had performed in Munich for the first half of the twentieth century and died in 1948. That same year, Joseph Ratzinger, himself a lifelong admirer of Valentin, made a self-declared "pilgrimage" to visit the grave of the great comic, walking the nine miles to and from the theological faculty in Fürstenried to the cemetery in Planegg.

At "Narrhalla,", Georg Lohmeier, a former school comrade of Ratzinger's, who had become a famous author in his own right, held the panegyric for the Cardinal. He flatly said he worked through Ratzinger's theological writings line by line and could find no justification for giving him the award. Then he said that he came across a newspaper interview where Ratzinger was asked when the Catholic Church would finally allow for female priests. The Cardinal's reply: "I am not authorized to make an 'our mother' out of the 'Our Father.'" On accepting the award, Ratzinger reminded the audience that for much of European history, the court fool or jester was often one of the few who had the privilege to speak the truth. "And since because of my career I am supposed to tell the truth, I am really glad that I have now been officially taken into the ranks of those that have the same privilege."[30] "And," he added during the applause, "the truth can never be harmful."[31]

There are dozens of other such stories floating about Bavaria. Once, after a festival Mass held in the Bavarian forest, near the border with the Czech Republic, he visited the Benedictine monastery of Metten. One of the monks, a well-known author of children's books, was introduced to him and declared proudly, "We have a Cardinal here, too," (referring to Cardinal Paul Augustine Mayer, a member of their community who took holy orders there, later became abbot, and then received a red hat). Ratzinger's response: "Does he just get in the way?" *(Liegt er nur rum?*—a Bavarian phrase, usually referring to old people and things that just make trouble or are otherwise annoying).

In a television interview in 2006, one in which the Pope spoke to a group of journalists without any preparation or restriction on what might be asked—this is extremely rare in the history of the Vatican—Benedict said very truthfully that he was not one who thinks of jokes all the time, to say nothing of telling them, but he tries to take the impossible array of tasks and responsibilities the papacy demands as lightly as he can. This is typical of his sense of humor, which is solidly rooted in understatement. It is true; he is not a joke teller, but he has a taste for delicious irony, accompanied by a slight smile and a stoic delivery. I cannot resist relating a famous example: After the publication of his autobiography, a journalist asked why there was no mention of women or romantic relationships. The Cardinal replied, "I had to keep the manuscript to one hundred pages."[32]

Despite his good humor, the relentless pressure from work took its toll on his health. In 1991, a fainting spell led to a fall in the bathroom, against the heater, gashing his forehead and leaving a visible scar.[33] Perhaps moments such as these moved him to ask the Pope to accept his resignation. In a televised interview in 1997, when asked what he was afraid of, Ratzinger said, "Perhaps the dentist, and all medical treatments." He went on to say that his perennial fear was of misspeaking on an important issue, of formulating an answer in such a way that it would be badly misunderstood. "Then naturally I think also of the Last Judgment."[34] These were the stresses of being the Prefect of the CDF.

Nothing, however, weighed on him like the loss of his sister, who succumbed to a stroke on November 2, 1991, while she and her brother were visiting Georg in Regensburg. Maria had lived with her brother for thirty-four years, keeping his house and supporting him in his career. We should not forget that her wages also supported his early education at the seminary in Traunstein. Margarete Richardi spoke of her as an intelligent and lively woman who was true to her brother, although she never wanted to occupy the foreground. "She always accompanied him, she was always there, and she could be quite resolute."[35] When she died, he lost a loved companion in his daily life. She had never come to like Rome very much, and missed her Bavarian homeland, but she had acted on her brother's needs instead of her own wishes. The published death announcement said that she had served him "with tireless devotion, great goodness, and humility." Joseph and Georg said her requiem Mass in the cathedral at Regensburg, and laid her remains to rest in the family grave near their house in Pentling.[37]

After Maria's death, Joseph increased his annual visits to the family home in Pentling from three (just after Christmas, at Pentecost, and late July to late August) to four (adding early November), and Georg came to Rome at least once a year. During their time in Pentling, the brothers would usually take at least one day trip per year to Traunstein, Tittmoning, Altötting, and other places that served as the homes of their youth. Joseph chose St. Michael's Seminary in Traunstein to celebrate his seventy-fifth birthday and the silver anniversary of his being named a cardinal. Joseph would also come from Rome to celebrate his brother's special birthdays (seventy, seventy-five, eighty, etc.).

Since April 2005, however, the roles have reversed; now Georg comes to Rome a few times per year and spends part of the summer vacation in Castel Gandolfo, because Joseph can no longer go home without causing a tremendous uproar. It must be said in no uncertain terms that becoming Pope was not part of his plans.

THE GUILLOTINE - 2005

*"When, little by little, the trend of the voting led me to understand that,
in a manner of speaking, the guillotine was going to fall on me,
my head began to spin."*

—*Pope Benedict XVI*

On April 2, 2005, the amazing life of Pope John Paul II came to an end. This man had inspired hundreds of millions, perhaps even billions of people; in him they saw the source of hope, joy, and love, and at the same time, a man frequently sunk in agony. On the day before he died, Cardinal Ratzinger left Rome for nearby Subiaco, where he had been invited to the Monastery of St. Scholastica to make a speech and receive the St. Benedict Prize, given "for the promotion of life and the family in Europe."[1] A prophetic gesture to say the least.

Six days later Ratzinger, as dean of the College of Cardinals, presided over the requiem Mass for the deceased Pope at what has been deemed "the best attended funeral in the history of the world . . . [where] Christian, Jewish, and Muslim leaders appeared in a show of unity."[2] Two hundred political leaders came in from around the world, in addition to around two million mourners. In the days before and after, people around the world began calling the deceased "the Great," and cheered at the funeral en masse for his immediate sanctification. *"Santo subito!"*

On April 16, Cardinal Ratzinger turned seventy-eight years old. He celebrated quietly in his household with only a few friends. He told Josef Clemens, his former secretary and now a bishop, "I am somewhat nervous."[3] Perhaps on that day the cardinal was trying to take solace in his advanced age, as a kind of protection against the papal office. If it were to fall on him, he would be the oldest cardinal to become Pope since 1730.[4] When Ratzinger opened the conclave on April 18, he addressed the Cardinal College and the whole Church with unforgettable words:

> *Christ's mercy is not a grace that comes cheap, nor does it imply the trivialization of evil. Christ carries the full weight of evil and all its destructive force in his body and in his soul. He burns and transforms evil in suffering, in the fire of his suffering love. . . .*
>
> *How many winds of doctrine have we known in recent decades, how many ideological currents, how many ways of thinking. The small boat of the thought of many Christians has often been tossed about by these waves—flung from one extreme to another: from Marxism to liberalism, even to libertinism; from collectivism to radical individualism; from atheism to a vague religious mysticism; from agnosticism to syncretism, and so forth. Every day new sects spring up, and what St Paul says about human deception and the trickery that strives to entice people into error (cf. Eph 4:14) comes true.*
>
> *Today, having a clear faith based on the Creed of the Church is often labeled as fundamentalism. Whereas relativism, that is, letting oneself be "tossed here and there, carried about by every wind of doctrine," seems the only attitude that can cope with modern times. We are building a dictatorship of relativism that does not recognize anything as definitive and whose ultimate goal consists solely of one's own ego and desires.*
>
> *We, however, have a different goal: the Son of God, the true man. He is the measure of true humanism. An "adult" faith is not a faith that follows the trends of fashion and the latest novelty; a mature adult faith is deeply rooted in friendship with Christ. It is this friendship that opens us up to all that is good and gives us a criterion by which to distinguish the true from the false, and deceit from truth.[5]*

The assembled cardinals must have known whom they were dealing with and what kind of Pope he would be, if they were considering him as John Paul II's successor. About twenty-four hours later, the selection process was complete.

Joseph Ratzinger never desired to become Pope. There was no campaigning on his part except from doing his duty and speaking his mind. Ratzinger had often described himself as "a man of the second row," a supporter rather than a leader.[6] Shortly before the conclave began, Cardinal Meisner of Cologne told him, "Joseph, you must become Pope." Ratzinger covered his face with his hands and said, "Are you crazy?" Meisner said later that as he left, Ratzinger looked utterly distraught.[7] During the conclave, when the voting was pointing to Ratzinger's succession, one of the cardinals sent him a note, reminding him of his self-stated commitment to be the Lord's pack animal: come what may, he should not shrink from the call to serve. Benedict told a group of German pilgrims a week after the election, "I was convinced that I had already carried out my life's work and could look forward to ending my days peacefully. With profound conviction I said to the Lord: Do not do this to me!"[8] According to a cardinal, in the Sistine Chapel there was a "great collective sigh of relief" when Ratzinger accepted the new charge, which clearly shows that many of his supporters were not sure that he *would*.[9] His brother, Georg, was "shaken" when he saw his brother appear on the high balcony as St. Peter's successor. The result shocked him, he said in an interview; it totally upset their plans for retirement and placed an enormous burden upon his brother, whose health had been delicate through much of his life.

A number of journalists and papal biographers have written interesting accounts of the conclave of 2005, but the fact remains that none of them were witnesses of the closed-door proceedings.[10] These writings can only be based on conversations before, conjecture during, and limited anecdote after the actual event. What happened in the Sistine Chapel is actually nobody's business but the cardinals'. The election of the Pope is one of their roles in Church governance and has been so for about a thousand years. It is essentially a private event, and the voting procedure is purely democratic. The facts speak plainly for themselves. On Monday, April 18, there was one ballot in the evening. The day after there were three, with the result that Cardinal Ratzinger met or exceeded the required two-thirds majority. The timing made it one of the three shortest conclaves in modern history. That in itself is notable evidence of unity of opinion within the college. Cardinal Ratzinger was known to them all, personally and through his writings. There can have been no doubt where he stood on everything to do with the Church and her role in the world, and during the funeral of John Paul II, they had a chance to see him perform on the world stage. When they all prayerfully asked the Holy Spirit for guidance in making their selection, all they had to do was to look up at their dean.

When he was asked what name he would take, he chose the name Benedict, as he had publicly recommended some time ago for whomever would be the next Pope. There were a number of good reasons. Not only does the name sound well in a number of world languages—Benedetto, Benito, Benoît, Benedikt, etc.—but he has a high regard for the last Pope with that name—Benedict XV—who tirelessly called for peace during the relentless slaughter of the World War I. Furthermore, Saint Benedict of Nursia is the co-patron of Europe, and the monastic order he founded is one of the taproots for the Christianization of the West. And we should not neglect another reason: the Pope's homeland is Benedictine. The great cloisters of Ettal in the Alps, Andechs by the Ammersee, St. Bonifaz in Munich, Metten, Niederalteich, and Weltenburg on the Danube, with their ancient tradition of *ora et labora* (work and prayer), first spread by Irish and Gallic missionaries among the Celtic peoples, should impress every pilgrim who comes to Bavaria.[11]

The cardinals then came in turn to kneel before the Pope and promise him their loyalty and obedience. At this time, his personal secretary, Georg Gänswein, entered the Sistine Chapel and beheld his boss, now dressed in papal garments. "His face was almost as white as his new, white cassock and the skullcap on his head. He looked terribly worn out. . . . And the days that followed were rather like a tidal wave."[12]

Later that same day, after a simple dinner and a glass of champagne with the cardinals, Pope Benedict called his brother, Georg, repeatedly at his apartment in Regensburg, but no one answered the phone. Georg had watched it all happen on television, and journalists had started calling the moment his brother's name was announced. By evening, Georg had had more than enough of the same questions. The day after when the housekeeper, Mrs. Heindl, finally picked up the receiver, she could barely utter a word at the thought of having the Pope on the phone.[13]

FIRST WORDS, FIRST THINGS

Benedict's first words as Pope, spoken from the balcony of St. Peter's were, "Dear Brothers and Sisters, after the great Pope, John Paul II, the cardinals have elected me, a simple and humble worker in the Lord's vineyard." This statement came from his heart, because that is exactly who he is and knows himself to be. His whole life long he never tried to be anything else.

"The fact that the Lord can work and act even with insufficient means consoles me, and above all I entrust myself to your prayers." Above all we must remember that Peter was not named "the rock" because of who he was. Actually he was not very rocklike at all. He was impetuous, emotional, and unsteady in his faith, sinking into turgid waters and denying Christ three times. And it is silly to say that he was completely different after the Resurrection and Pentecost; he was still the same person, albeit with a fuller understanding of his faith and vocation. Christ named Peter "the rock" as a *commission*; the title designates a ministry. Many of the Popes from the last two thousand years have been woefully inadequate to the task, but the Church has survived nonetheless. Bearing that historical reality in mind, Benedict found consolation in the immensity of his new duties. He also knows the only thing, apart from God's grace, that can help him live up to expectations is the love and prayers of the faithful.

"In the joy of the resurrected Lord, we go on with his help. He is going to help us and Mary will be on our side. Thank you."

The day after (a Wednesday), the Pope came to breakfast with the cardinals in their guesthouse, and there was no sign of new pretensions. Cardinal Schönborn complimented him on his white outfit, and the pontiff replied with a laugh, "I will need time to get used to them." At Mass later that day he delivered an address to the cardinals in Latin, which he had somehow managed to write during the turbulent hours following his election the day before. In it he declared his total loyalty to Christ, his promise to proclaim "the living presence of Christ to the whole world," and his commitment to the resolutions of the Second Vatican Council. This should have surprised none of them. He continued:

> *The Church of today must revive her awareness of the duty to re-propose to the world the voice of the One who said: "I am the light of the world. No follower of mine shall ever walk in darkness; no, he shall possess the light of life" (Jn 8:12). In carrying out his ministry, the new Pope knows that his task is to make Christ's light shine out before the men and women of today: not his own light, but Christ's.[15]*

Benedict has made it clear from the beginning: he does not want people to see him, but the way, the truth, and the life. If he does not bring Christ to people and people to Christ, then he has failed in his ministry. It is no easy task.

After Mass he visited his old office and the staff of the CDF, greeting each person individually—which was not required by papal etiquette, but that was not going to stop him from showing appreciation where it was due. That same morning, he was shown his apartments-to-be, on the fourth floor of the papal palace. Renovation was sorely needed. John Paul II had lived simply, to say the least; his black and white television dated from the 1970s, and the few rooms that had any electricity had wiring from the 1930s, not that Benedict has any interest in technology, apart from his stereo and classical music recordings.

In the afternoon on Thursday and Friday, he left the Vatican to go to his old apartment of twenty-something years. There he played the same piano he has owned since his stint on the faculty at Freising, and he consulted his library for the writing of his homily at the Inauguration Mass.[16] He arranged for the transfer of his belongings—above all his piano, the old walnut desk (a family heirloom), and his indispensable, beloved library. On his way out, he rang his neighbors' doorbells to say farewell.[17]

For the Inauguration Mass, Benedict chose to wear the same golden vestments that John Paul II had used, as a definite sign of continuity between his pontificate and the last. During the ceremony he put on the fisherman's ring, symbolizing the chief purpose of his life, and that of every priest—to bring souls closer to God. He also received his special pallium, a simple stretch of woven wool cloth that has a number of meanings. For one, it is meant to remind everyone that a bishop carries the yoke of Christ's will, for the good of the people under his care. The material from which it is made can create the image of the lost, wounded, or diseased lamb, borne around the bishop's neck, being carried back to the safety of the flock. The contour and appearance of Benedict's pallium is strikingly similar to those worn by the Popes of the fourth century, and the title for the distributed, printed text of the Mass was "Inauguration of the Petrine Ministry of the Bishop of Rome," with no mention of "Supreme Pontiff" or the other grand papal titles. These choices clearly demonstrate his adherence to the mission and tradition of the ancient Church.

That continuity extends to himself as well. For his papal insignia he selected the same symbols that he used as the archbishop of Freising and Munich: the Moor's head, the bear, and the shell. He kept the two crossed keys, which clearly identifies him as the successor to Peter, to whom Christ gave the assignment to bind and loose (which basically means to establish disciplinary rules within the Church), but he scrapped the triple tiara, the three-tiered, beehive-shaped crown in use since the Middle Ages. He is the first Pope in modern times to do so. Instead, on the top of his coat of arms is a bishop's miter—Ratzinger had been a bishop since 1977—with three golden bands referring to the traditional three functions of the Pope: as teacher, priest, and shepherd of souls. But the message is clear: this Pope will be what he always was, a bishop, not a worldly prince or king.

In his homily for the Inauguration Mass, which was attended by almost as many world leaders as the Requiem for John Paul II, Benedict made clear that his pontificate is not about himself.

And now, at this moment, weak servant of God that I am, I must assume this enormous task, which truly exceeds all human capacity. How can I do this? How will I be able to do it? All of you, my dear friends, have just invoked the entire host of Saints, represented by some of the great names in the history of God's dealings with mankind. In this way, I too can say with renewed conviction: I am not alone. I do not have to carry alone what in truth I could never carry alone. All the Saints of God are there to protect me, to sustain me and to carry me. And your prayers, my dear friends, your indulgence, your love, your faith and your hope accompany me.

My real program of governance is not to do my own will, not to pursue my own ideas, but to listen, together with the whole Church, to the word and the will of the Lord, to be guided by Him, so that He himself will lead the Church at this hour of our history.

Turning the audience's focus away from himself, he used this moment on the world stage to make an appeal for Christ.

Are we not perhaps all afraid in some way? If we let Christ enter fully into our lives, if we open ourselves totally to him, are we not

*afraid that He might take something away from us? Are we not
perhaps afraid to give up something significant, something unique,
something that makes life so beautiful? Do we not then risk ending up
diminished and deprived of our freedom? . . . No! If we let Christ into
our lives, we lose nothing, nothing, absolutely nothing of what makes
life free, beautiful and great. No! Only in this friendship are the doors
of life opened wide. Only in this friendship is the great potential of
human existence truly revealed. Only in this friendship do we experience beauty and liberation.*[18]

Typical Ratzinger. He asks tough questions and answers them clearly and
directly, not shying from a plain "no" where one is needed. After the Mass, he
rode through the cheering crowds in his roofless white car, imparting blessings
left and right. He looked genuinely happy, but more beleaguered than at ease.
Who wouldn't have?

It was a great day for all those who knew and loved him for who he is and
what he does. But in a more general sense, it was a good day for Germany
as well, because it was a sign that country has finally returned to normality,
despite the horrid memory of the World War II. It had been a little less than
a thousand years since a Bavarian led the Church. The last was Damasus II,
elected July 17, 1048, who reigned for all of twenty-three days. The last Pope
from Germany was Victor II, who hailed from Swabia in the southwest, who
was elected in 1055 at the age of thirty-seven. Those were the days when Holy
Roman Emperors installed Popes in Rome favorable to their interests, and
deposed them when they failed to please. A nasty fever ended Victor's pontificate little more than two years after it began. Adrian VI, who served from
1522-23, hailed from the Low Countries and was the last non-Italian Pope
until John Paul II. Technically Adrian was from the Holy Roman Empire,
which was commonly referred to as "Germany" during that era, but he was a
Dutchman, not what one these days would call *deutsch*.

"IL TEDESCO"—THE GERMAN POPE

Benedict then had to get down to the business of being the Pope. The last
thing he had on his mind was "germanizing" the Vatican, subjecting it to
the legendary German obsession with order and control. It is a distaste-

ful stereotype, but like all generalizations, complimentary and otherwise, it did not come out of nowhere. When Cardinal Ratzinger was interviewed in the 1980s, he spoke openly about the Vatican's reputation for slowness, and although he acknowledged that it could be a problem, on the whole he defended the virtue of delay with regard to certain difficulties, particularly those that will settle themselves with the passage of time.[19]

The papal palace now has a Germanic accent, but Benedict has made no attempt to increase German influence at the Vatican or in the Church as a whole. When he named fifteen new cardinals in March 2006, not one was from Germany. Italian is the language of the papal staff and household—Benedict's Italian is better than fluent, although it carries a distinctly Bavarian accent. The rule, however, about receiving only heads of state has been relaxed when it comes to Germans. He has received a half-dozen German minister presidents (state governors), including, naturally, Edmund Stoiber of Bavaria, on more than one occasion. Nonetheless, to quote an unnamed monsignor, "His love for his homeland has no influence in his policy."[20]

In the papal household, only one is German besides the Pope: Georg Gänswein, one of two secretaries (the other being from Malta, Alfred Xuereb). The four housekeepers and one personal attendant are Italian. Gänswein's daily proximity to the Pope has made him a target of massive media attention, to say nothing of his good looks and athletic build, which have made him the target of nasty rumors and the occasional, deranged love letter. Ratzinger's former housekeeper, Ingrid Stampa, a former professor of music from Hamburg, could not move with him into the papal palace because she is not a member of a religious order, but she still works as a Vatican employee.[21]

Although not a member of the papal household, Thaddäus Joseph Kühnel, a bank director in Munich, serves the Pope as his unofficial Bavarian courier. Kühnel has known Ratzinger for three decades and driven him all around Bavaria during his visits, to the tune of 10,000 km, so he claims. During their many hours together, they talked and laughed—usually at Karl Valentin's stories and jokes, quoted verbatim by Ratzinger—but were mostly silent. Often during these stretches of silence, Ratzinger would compose the homilies or speeches he was about to give. "He does everything in his head," Kühnel said. "He has a memory like a computer." In addition to chauffeuring, at Christmas and Easter time Kühnel brings to Rome some of the Pope's favorite, simple, old-fashioned Bavarian products from Munich: Adelholzener mineral water, beer from Cloister Andechs, and gingerbread, marzipan, and beeswax candles from Nuremberg. He drives right into the Vatican—the Swiss guards have known him for twenty years—and rides the elevator straight to the papal apartments. The Pope greets him with the words, "Mr. Kühnel, now we really have to catch up!"[22] In December 2005, Kühnel also delivered forty-two advent wreaths and seven Christmas trees, obviously intended for other people at the Vatican besides Benedict. "The Pope," he says, "delights in all the Bavarian things I bring him. He needs this connection to his homeland." When asked what is Bavarian about the Pope, Kühnel responds without delay, "His speech, mentality, love of homeland, humility—and his cleverness."[23]

Based on interviews with his brother and his secretary, and on a special, behind-the-scenes documentary prepared for German television, it is quite clear that the Holy Father is doing about as well as an octogenarian can hope to in his position. A modest, disciplined, orderly lifestyle is part of it, and he knows that he has to heed his limits. A typical day begins with rising between 5 and 6 a.m., Mass every morning in the papal chapel between 7 and 8, with his two secretaries concelebrating, before the tiny congregation of his four housekeepers and his personal attendant. Benedict then has some time for private prayer to prepare himself to face the duties of the day. After a light breakfast, he goes to his study to get to work.

Around 11 a.m., in the audience hall on a lower floor, he receives official visitors, mainly political figures, in front of a legion of journalists and cameramen. To accommodate his advanced age—John Paul was fifty-eight when he became Pope, Benedict seventy-eight—he spends less time with VIPs, and he has delegated the celebration of beatifications to another cardinal. Only heads of state and their spouses get audiences, and not every government minister or secretary. First Lady Laura Bush and her daughter had all of fifteen minutes, and Condoleezza Rice's request was turned down, possibly because the Pope was on vacation and no emergency was involved. Sometimes he withdraws with his guests into an adjacent chamber for official, private conversations.

Lunch is normally taken at 1:30 p.m. with a minimum of company or in private whenever possible. The Pope prefers lots of fruits and vegetables, simple and light Italian fare rather than heavier food. But it is well known that he has a weakness for occasional Bavarian *Mehlspeisen*, batter-based dishes like *Kaiserschmarrn* or "Emperor's rubbish," thin pancakes, and different kinds of dumplings. If he drinks beer or wine, it is in small amounts. Instead of coffee, the Pope prefers herbal and fruit teas.

The rest of the afternoon, if there are no liturgies or general audiences, is mostly given to working and writing in his private office, its walls lined with shelves of his beloved books. There he completes the administrative tasks of the day, working through documents, files, and papers "at lightning speed," according to Georg Gänswein. The Pope's furious pace of work is complemented by his "elephantine memory."[24] Unlike his predecessor, Benedict reviews the files of all candidates under consideration for episcopal appointments. He meets directly with the leaders of the dicasteries (Church governing agencies) and several of the congregations in the Roman Curia, the central Catholic bureaucracy located at the Vatican. More diplomatic functions are left to the Vatican's secretary of state.

A walk in the fresh air, accompanied by his secretaries, is part of the papal routine, praying the Rosary as they go. The many gardens, Benedict once said, are his favorite part of the Vatican. If time does not allow for a tour around one of them, there is always the roof terrace atop the papal palace, amid potted orange trees, blooming flower boxes, and small trickling fountains. The papal physician, Dr. Buzzonetti, supplied a stationary bike to the papal palace for days with bad weather, but it is questionable how much Benedict uses it. His favorite exercise above all is to hike in the mountains, but opportunities are severely restricted to maybe a few days in the summertime. His health is good and stable for a man of nearly eighty-one at the time of this writing. He had two small strokes in the past, and a mild heart condition, supposedly, for which it is said he needs to take a blood thinner. An hour-long afternoon nap helps to keep him in good stead.

By 7 p.m. the day's meetings are over, and the Pope prays from the breviary. Dinner is at 7:30, and then he withdraws to his living room. On occasion he watches the local eight o'clock Italian newscast, or takes another walk. He rarely gets to play his old piano, but when he does, Mozart sonatas are the music of choice. Why Mozart? "I just simply love him," Benedict has said.

"There is nothing artificial in it; it does not pander. This music is simply beautiful, just as creation is beautiful."[25] His brother said in an interview that there was talk of getting a Steinway for the papal apartment at the Vatican, "but my brother says it's not worth it. For one thing he doesn't have much time, and also he gauges his own abilities realistically. For his own playing, his old piano is good enough."

At night, a member of the Swiss Guard locks all the doors in the papal palace. If the Pope still has enough energy and concentration, he goes back to his desk to work on whatever project is most pressing or to commit to writing the ideas that probably come to him all the time. Finally he prays the rest of the breviary and retires by 10:30 or 11 p.m. at the latest. When the light in the window (second from the left on the east side of the palace, fourth floor) goes out, the Pope has brought yet another full day to an end.[26]

Benedict talks on the phone with his brother every week. The Pope does the calling, because Georg is easier to reach. Friends of theirs installed a second line at Georg's apartment, so his brother can always get through to him. Their conversations are as they always were; they talk about the weather, how they are doing, mostly everyday matters, just touching base. Georg comes to visit four times per year, and lodges on the fifth floor. He concelebrates at daily Mass, which he thoroughly enjoys, and eats with the papal "family." He cannot read due to vision problems, so someone at the Vatican takes the time to read to him in the morning and afternoon. The time he gets to spend with his brother outside of Mass and mealtime is very short. Georg said he would never move to Rome, because he would feel like a burden. Besides, he added, "I have a nice apartment [in Regensburg] and am known here."

A NEW PONTIFICATE

Comparisons between Benedict and his superlative predecessor are unnecessary but inevitable, and he is measuring up to the task. In the first five months of his pontificate, an estimated 600,000 people attended his Sunday Angelus prayer and address, and his general audiences on average attract double the number of people as John Paul II's. A Vatican specialist is quoted saying, "John Paul II opened people's hearts; Benedict fills them."[27] Another commentator observed that John Paul's was a papacy of the grand gesture, whereas

Benedict's is one of the word. People were fascinated watching John Paul, a mystic with great charisma, where they seem to be more keen to listen to Benedict, one of the great intellectual lights of the past decades. But we should not take any of this too far, lest we begin to mistake appearance for substance. The two are in essence the same.

What principles or agenda guide this pontificate? What is the Pope's primary goal and purpose? The answer to these questions, I am convinced, lies in his writings, for all to see, read, and reflect upon. In the Foreword to the *Compendium of the Catechism of the Catholic Church* (a brief digest or companion text to the weighty, 800-page Catechism), Benedict states that the purpose of the work is to "awaken in the Church of the third millennium renewed zeal for evangelization and education in the faith, which ought to characterize every community in the Church and every Christian believer, regardless of age or nationality."[28] Benedict XVI, a scholar and teacher for most of his life, supports all movements that enhance awareness, knowledge, respect, and love for the Catholic faith, wherever they are. Those branches of the Church that do not do so will be allowed to wither and fall off as the Spirit moves them to do.

First and foremost, Benedict wants to be a bridge-builder, which is actually the original meaning of the Latin *pontifex*. One of the Pope's honorary titles, inherited straight from the ancient Roman priesthood, is *pontifex maximus,* and Benedict is taking this role seriously. On the day after his election, he declared his commitment to ecumenism, which includes reestablishing unity with the Orthodox Church, a project dear to Benedict's heart, one that we will explore in the next chapter. His first official letter was to the head rabbi of Rome, congratulating him on his birthday and looking forward to continued dialogue. In the summer of 2005, he met Bernard Fellay, the excommunicated head of the Society of St. Pius X, the reactionary splinter group that has set itself against the reformed, vernacular Mass and the Second Vatican Council, in hopes of ending the schism with the self-proclaimed traditionalists. He also granted an audience to the prominent atheist Italian journalist, Oriana Fallaci, known for her antagonistic stance toward Islam in Europe.

Not long after, he invited Hans Küng, his former colleague at Tübingen, to Castel Gandolfo, the papal summer palace with its own farm and gardens, at the edge of an inland lake southeast of Rome. Küng, Germany's most famous the edge of an inland lake southeast of Rome. Küng, Germany's most famous dissident, the man who devoted much of his career to attacking the papacy, who for years had requested an audience with John Paul II and never got one, and who has said awful things about Joseph Ratzinger in the media, now came to dinner with the Pope. It was their first meeting since 1983. The press was left out of the loop until it was over. They strolled through the gardens, made a tour of the palace, and shared a long dinner, from which was heard frequent laughter.[29] The visit offered four hours of conversation about books, the Church, the role of reason in both religion and science, and Küng's pet project about the World Ethos: no peace on earth without peace between religions.[30] "There are not two Ratzingers," Küng said afterwards.

> *He has stayed the same person but what has changed is his role. He no longer has to control the teaching and censor the teachers. Now he is responsible for spreading the Christian message in the Church and in the world."[31]*

Father Andrew Greeley, an American Catholic writer and outspoken critic of the Vatican, said the meeting was "a powerful act of graciousness and humanity that moved some priests who knew both to tears."

Then there was the Twentieth World Youth Day in Cologne, in Germany's Rhineland. As this grand event began, German TV commentators asked viewers, "Will Benedict pass muster? Will he connect with the young? Will he have enough appeal, despite his age and reputation?" There was scarcely a doubt in my mind that he would; he's the *Pope*. John Paul II showed that a Pope could be nearly paralyzed, slunk in an oversized chair, slurring his speech to the point of incomprehensibility, and still excite huge crowds of young people. This was not because he was Karol Wojtyła, but because of his service as the Vicar of Christ.

Each ceremony seemed bigger and more ecstatic than the next, from Benedict's arrival on the banks of the Rhine to the evening vigil and holy Mass the next day, which were attended by about a million young people, Germany's largest religious service ever.[32] Time and again the Pope exhorted the young people not to hear him but Christ, to give Christ "the right of free speech during these days," to open their hearts to him, and to let him suffuse their lives with the "nuclear fission" of his love. "Only from the saints," he said, "only from God does true revolution come, the definitive way to change the world." The power of God, the transformative power of divine love, does not compete with "the noisy and ostentatious power of this world." He challenged them to place the Eucharist at the center of their lives and to pass on the great joy they find in Christ to others. "Form communities based on faith!" but he added, "It is also important to preserve communion with the Pope and with the bishops. It is they who guarantee that we are not seeking private paths, but instead are living as God's great family, founded by the Lord through the Twelve Apostles."[33]

There were quieter moments, too. Benedict requested Eucharistic Adoration, silent prayer before the consecrated Host, to be available for participants after the major liturgies and meetings. There were also a number of smaller gatherings, where the Pope encouraged a group of seminarians on their journey of faith, the meaning of which is "to serve the kingship of God in the world." In Cologne's synagogue, he confirmed the stance of the Second Vatican Council: "The Catholic Church is committed . . . to tolerance, respect, friendship and peace between all peoples, cultures and religions." But in their mutual dialogue, he added, no one should simply dismiss the significant differences that distinguish one from another. "Precisely in those areas, we need to show respect and love for one another." Finally, in a meeting with leaders of Germany's Muslim community, he highlighted the mutually held belief of Christianity and Islam that "the life of every human being is sacred," but he condemned terrorism as "perverse and cruel," a real threat to peace and civilization in our day. He thanked those present who had spoken out publicly against it and reaffirmed the Church's respect for Islam.

From the beginning to the end of World Youth Day, Benedict was thronged with clergymen, dignitaries, and people young and old. No camera caught him showing anyone anything but decent respect. At times he looked as awed as the young people in the gigantic congregations, and it must have been overwhelming. The well-organized event saw not a single instance of violence, vandalism, or other criminal behavior. The word I heard again and again was "amazing." Can you think of any other convergence of so many young people on a single city with such peaceful results? The archdiocese and city of Cologne could slap itself on the back for a job well done, but still, the Pope's visit was not totally without embarrassments. At one point, the world-famous soc-cer legend, Pelé, was brought forward to be introduced to the Pope. He was met with the question, "And you are Brazilian?" Sport was never Benedict's forte, and it really is not the best criteria for determining a person's worth, when you think about it. Even if you are Pelé.

For the plane ride back to Rome, the market community of Marktl am Inn and Lufthansa, the German national airline, arranged a light show for the Holy Father. Marktl's fire department directed its floods at the house of his birth, and the pilot altered the flight path and brought the plane down to 1,500 meters so the Pope could see it from the air. By 8:30 p.m. about 2,500 people had gathered in the square in front, and they cheered when they saw the plane's landing lights in the distance. The Pope came into the cockpit and addressed the townspeople over the radio. Together they prayed the Angelus, with the Pope leading from the plane. Stephan Semmelmayr, Marktl's director of tourism, said, "I never thought, even in my dreams, that the Holy Father himself was going to speak to us. It was the best moment of my whole life, except for the birth of my children."

What has come of it all? Hans Langendörfer, the secretary of the German Bishops' Conference, said that one need only go to a bookstore and glance at all the new titles about religion and religious topics. The statistics from 2005 show that fewer people in Germany are leaving the Catholic Church, more people are returning who had left, and there are still more converting. The name Benedikt, not uncommon for German boys, has made a huge leap in popularity, doubling its numbers among the newborn in 2005.

There is no question that Benedict XVI is connecting with people, both en masse and one at a time. Six months after his election, the Munich Philhar-monic and the Regensburg *Domspatzen* put on a concert before a crowd of seven thousand people. Among them was the well-known German actress, Veronika Ferres, a publicly committed Catholic. When introduced, Bene-dict told her how well he remembered her performance in Salzburg in Hugo von Hofmannsthal's *Jedermann*. She responded that her mother had always appreciated his sermons as archbishop of Munich, but she was long dead, having died "much too early." The Pope took both her hands, looked into her eyes, and changed his formal address to *du*, the familiar German *you*. "You know," he said, "she is here now, with us, and is watching us." Ferres was overwhelmed.[34]

⟨⟨⟨ CONTINUITY

By the end of 2005, Benedict XVI established a pattern of continuity—with his predecessor, with himself, the Second Vatican Council, and the whole history of the Roman Catholic Church. With regards to John Paul II, in an exclusive interview with Peter Seewald, Benedict said, "I hear him and I see him speak. We are close to each other in a new way."[35] Benedict will make no major departures from the teachings of the great Polish Pope. With regards to Benedict himself, all who knew him as Cardinal Ratzinger—his former housekeeper, secretaries, graduate students, cardinal colleagues, even some of the Swiss guards and members of the Vatican police—say the same thing: He is as he was. Reserved but not arrogant, friendly but not familiar, correct but not sanctimonious, interested in people, communicative, and a good listener: an authentic, humble human being.[36]

With the Second Vatican Council, it is normal for him to begin an address with a quotation from one of the documents. In doing so, he conveys to all that his position is *not his own,* but one belonging to the Church as a whole, as inspired by the Holy Spirit that keeps her alive. Vatican II, which completed the unfinished work of the First Vatican Council in the nineteenth century, will serve as the compass for the Church as it enters the twenty-first century and the third millennium.

In December 2005, Pope Benedict said in an address to the Curia, "We can look back with gratitude to the Second Vatican Council. If we read and accept it *guided by a correct interpretation,* it can become a great force in the ever necessary renewal of the Church."[37] No one should falsely interpret the phrase, "openness to the modern world," that is now commonplace in summing up the significance of the Council, as a Catholic pledge to embrace whatever comes down the road in the name of progress. "The Church itself," he said, "is conscious that it is fully in sync with the teachings of Jesus (cf Mt 22: 21), the Church of the early martyrs, and with all the martyrs." This identity, this foundation has not and cannot change. Although reform must certainly go on, it must be more akin to "renewal" than simple "change" or "novelty."

"True reform" for Benedict is a "multileveled continuity and discontinuity" that is based on permanent principles. Inability to discern the principles at work can lead to the confusion, for example, about religious freedom—which the Council wholeheartedly endorsed—and relativism. Religious freedom was clearly "a social and historical necessity," a legal arrangement in which the modern state provides for "the orderly and tolerant coexistence between citizens and for their freedom to exercise their religion." But when religious freedom is regarded as a metaphysical principle and people argue that it is proof that no one can really "find truth, [then] relativism becomes the canon."

Benedict's commitment to continuity, however, is not a rigid adhesion to all traditions in place at the Vatican. For one, he cancelled the Christmas charity concert in the Paul VI auditorium that had featured Italian and international pop stars since 1993 and moved it to Monaco. He also switched tailors, away from the family firm that has dressed the Pope since 1793, which caught the attention of the media. It is said that it had something to do with an excessively short cassock for his first audience. Personally, I doubt Benedict had much to do with that decision; clothing is not an area where he shows much interest. I remember a major U.S. television newscaster insinuating that when he wore the camauro (a red hat trimmed with white fur) for an outdoor audience in December 2005, he did so because he wanted people to think he was the real Santa Claus. Georg Ratzinger saw a similar newscast in Germany and asked his brother about it during their weekly phone conversation. The papal reply: "I just put it on because of the cold." There was nothing else to say.

What matters to Benedict is the truth, right thinking, and right teaching; but without love, none of these are worth anything. On Christmas Day 2005, the Pope released his first encyclical, a letter addressed to all members of the Catholic Church, laymen and clergy, entitled *Deus Caritas Est,* or "God is Love." The main message was as simple and as old as the gospel itself: Christ Jesus, the incarnate God, is the reality of love. What is unique about the encyclical is the Pope's approach. "Fundamentally, 'love' is a single reality," Benedict writes, "but with different dimensions." The Pope invokes two ancient Greek and biblical concepts of love: *eros* and *agape. Eros,* the obvious root of eroticism, is that intoxicating love that yearns, madly at times, and seeks to conquer. *Agape,* however, wants to give, not to grasp; *agape,* self-giving love, cares more about the beloved than oneself. *Agape* directs, disciplines, and saves *eros,* that without *agape* remains self-gratifying and, therefore, ultimately empty. Trying to have one without the other will lead nowhere, while the two together bring us to God. *Eros* and *agape* belong to both God and man. God wants nothing more but that we should love him as he loves us. God's love is totally excessive—look at the extent of the natural world and the whole of the universe—he gave us everything, even the free will to decide to give him nothing in return. Love, therefore, is a commandment, in worship and in relationship. We owe God nothing less, and we are the only creatures that can give it to him.

11

$\mathcal{R}$ESCUING *the* $\mathcal{W}$EST – 2006

"On the one side, there is the interior opening up of the human soul to God; but on the other side, there is the stronger attraction of our needs and our immediate experiences. Man is the battlefield where these two contend with each other."

—*Pope Benedict XVI,* Christianity and the Crisis of Cultures

The first full calendar year of the new pontificate was as busy and eventful as any under Benedict's predecessor. Attendance at papal events and liturgies continued to burgeon. Deutsche Welle, a German international news service, hardly known for being partial to the papacy, reported that 500,000 people came to Rome for Easter, many more than in the past several years. Benedict's weekly audiences have been swamped, far exceeding those of his predecessor by the tens of thousands. Some wags have said it is due to Benedict's having lifted the long-standing ban on picnicking in St. Peter's Square, but this makes little sense when taken in account with the long hours of waiting at security checkpoints. Deutsche Welle estimated that Benedict XVI spoke before four million people in his first year alone. Benedict is drawing the masses to him, chiefly by his clear, moving speech. He is doing everything in his power to win the hearts of all people, but especially the young, over to Christ and his Church.

Benedict authorized some reforms in the Roman Curia in order to streamline the business of the Holy See, though none were revolutionary or unexpected. It is common knowledge that John Paul II treated the Roman Curia with benign neglect. He came to the papacy from a Polish diocese; Ratzinger, however, had more than two decades of direct experience behind him. In 2006, all Vatican communications were placed under one office, instead of leaving the various media—print, radio, TV, Internet—to their own devices. This arrangement should cut down on occasionally contradictory statements emanating from the Holy See.

Then there were the apostolic journeys. The Pope seems to garner the most attention, in the media at least, when he visits another country. Soon after his elevation, Benedict XVI said that he thought John Paul II's record of 104 apostolic voyages in twenty-six years was unsurpassable, and he indicated that he would make no attempt to maintain his predecessor's rate of travel. But John Paul's achievement averages out to about four trips in a year on average, and Benedict, despite his eighty-plus years, has actually matched it. In 2006 he traveled beyond Italy to Poland, Spain, Bavaria, and Turkey. For the first two journeys, he was honoring commitments made by his predecessor. The latter two were arranged on his own initiative. The four voyages were very different from one another in tone and content, but taken together as a whole, they reveal the priorities of Benedict's pontificate: peace, reconciliation, protection of human life in the family, and interreligious dialogue.

POLAND: MAY 25–28, 2006

This journey the Pope made as a "duty of gratitude" to Pope John Paul II. The Polish people received him enthusiastically, knowing full well of his close friendship with his Polish predecessor. The Polish police estimated that three million people saw him directly, and the returns from a poll said that 55 percent thought of Benedict as *"our* Pope." After jubilant receptions in Warsaw, Wadowice, his predecessor's birthplace, the Marian shrine in Częstochowa, and Krakow, Benedict went to the memorial site of the concentration camp at Auschwitz-Birkenau, where well over a million people were murdered during World War II.

The gray clouds above threatened to resume raining at any moment. He left the black limo and entered alone, through the old iron gate, inscribed with the grand lie of the place, "Work brings freedom." He walked alone over the gravel path, in silence but for the sound of a distant tolling church bell. He prayed before the firing squad wall, lit a candle for the dead, and went to greet a small group of thirty-two former prisoners, one after the other, taking his time to listen to them. Some gave him pictures; most spoke German. Next he entered the cell of St. Maximilian Kolbe, the Franciscan who gave his life for a Polish family man facing execution. He emerged to join the others in prayer.

Only a few paces from the site of the crematoria, the Pope delivered his speech in measured tones; his face was somber, but with no trace of melodrama. He chose to give the address in German, instead of the papal Italian, or French and English, the main languages of world diplomacy. The gesture made it clear that he was coming not only as head of the Catholic Church, but as a son of Germany. He said it was a duty for the truth, for those who suffered here, a duty before God. "I could not fail to come here. I had to come."[1]

Everyone knows today that the camp at Auschwitz was part of a system meant to murder all the Jews of Europe, the Polish elite, the Roma, the Sinti, and others deemed "unworthy of life," and many people throughout the world were waiting to hear what Benedict would say about it. No words can really do justice to the barbarities that went on in that place, and the Pope tried to sum it up in a single sentence:

> *A horde of criminals rose to power by false promises of future greatness and the recovery of the nation's honor, prominence, and prosperity, but also through terror and intimidation, with the result that our people were used and abused as an instrument of their thirst for destruction and power.*

Criticism was almost instantaneous. Why had Benedict not implicated all the German people? Why had he not apologized on behalf of the Catholic Church for fomenting anti-Semitism for centuries? Some commentators, however, noticed that the speech was meant to answer a different question.

"Where was God in those days?" Benedict asked, "Why was he silent? How could he permit this endless slaughter, this triumph of evil?" The answer: We must not, cannot judge God.

> *We cannot peer into God's mysterious plan—we see only piecemeal, and we would be wrong to set ourselves up as judges of God and history. Then we would not be defending man, but only contributing to his downfall. No—when all is said and done, we must continue to cry out humbly yet insistently to God: Rouse yourself! Do not forget mankind, your creature! And our cry to God must also be a cry that pierces our very heart, a cry that awakens within us God's hidden*

presence—so that his power, the power he has planted in our hearts, will not be buried or choked within us by the mire of selfishness, pusillanimity, indifference or opportunism.

Ratzinger has argued for decades that we really have no choice. If we put God on trial, then we would be headed down the path that leads to an ideology not terribly unlike Nazism, one that is cynical toward religion, based on atheism, relativism, and subjectivism, preferring raw feeling over rational thought, self-empowerment at the expense of the weakest, and besotted with the superficial glamour of physical power. The only faith it has is in technology that will bring about a future utopia.

If we blame God for what happened in the 1940s, then we will not believe in the power of forgiveness. Auschwitz should remind us that there can be no hope for the future of mankind on earth without forgiveness and reconciliation. Reconciliation, especially between Jews and Christians, is the only way to bury the horrors of the past. The Pope cited a number of organizations and initiatives that promote dialogue, prayer, education, and mutual understanding. "So," he concluded, "there is hope that this place of horror will gradually become a place for constructive thinking, and that remembrance will foster resistance to evil and the triumph of love."

Szewach Weiss, the former Israeli ambassador to Poland and chairman of the Yad Vashem (a Holocaust museum) Council, called it a "wise speech." One of the survivors present, Marta Domagala, tattooed with the number 59074, said, "Yes, we forgave a long time ago. We couldn't go on living with hate in our hearts." When asked by a reporter how she felt that the Pope did not *ask* for forgiveness on behalf of the German people and the whole Church, she said, "But we are all children of God." The tears came. "Benedict is a good man."[2]

Just before the Pope's speech, a rainbow appeared in the sky on the horizon above the concentration camp; on television it was plainly visible to the whole world. The remarkable timing of that perfectly natural phenomenon rendered it a symbol of the presence and promise of God. For Benedict it was a perfect confirmation of his message of peace through forgiveness.

⚓ SPAIN: JULY 9–10, 2006

On a summer weekend, Pope Benedict came to Spain for the conclusion
of the nine-day Catholic World Family Convention in Valencia on the
country's sunny east coast. When he arrived at the airport, he stated un-
equivocally that the family is part of God's plan of love, and the church
must declare and promote the family's significance. After being greeted
by the King and Queen of Spain, the Pope made his way toward the
center of town, cheered by tens of thousands of onlookers. He stopped
at a subway station called "Jesus" and prayed for the forty-two people
who died on the Monday before in a train that was going twice as fast as
it should.

Benedict then met Jose Luis Rodriguez Zapatero, Spain's socialist prime
minister, whose government had recently instituted gay marriage and made
divorce and abortion easier to obtain. Their private conversation was probably
"friendly and polite," as a government spokesman said, but also a bit strained.
That same day, when asked about divorce, abortion, euthanasia, and stem-cell
research, the Pope said, "There are some things where the Church has to say
No." At any rate, on Sunday, Benedict celebrated a holy Mass attended by
roughly a million people, but Zapatero did not show up. This was an un-
fortunate choice, considering that Fidel Castro, Daniel Ortega, and General
Jaruzelski, despite their animosities toward the Church, had all attended when
the Pope came to town in their countries, but Spain has a long, tragic history
of struggle between those who love the Church and her teachings and those
who hate them.

At the Mass, Benedict made a plea for the maintenance of the natural family
and its attendant, traditional values. Family life, he said was not a subjective
idea to be molded as certain organizations wish it to be. It is what it has been
and always shall be. The union of man and woman and the new life that
union can produce is nature's creation. It is not an arbitrary sociopolitical
construct; it comes from God, as does each one of us. As long as the marriage stands on the bedrock of true, self-giving love, the family is simply the
best structure for human growth and development, both as individuals and
members of society. No other combination comes close. The Pope's presence
and his words at this convention highlight his struggle for the long-term vi-

ability of Europe against the forces of the culture of death and the dictatorship of relativism.

The media, in some countries, ably depicted the divide. A German anchorman stated plainly that a million came to Mass, and showed a few seconds of the Pope's gesturing appreciatively before the massive gathering, adding that the Pope took the opportunity to convey *"his* version" of marriage and family. The next clip cut away to a marriage ceremony for two gay men, taking place at the same time in a small room somewhere in Valencia with about a dozen onlookers. "Others, meanwhile, have *their* version," said the commentator. The gay ceremony was given the exact amount of airtime as the Catholic.

Besides the gross distortion with regard to numbers, this particular media service got something else wildly wrong. The Pope is not in a position to preach *his* own private view on the matter of marriage, family, and life. Ratzinger has described the Pope's role as the first preserver of Christian memory, the living Church across time. There is really very little any Pope can do to change Church teachings on such fundamental aspects of human life.

Still, in Benedict's two speeches that weekend in Valencia, he did not say a negative word about the recent, liberalizing changes in Spanish law. Later, in a televised interview with German journalists, he was asked why he did not. With an impish grin he said, "When you are given two opportunities to speak for twenty minutes, that is not the time to start hurling Nos about." The Church's message, he explained, is much greater, more uplifting and ennobling than a list of thou-shalt-nots.

Just minutes before the blurb about the Holy Father, when the news show reported on a fan rally for the German national soccer team, the commentator said in a thrilled tone of voice that nearly a *million* people had shown up to cheer the nation's heroes. Wherever the Pope goes or has gone in the last couple of decades, crowds of such a size are to be expected.

MANOPPELLO: SEPTEMBER 1, 2006

Before he made the next apostolic journey to his Bavarian homeland, the Pope left Rome for Manoppello, a small town in Abruzzo, a region of central Italy in the Apennine Mountains. His intention was to pay a "private" visit to an image of Jesus Christ on a piece of linen cloth, the Veil of Veronica, which is every bit as mysterious and controversial as the Shroud of Turin. The image is kept in the church of a Capuchin friary, called the Sanctuary of the Sacred Face, which has more or less remained off the itinerary of most pilgrims. What is controversial about the gesture is that the Vatican itself has a similar relic by the same name. The Pope's gesture indicates where he thinks the most trustworthy version resides. "The Pope—this is like a bomb," said Brother Emiliano, one of the younger Capuchin friars, through his long, full, dark beard. But there was more to the visit than giving credence to a relic. "Benedict XVI," the friar continued, "would like us Christians to rediscover that God has a human face. In Jesus he became one of us."[3]

Benedict XVI arrived by helicopter, made his way to the church, prayed before the image, was presented with a painted copy to take back to Rome with him. He made an address to the gathered clergy, seminarians, faithful, and children receiving first Communion, and spoke of the saints, those who search for the "face" of God.

> *This is the experience of God's true friends, the saints who, in the brethren, especially the poorest and neediest, recognized and loved the Face of that God, lovingly contemplated for hours in prayer. For us they are encouraging examples to imitate; they assure us that if we follow this path, the way of love, with fidelity, we too, as the Psalmist sings, will be satisfied with God's presence (cf. Ps 17[16]: 15).*

And who are the ones who follow this path? What does one need to see God's "face"? Benedict's answer: The way is open for anyone with clean hands and a pure heart.

> *Clean hands, that is, a life illumined by the truth of love that overcomes indifference, doubt, falsehood, and selfishness; and pure hearts are essential too, hearts enraptured by divine beauty, as the Little Teresa of Lisieux says in her prayer to the Holy Face, hearts stamped with the hallmark of the Face of Christ.*

The visit to Manoppello was really not about the vying authenticity of relics. The Pope's message is clear: the way to God is through love, pure, clean, unadulterated, undivided, and unlimited. It would not be going too far to say that what he said here is consistent with what he says everywhere else.

·⟨≼ BAVARIA: SEPTEMBER 9–14, 2006

The return to Bavaria was a complete success, in more ways than one. Germany was still aglow from the World Cup in soccer that took place all across the country during the month of June. Everywhere in the land, people celebrated, at home and in public, in ever increasing numbers. There were no disasters, no terrorism, and only a couple of cases of rowdy behavior, and the German national team made it to third place. One of the main slogans was, "the world staying with friends" *(Die Welt zu Gast bei Freunden)*, and everywhere people were exhorted to go out of their way to be welcoming to foreigners. In the city of Munich, the bus, tram, and taxi drivers and the hotel, restaurant, and security personnel took a mandatory course in politeness, an attribute sometimes lacking among Bavarians. When my wife and I finished lunch at a Munich beer hall, the waiter asked resolutely, *before* gathering the plates, "Did it taste good?" My wife looked at me in mild amazement. She couldn't remember such a thing ever happening before. Even the weather was sensational that September. The usual phrase for several days of cloudless blue skies, a mild breeze, and temperatures in the mid-seventies is *Kaiserwetter* (weather fit for an emperor), but in 2006 the new word was *Papstwetter!*

Benedict XVI arrived in Germany in triumph. People turned out in droves to see him, despite security measures that gave ample reason to stay away. In the town of Freising, where he made his last stop, those who lived along his planned route of entry were told not to leave their homes for six hours; all the manhole covers were welded shut; and no one was allowed to enter or leave the area for a few hours before his convoy even drew near. The radio announcements by some authorities made it sound like they wanted people to keep clear of the area. Whole highways were shut down near Regensburg, and production at the BMW and Siemens plants, with their 16,000 workers, came to a halt for a day. Not even a strike has accomplished that. It was a little extreme if not somewhat paranoid, but better safe than sorry. As it was, there were no traffic disasters and no criminal incidents. In spite of the inconvenience, hundreds of parishes organized little pilgrimages to take part in the liturgies or to greet him as he entered a destination. Millions watched him via television.

Local newspapers and parish publications gushed out stories of the readers' experiences in addition to the Pope's words and actions. Bookstores and tourist shops burst with colorful papal memorabilia such as flags and banners, candles, coins, cups, T-shirts and other clothing, beer, water, and cookies, cards, pamphlets, books, necklaces, watches, and even teddy bears, plastic figurines, and nutcrackers, to say nothing of the rosaries. New music, mainly for organ and choir, was composed for the occasion and performed at numerous venues. For a Bavarian Pope to visit his homeland is simply a millennial event.

After arriving in Munich, his tour took him to Altötting by way of Marktl am Inn, Regensburg, and finally Freising, "those places that I love dearly . . . my native land."[4] But the real purpose of the trip was not for nostalgia's sake, but "to reaffirm and confirm, as the successor of the apostle Peter, the close bonds that unite the See of Rome with the Church in Germany." He wanted to remind all baptized Catholics that they are not merely members of the Church in Germany, but through Rome, in communion with the world of believers.

At the outdoor Sunday Mass in Munich, he warned all attending against a deafness to God that so easily comes with life in a secular society. At the cathedral in Munich, he exhorted parents and children to remember that God is close to us, not beyond the material universe. Sharing faith, worshipping as a family, on a weekly, daily basis will make family life more beautiful and stronger, he said. In Altötting he highlighted the Blessed Virgin's role in the Church: quite simply, "Mary leads us to Jesus." And in Regensburg he explained the meaning of the visit's motto, "Those who believe are never alone," an important message for Germany, where roughly half the population is single. At his last stop, in the cathedral in Freising where he was ordained a priest, he put his prepared text aside and spoke from the heart, encouraging the gathered clergy to nurture their inner spirituality so as not to let the ceaseless work of parish life get between them and Christ.

Of all the places he visited in Bavaria, I am certain that Regensburg was the most meaningful for him. He was able to hear his brother conduct another performance by the *Domspatzen*, he celebrated a grand, outdoor Mass and gathered in prayer in St. Peter's Cathedral with members of the Orthodox and Protestant confessions. The ecumenical gathering prayed for unity and for the strength to preach the Gospel "in a total and clear manner without toning it down and, above all, by conducting ourselves with sincere love." He also was able to spend an afternoon and evening in private with his brother at their house in Pentling, with its same furniture from the seventies. If it was not quite like old times, then it was as close as he will ever be able to get. Rupert and Therese Hofbauer, who have been looking after his house and yard for thirty years, greeted him and said he was "very moved" to be at his home again. Finally, in Regensburg, he delivered a lecture before a capacity crowd of scholars and students at his former university that he said was "an especially beautiful experience," but with an outcome he never expected.

⇌ THE REGENSBURG ADDRESS

The Pope's address in the Aula Magna, the massive concrete lecture hall at the University of Regensburg, has now become an event of world significance. If there is a turning point in this pontificate thus far, it is September 12, 2006.

His talk was composed and directed to a scholarly audience of professional researchers, thinkers, and teachers. The language is lofty and the ideas complex, but the message is clear and pertinent to all who would sit up and take note. In this work, entitled "Faith, Reason, and the University: Memories and Reflections," one can experience the Pope's intellectual powers operating at full throttle.[5]

After some opening reminiscences of his years as a professor of theology, he introduced the idea of reason—that exclusively human faculty known as "rationality"—that should unite all fields of inquiry and knowledge. During his years in Bonn, the university community periodically held discussions about their own fields and the role of reason therein. All questions were entertained, naturally including those challenging the existence of God. "Even in the face of such radical skepticism," Benedict said, "it is still necessary and reasonable to raise the question of God through the use of reason, and to do so in the context of the tradition of the Christian faith: this, within the university as a whole, was accepted without question." The discussions, it is fair to say, were held in the spirit of an intellectual community united by the search for truth.

The Pope's speech then turned to a recently published document, originally written in Greek, around the year 1400, in the form of a dialogue between a well-read Byzantine Emperor and a Persian scholar. The discussion covered a number of topics of interest to both Christianity and Islam, and sparked the Pope's interest in its treatment of the relationship between reason and faith. When it came to the role of violence, the emperor attacked in a way, the Pope said, we find shocking today:

> *"Show me just what Mohammed brought that was new, and there you will find things only evil and inhuman, such as his command to spread by the sword the faith he preached." The emperor, after having expressed himself so forcefully, goes on to explain in detail the reasons why spreading the faith through violence is something unreasonable. Violence is incompatible with the nature of God and the nature of the soul. "God," he says, "is not pleased by blood—and not acting reasonably is contrary to God's nature. Faith is born of the soul, not the body. Whoever would lead someone to faith needs the ability to speak well and to reason properly, without violence and threats. . . . To convince a reasonable soul, one does not need a strong arm, or weapons of any kind, or any other means of threatening a person with death. . . .*

The speech continued from there, highlighting the stormy history of the role of reason in interpretation of the Christian faith across the centuries. In describing the nexus of faith and reason, Benedict exhorted his audience not to define the latter so that there would be no room left for the former. He made a plea for a genuine, intense dialogue between the experimental, material sciences on the one hand and philosophy and theology on the other, for the sake of finding true answers to the great questions of humanity—those relevant to all cultures in the world, today and across recorded time. It was a stunning condensation of a lifetime of learning.

What happened afterward is a testimony to the awesome, terrible power of television. Some enterprising studio surgically removed the few seconds of the Pope reading the first twenty to thirty words of the passage quoted above, leaving out the qualifications before and the explanation after, to say nothing of the context of the speech as a whole. Virtually every network showed it. The clip gave the impression that the Pope had given a speech about the failings of Islam, which of course had nothing to do with his central thesis.

The immediate response from members of the Muslim community, as depicted by the same media industry, was predictably outraged and in places, outrageous. It is hardly likely that the people involved had read the Pope's speech in its entirety, let alone understood the quotation in its context. A translation into English had yet to appear, to say nothing of Arabic and other Middle and Near Eastern languages. The airwaves showed again and again the scant seconds where the Pope appears to declare Islam evil and inhuman. Mobs marched in the streets of more than one Middle Eastern city, burned effigies, and issued death threats. It was a remarkable display of perfectly unreasonable behavior. All this took Benedict completely by surprise. He first heard of the violence when he had left Bavaria and reached the airport in Rome.[6]

Very prominent people and whole institutions were taken in. The Parliament of Pakistan officially condemned the speech, and Mohammed Akef, a Sunni leader in Cairo, said the Pope "endangers world peace." The King of Morocco recalled his ambassador to the Vatican, and Ali Bardakoglu, the head of Turkey's Religious Affairs Directorate, told the press he was personally offended and demanded that the Pope take back his remarks and issue an apology. Later, however, Bardakoglu admitted to the Turkish newspaper *Hürriyet* that he had neither read the speech nor known about the context. He ended up revoking his own criticism. Cooler heads in the Islamic world were reticent.

Naturally, looking back on it, one can say that the Pope should have interrupted his quotation mid-sentence to add yet another disqualifier, so that he could not be caught on film attacking Islam, but one should also remember that the speech itself, as written and delivered, contains no cause for offense. *The Pope made no attack on Islam.* The Holy See was nonetheless quick to respond to international calls for an apology. In an official statement, read by a Vatican cardinal, the Pope said exactly what the situation demanded: he conveyed deep regret that the speech could have offended the feelings of Muslims. He reiterated what he said during the same trip to Germany: that it is wrong for Western secular society to confuse freedom of expression with the right to insult God and all that people call holy. The Pope spoke of his respect and esteem for Islam and the people of that faith, and added that it will help them and everyone to get over this difficult misunderstanding if they make the effort to look into what he actually said. On September 17, he voiced a direct apology in his Sunday address from the Vatican, adding, "These (words) were in fact a quotation from a medieval text which do not in any way express my personal thought."

Still, some good came from all the ruckus. Many more people in the world became aware of the Pope's visit to Germany, and of that marvelous speech to the university community, with its uplifting call for an open, exciting dialogue between religion and science in the common quest for truth. "The true meaning of my address," Benedict said when he issued his apology, "in its totality was and is an invitation to frank and sincere dialogue, with great mutual respect."

In the days and weeks that followed, the negative media coverage did not let up. It seemed as if every homemade firebomb and isolated potshot aimed at a Christian church, despite its denomination, across the Middle East got coverage on the evening news, although there were no injuries involved anywhere. On September 16, the murder of an Italian nun in Somalia was instantly attributed to the Pope's impolitic choice of quotations. That her last words were, "I forgive," (said three times) received considerably less attention. On October 3, a twenty-eight-year-old Turk named Hakan Ekinci hijacked a plane in his homeland and, with 113 other people on board, forced it to fly to Italy where it landed in Brindisi. Unarmed and unstable, he said he had a message for the Pope. After two hours he surrendered. The initial reports in the world media were all more or less the same: young Islamic Turks were hijacking planes as a protest against the Pope's words about Islam and against his intended visit to Turkey in November 2006. But it was all rubbish. Italian and Turkish governmental authorities quickly clarified the situation: Ekinci was a Turkish Christian, protesting state discrimination against him and members of his religious community, in the vain hope that the Pope would be able to grant him political asylum. Reality aside, the story gave plenty of opportunity for ominous predictions for the Pope's apostolic visit to Turkey, planned for later November.

We have to remind ourselves that all the fuss was due to a wonderful piece of academic rhetoric, which, as time passes, is showing positive effects. By the year's end, the famous School of General Rhetoric at the University at Tübingen in Germany declared Benedict's speech the "Address of the Year," based on its construction, courage, relevance, and significance.[7] Some famous German authors and politicians heartily and publicly agreed. In October 2007, a group of 138 Muslim scholars, religious and political leaders from Turkey, Iran, Egypt, the Balkan states, and central Asian countries sent the Pope a cosigned letter asking to join them in promoting peace, moderation, and mutual understanding between their two great world religions.[8] Benedict's speech may have longer reaching and better consequences than he hoped for. No matter what, it will remain one of many highlights in his apostolic journey to his Bavarian homeland.

Despite covering half the state of Bavaria, he did not go everywhere he wanted to. Traunstein made its bid to get on the itinerary, but failed to come through, although they had commissioned and installed a special, massive "Benedict Bell" in the church tower for the occasion. The city voted nonetheless to make him an *Ehrenbürger*, and a delegation came later to Rome to hand over the document. Benedict accepted graciously and said what he most appreciated in Traunstein was "the triad of *liberalitas, humanitas,* and *christianitas bavarica."* (These Latin words were later engraved on a church bell that was presented to the Pope during his visit to Bavaria in 2006.) He also told the delegation, "Not just once per week do my thoughts go back to Traunstein, but again and again."[9]

The immediate results of the visit are encouraging. In Germany in 2006 more than 200,000 children chose to receive confirmation at Easter time, far more than in recent years.

✈ TURKEY: NOVEMBER 28 TO DECEMBER 1, 2006

The Pope was nervous, and one could see it. He left the plane in Ankara wearing the white papal cassock, but the golden crucifix around his neck was hidden from view. Preceded by numerous death threats and grave warnings, he arrived as the head of one of the world's smallest states. There were no cheering crowds, bands, or the usual pomp and circumstance. A poll indicated that only 10 percent of the population was happy about his coming. Three thousand additional police officers were sent to keep order in Ankara, and sharpshooters were placed on nearby rooftops. The contrast with the last trip could not have been more extreme. But Benedict was undaunted. Everywhere he went he refused to wear the recommended bulletproof vest.

Benedict was taken to a small reception room in the airport where members of the Turkish political establishment greeted him civilly but without warmth. The Turkish prime minister and president almost certainly asked him about the long-standing Turkish bid to join the European Union, a project that Cardinal Ratzinger (as late as 2004) had considered unwise. Because of its Islamic religion and culture, he said that Turkey stands in "permanent contrast" with Europe. Obviously Pope Benedict wanted to avoid this hot-button political issue, principally because it had nothing to do with the purpose of his visit. Without endorsing or denigrating the plan, Pope Benedict wished them luck with it, taking the opportunity to clarify that the Catholic Church is not a political entity and aspires to no political power as such. That being said, however, she is always concerned about the sanctity of human dignity all throughout the world.

When Benedict met Ali Bardakoglu, the president for religious affairs, the atmosphere was tense. The Pope smiled cordially at the man who had publicly condemned his Regensburg address without having read it, and Bardakoglu showed virtually none of the easy warmth typical of Turkish hospitality. His face was grave throughout the encounter, and he only occasionally looked the Pope in the eye. His demeanor said clearly, "This man is no friend of mine or Turkey's." Turkey, it must be said, is an overwhelmingly Muslim country, but the constituted government is entirely secular and hostile to any Islamic political arrangement, from the Saudi Wahhabist monarchy and Iran's Shi'ite government to the Taliban and Al-Qaeda. Turkey's political establishment is decidedly more pro-Western than Middle Eastern.

But Benedict brought him around. Later that day, the two made speeches before the diplomatic corps in Ankara. The Pope praised the guarantees for religious freedom in Turkey's secular constitution, adding,

> *Naturally it is my hope that believers, whichever religious commu-*
> *nity they belong to, will continue to benefit from these rights. . . . This*

assumes, of course, that religions do not seek to exercise direct political power, as that is not their province, and it also assumes that they utterly refuse to sanction recourse to violence as a legitimate expression of religion.

When it was Bardakoglu's turn to speak, he really had no choice but to agree. The occasion became the moment where the head of the Catholic Church and Turkey's highest religious official spoke together against all those who condone violence in the name of religion—Islamic and otherwise. Later Bardakoglu put it into writing:

The great problems of the world do not arise from religious differences. . . . The problems develop when religious differences are exploited to legitimize political conflict, and so the problems become more complex and at the same time insoluble.[10]

In the rest of his speech, the Pope expressed his esteem for Islam, particularly its belief, shared with Christianity, not only in one God, but also in the sanctity of human life, peace, and justice. He also made an appeal for real, thorough-going religious freedom in Turkey, on behalf of the tiny Christian minority, both Catholic and Orthodox. While there is no legislation in Turkey banning conversion to Catholicism, it is only allowable for those of eighteen years or older. There are restrictions on Christian schools; Turkey also has no Catholic seminary, and the Orthodox seminary was shut down thirty years ago. After discussing religious freedom with the secular Turkish government in Ankara, the hardest part of the journey was over.

The following day Benedict could relax; he traveled to Ephesus, right near the Aegean coast, where he was in his element. He greeted a small gathering of Catholic faithful at the Shrine of the Mary's House and celebrated holy Mass. He returned to Istanbul on November 30 to celebrate the feast of the apostle St. Andrew, the brother of Simon Peter, with the Ecumenical Patriarch of Constantinople, Bartholomew I, one of the foremost spiritual leaders of the world's 300 million Orthodox Christians. Together they celebrated the liturgy, and together they imparted their blessings at the end. The two were visibly moved by the encounter, and they both took the opportunity to sign a "Joint Declaration" of their commitment to ecumenical dialogue with the goal of "the reestablishment of full communion between Catholics and Orthodox."

Achieving "full and visible unity" with the Orthodox Church is a stated goal of this pontificate, and it is not a new story. Paul VI and John Paul II worked for the same goal, and progress has been made toward it. As impossible as it may seem, after about a thousand years of division, one must remember that the Catholic and Orthodox religions both maintain an apostolic succession and priestly vocations, have a real Eucharist, and seven sacraments. One of the major sticking points is the business of primacy among the patriarchs and the special role of the Pope in the leadership of the universal Church. Before leaving Turkey, the Pope celebrated a Mass in the Latin Cathedral of the Holy Spirit in Istanbul, with the Ecumenical Patriarch, the Armenian Patriarch Mesrob II, the Syro-Orthodox Metropolitan Mor Filuksinos, and Protestant religious leaders attending. Different Christians prayed together, in spite of their differing languages, views, and rites.

The trip ended on an unplanned high point for all that took place in the Sultan Ahmed Mosque (also known as the Blue Mosque) in Istanbul, the most prominent religious building in the city. The minarets were decorated with lights to mark the Pope's visit, and the Pope removed his shoes before entering as a basic sign of respect. When Mustafa Cagrici, the gran mufti of Turkey, led his guest through the various parts of the seventeenth-century structure, his demeanor showed real, hospitable joy at the opportunity. Pausing at one point, the gran mufti said that he would take a moment to pray and turned to face Mecca. The Pope joined him spontaneously.

> *Remaining recollected for a few minutes in that place of prayer,*
> *I turned to the only Lord of heaven and earth, merciful Father*
> *of the whole of humanity, and implored that all believers might*
> *recognize themselves as creatures and give witnesses of authentic*
> *fraternity![11]*

Everyone remained still, except for the photographers and cameramen who scurried about in the background, trying to immortalize the moment in two dimensions. But it was a splendid gesture: two religious leaders—one Christian and one Muslim—praying at once to the one God under the same roof. The Turkish press ran headlines like "A Historic Prayer," "Peace in Istanbul," and even "The Pope Conquers Hearts and Minds."[12]

When Benedict visited the Hagia Sophia, the former basilica of Constantinople and now a museum, he wrote in its golden book, "In our diversity, we stand together in faith in the One God. May God enlighten us and lead us to the way of love and peace!" On the day he left Turkey, one of the largest national newspapers proclaimed, "He came as Pope. He returns as Father."

FAITH AND REASON

In December 2006 Benedict delivered an address before the Roman Curia that reviewed the journeys and events of the past year and looked forward to the future. In line with his address at Regensburg he said, "The relationship between faith and reason is a serious challenge for the present prevailing culture in the Western world." The problem with a reason that is solely based on material and experimental fact is that it subverts morality. While modern science has brought humanity enormous technological possibilities and capabilities—and we all know what they are—it simultaneously enables a number of appalling abuses. According to Benedict:

> *It must be admitted that the tendency to consider true only that which can be experienced constitutes a limitation for human reason and produces a terrible schizophrenia, evident to all, because of which rationalism and materialism, and hypertechnology and unbridled instincts, coexist.*

In his Christmas Day message, Benedict raised the same issue in the form of a question:

> *Does a "Savior" still have any value and meaning for the men and women of the third millennium? Is a "Savior" still needed by a humanity which has reached the moon and Mars and is prepared to conquer the universe; for a humanity which knows no limits in its pursuit of nature's secrets and which has succeeded even in deciphering the marvelous codes of the human genome? Is a Savior needed by a humanity which has invented interactive communication, which navigates in the virtual ocean of the Internet and, thanks to the most advanced modern communications technologies, has now made the Earth, our great common home, a global village? This humanity of*

the 21st century appears as a sure and self-sufficient master of its own destiny, the avid proponent of uncontested triumphs.

"So it would seem," he continued, "yet this is not the case." People all over the world suffer from hunger, thirst, slavery, oppression, hatred, and the violence of chaos and war. Others, among the rich and the supposedly free, enslave themselves to food, money, entertainment, drugs, and material possessions, rendering their own lives a kind of commodity. What then must we do?

The answer, according to the Pope, is what you would expect: listen to Christ. He has the message of good will, hope, reconciliation, and love. He shows the way, of "reasonableness and moderation," to tame the appetite, calm all strife, and find the way out of endless conflict.

God became man in Jesus Christ. He brings to all the love of the Father in heaven. He is the Savior of the world! Do not be afraid, open your hearts to him and receive him, so that his Kingdom of love and peace may become the common legacy of each man and woman.

In 2006, across Europe from west to east and north to south, Benedict exhorted people to open themselves to reason. They must regard human rationality as a gift of the Divine and perfectly embodied in Jesus Christ. Faith and reason are compatible and good, just as one without the other is dangerous. No one, he claimed, will lose anything worthwhile by following the path laid down by Jesus and his apostles, to the present day. In 2007, the Pope endeavored to show the world that that path is one of love.

12

THE MESSAGE of LOVE – 2007

"God is love, and he who abides in love abides in God,
and God abides in him."

–1 John: 4:16

"Love – caritas – will always prove necessary, even in the most just society.
There is no ordering of the State so just that it can eliminate the need
for a service of love. Whoever wants to eliminate love is preparing
to eliminate man as such."

–Pope Benedict XVI, Deus Caritas Est

Some of the numbers coming in from 2006 indicate that Pope Benedict XVI is the most popular pontiff in history. The prefecture of the pontifical household reported that 3.2 million people came to see the Pope at the Vatican and his summer residences in 2006, mainly for general and special audiences, various liturgies, and prayer services. These numbers are on the rise from 2005, and do not include the apostolic visits abroad and in different parts of Italy. What is drawing so many people to these audiences is not a charismatic pantomime or a compelling ringmaster, but a man who asks life's most important questions and then gives good, persuasive, uplifting answers. At the audiences, Benedict has effectively been telling the story of the faith, about the first apostles, martyrs, and saints of the Church in the first four centuries after the death of Christ. In each of these short expositions, the Holy Father lays out the contribution of each man, in word and deed, to the Catholic faith. Following them on zenit.org is like taking a course in Church history and patristic theology from one of the world's foremost authorities on the subject.

The topic chosen for the audiences shows how this Pope is not using his pontificate as a chance to sit back and enjoy the adulation until death overtakes him. For Benedict, the pontificate is a culmination of his life's work, which spans the era from before, during, and after the Second Vatican Council. Benedict's pontificate is about consolidation, always true to holy Scripture and Catholic tradition. In his own final years, he is dedicated to showing the Church the way into her future. The best way is the path of love.

The Pope's devotion to Christ's message of love is what drove him on during his second full calendar year, and it led to a number of surprises. On January 4, he visited a soup kitchen near the Colosseum in Rome, where he spoke with the volunteers and a large group of its beneficiaries. Referring to the center's Nativity scene, he said that the coming of Jesus reminds us to love in this world and tells us how to do it. "Here," he said, "one can experience that, when we love our neighbor, we know God better."[1] He made a present of 10,000 blankets and 2,000 coats and received in return an apron and a collection of drawings by the children who come to the center.[2] Three days later he baptized thirteen babies in the Sistine Chapel, giving an improvised homily on the meaning of the sacrament. "Every child who is born," he said, "brings us God's smile and invites us to recognize that life is his gift, a gift to be welcomed with love and preserved with care, always and at every moment."[3]

One of the first surprises of 2007 came with the establishment in February of an official Vatican soccer club and competition, the "Clericus Cup." That Benedict, who avoided team sports whenever possible throughout his whole life, should have been the Pope to set up the papal team is astounding. And chances are that the team will be good. There are a number of seminarians who come from soccer countries like Brazil and Argentina, to say nothing of Italy, Spain, and many others, and these young men devote their free time to sports. It is certain that the club will not be like any other. Games on Sunday are forbidden, and players who curse and swear are asked to leave the field.[4]

In February, Benedict released a document about the Eucharist, the sacrament of love in the Church, appropriately entitled, *Sacramentum Caritatis*. This sacrament, according to Benedict, "makes manifest that 'greater' love which led (Christ) to 'lay down his life for his friends.'" Based on fifty propositions coming from the Synod of Bishops held in October 2005, the 130-page text also contains several points that have appeared in Benedict's writings over the last decades. One can look at the document as a clarification of potential confusions that came in the wake of liturgical reform during and after Vatican II.

Sacramentum Caritatis entails a number of basic ways to make sure the celebration of the Eucharist is appropriately devout. To begin with, celebrants should follow the norms and give the best homily they can about the word of God, without getting sidetracked on other topics. At the sign of peace, sobriety befits the occasion better than plunging into the congregation, which can be rather disruptive. The document recommends greater use of Latin and Gregorian chant, and all music should be properly devout rather than merely popular. The tabernacle should be up, front, and center in the church. It should be the central focus of the worship space, and not the celebrant's chair, mounted royally on a dais, as demeaning as the pastor might feel it to be. Confession and penance remains a crucial prerequisite so to speak, in line with Jesus' own constant call for all to repent. Celibacy for priests is a "priceless treasure," and hard as it might sound to postmodern ears, those who discontinue their marriages and start new ones really cannot partake in Communion. Christ is the center of the Eucharist and the selfless, unconditional love he and his followers share. Everything else pales in comparison. Nothing anyone does should risk denigrating it.

Sacramentum Caritatis, therefore, complements Benedict's first encyclical, *Deus Caritas Est.* The Eucharist is the sacrament of love, just as God himself is love itself. We do not make the Eucharist in our parishes and communities, rather it should make us, forming us into the devoted, obedient followers of Christ that God longs for us all to be.

THE BEST SELLER

Deus Caritas Est was one of the all-time top-selling works by a Pope, with 1.5 million copies in print in Italy, three reprints in German and Spanish, and translations in Russian, Chinese, and Latin, in addition to other major European languages. But his book *Jesus of Nazareth,* the first of two, topped those figures in one month. How he found time to write it is a thing of wonder in itself; it is said that he mainly worked on it during his summer "vacation" in 2005, in the Aosta valley in the Italian Alps, and whenever he had a spare minute thereafter. I would not doubt that it was done in a single draft, and it bears his former and papal names. It is a continuation of the pattern he established as a cardinal: although he occupies a high office in the Church, he will continue to publish as a private individual. His book about Jesus Christ, he said, is just an expression of his private opinion, his "personal search 'for the Face of the Lord,'" and is in no way a statement of papal authority.

The book's main contention is that the tendency to separate the so-called "historical" Jesus from the Jesus in the four Gospels is a mistake; it leads to a cacophony of rival historical theories. Claiming to use the methods of historical scholarship, anyone can come up with the Jesus that pleases him: the teacher, the revolutionary, the hippie, the healer, the racist taskmaster, the man of virtue, so on and so forth. Just recently I came across a new book that argues that Jesus and the early disciples were basically ancient rock stars, master orchestrators of ecstatic, charismatic, religious events, which is supposed to explain the birth and growth of Christianity. The idea is totally bizarre, but not one of the sillier ones out there. Let's avoid *The Da Vinci Code* altogether. The Pope's contention is that Jesus as depicted in Scripture is the Jesus of historical fact.

Benedict paints for us the picture of Jesus as the "new Moses," the man who knew the Jewish Torah front to back and whose life tells the truth about God to all people. The Pope explains the temptations, the Sermon on the Mount, the beatitudes, some key parables, and the Our Father as Jesus' way to explain to all people across time about who he really was. He *was* and *is* the Kingdom of God he constantly proclaimed. The book also explains Jesus' gathering of the disciples, especially the apostles Peter and John, the Transfiguration as a "prayer event," and Jesus' self-description as the Son of Man. None of these make any sense without looking at the whole of Scripture and Jesus' crucifixion. The Pope intends for treatment of Jesus' birth, passion, death, and resurrection to appear in the next volume. To put it simply, for Benedict, Jesus is the man who makes sense of human history.

In this book, the Pope does not try to explain in scientific terms how a virgin can give birth to a son, how a man can turn water into wine, work miracles, and rise from the dead, because he can't. No one can. Experimental science, despite its many wonderful achievements over the last two centuries, cannot explain the historical questions relating to life in general. Where did a cell come from? How did life come about on earth? How did light and matter come about? What accounts for human rationality? The normal answer to these questions usually is either "By accident," or "Some higher power is somehow responsible." If the former is right, then everything happens strictly by chance, so nothing can mean anything. If the latter is right, then everything bears a significance greater than itself.

A BAVARIAN BIRTHDAY

Popes have not ordinarily had public celebrations for their birthdays, but Pope Benedict broke this mold as he has others. On Divine Mercy Sunday, April 15, he celebrated Mass before a crowd of 50,000 in St. Peter's Square, and gave a homily about his own life, not in order to tell a good story, but to illustrate how God's mercy can act in the life of a simple man. He gave thanks for his birth and baptism on Holy Saturday, for his excellent, loving father and mother who taught him so much about the faith and life itself, for his brother and sister, friends, colleagues, and the great family that is God's Church. Above all, he thanked God for his priestly vocation and the special relationship it gives him with the faithful of the world.

Early Monday morning, April 16, 2007, a brass band from Geisenhausen in Bavaria filled a largely empty St. Peter's Square. Soon enough tens of thousands of people came out under the clear blue sky to congratulate the Pope on reaching the completion of his eightieth year. He spoke to the crowds warmly, remembering his parents and siblings who had stayed so close to him over the years. He told those waving the Bavarian flag and wearing the traditional Bavarian costumes that the sight lifted his heart and made him happy. The rest of the day was given to receiving a load of gifts: a gilded processional cross from Burgos in Spain, a decorated book of the Gospels from the Archdiocese of Munich and Freising, documents for a new state-sponsored prize in studies of his theological corpus, personally delivered by Edmund Stoiber, the minister president of Bavaria, a new musical setting of the Mass composed in his honor, and the news that a museum dedicated to his life and vocation was opened and consecrated in Marktl am Inn. Congratulations came in from political and religious leaders from all across the globe.

Other gifts were less grand but well-meaning nonetheless. There were pastries from Salerno and a huge marzipan cake decorated with papal insignia from Schleswig-Holstein in northern Germany. Admirers sent flowers, birthday cards, and music recordings, and one unnamed Italian sent him a huge teddy bear. Most of these items the Pope passed on to the less fortunate; the bear went to the Bambino Gesu children's hospital in Rome. Finally, in the evening there was a concert in the Vatican's main auditorium by the Stuttgart Radio Symphony Orchestra. The Pope, for his part, gave presents in return. All Vatican employees received the day off and a €500 gift. All monetary gifts received by the Holy Father were sent to Catholic communities in the Holy Land, Africa, and other areas in need.

ST. AUGUSTINE

On the next Sunday in April, Benedict paid a visit to someone he has loved since his days at the seminary and the university, one of the greatest minds in the history of the West—St. Augustine of Hippo. The Pope flew by helicopter to Pavia, which lies just south of Milan in northern Italy, celebrated Mass, and prayed at the tomb of the saint. Augustine, one of the four Fathers of the Church, who watched the disintegration of the Roman Empire and died in 430, was the first to show how God, who is love, works in human history. History, he showed, is driven by two kinds of love: the first is love of self, which leads to all the sins, all the wars, all the human disasters that have and will always plague us across time. Love of self, Augustine said, inevitably leads to hatred of God and thus of mankind, his creation. The other love—love of God—leads all mankind toward renunciation of self, toward selflessness, toward love of one's neighbor, forgiveness, reconciliation, and therefore peace and redemption. In God's love, we have hope—for each other, for the future of the world, for all mankind.

In a homily based on the readings from the Eucharistic celebration, Benedict discussed conversion, and what it meant to be a "convert." "One of the greatest converts in the history of the Church," he said, was St. Augustine. His conversion, which entailed his baptism in 387 by St. Ambrose, the bishop of Milan, was not a single event but part of a process, a journey. Being received into the journey was a benchmark in Augustine's life, in some ways an end, and in more ways a beginning. The Pope delineated three aspects of Christian conversion. The first is the move toward the faith, toward the great Yes that allows Christ to enter one's life. For Augustine, who was very much a man of his time, it was a difficult path to take, because it flew in the face of so many aspects of the prevalent, pagan culture. The second step, the Pope said, is when a person, through constant struggle and suffering gets beyond the concern with his own perfection, and devotes himself to others and their needs. For Augustine this meant his ordination to the priesthood. Finally, the third move is an intense period of studying Holy Scripture, during which the convert recasts his life and history in the light of Jesus' teachings. The main point of all this is that Christ enables conversion; he wipes away the stain of sin and shows us the right relationship to have with God and creation.

At Vespers, standing before the tomb of St. Augustine, Benedict said that his *Deus Caritas Est* is "deeply indebted to the thought of St. Augustine, who was in love with the Love of God, and sang of it, meditated upon it, preached it in all his writings and above all witnessed to it in his pastoral ministry." The truth that God is love is the starting point for everything the Church does, all actions and teachings. If that love goes, then nothing makes sense; nothing has intrinsic value. "Serving Christ," he said, "is first of all a question of love." And young people, he added, especially need to hear that truth proclaimed, so that they may find freedom and joy in Christ.[5]

✈ BRAZIL: MAY 9-13

In May 2007, Benedict XVI made his first apostolic journey to the western hemisphere. The American media coverage was typical. Never mind that tens of thousands turn out to line the street wherever he goes. Never mind that nearly a half million people show up for Mass on a Friday morning. Never mind that a stadium full of young people explodes in unrestrained joy at his arrival, without indulging in perhaps a single instance of drug abuse, random violence, or casual, uncommitted, exploitive sex. Days before his arrival, a lead article declared "As Pope Heads to Brazil, a Rival Theology Persists," referencing liberation theology that has been on the wane since the 1990s. Then there was "Pope Stresses Opposition to Abortion" and, even better, "Brazil Welcomes Pope but Questions His Perspective."

The American press is certainly not alone. Some German publications focus more on the Protestant sects that are multiplying across the face of Latin America, giving them and their message much more space than the Catholic, which was depicted as the wretched old monolith, the laity disheartened, the clergy lackluster, a ship sinking in a sea of tax-free, private religious initiatives that offer emotional highs instead of lasting theological truths.

This is not to say that no challenges awaited the Pope on this journey. In February 2007 he articulated the ones he wished to address in conjunction with the General Conference of the Episcopate in Latin America and the Caribbean, above all, a "growing hedonist secularism," which we know all too well in the USA. In Latin America live about half of the world's Catholics, about 480 million. Although the tourist industry depicts Brazil as one limitless beach or a nonstop Rio Mardi Gras binge, the culture of the country and the region has been traditionally, thoroughly Catholic.

All across Latin America, however, there has been an explosion in the number of Pentecostal churches year after year; the protestantization of the populace is well underway. This is not necessarily bad by any means, but it does mean that the Catholic Church is facing a strengthening competition, which is, historically speaking, probably a good thing. In the centuries where the Catholic Church was the only religious alternative, she and her clergy were not always known for their best behavior. Being presented with rivalry will most likely inspire her sons and daughters to stand by her and proclaim her message of truth in their lives and words. In addition to proselytism from the sects, in Latin America one finds an increasing incidence of new legislation that legalizes abortion and undermines marriage to say nothing of the perennial problem of mass poverty and its attendant woes, especially in terms of education, crime, migration, religious liberty, and the manipulation of public opinion. In all these areas, the stronger the family, the better it is for individuals, communities, and states as a whole.

In Brazil, Benedict kept to his schedule as closely as he could. When the Holy Father flies, it bears mentioning, he revels in none of the luxuries available in the average corporate jet. There is no couch, wet bar, or shower. The Vatican owns no airplane. The Pope flies to his destination in a normal Alitalia machine with no special outfit, and he returns using an airline of the country he has visited. His one privilege is to sit in the front row, sometimes alone. Near him sit the cardinals, bishops, and dignitaries accompanying him, and behind them, separated by a curtain, is a teaming horde of international journalists whose job it is to cover the journey. At takeoff and landing, flight attendants sit on the fold-down benches as in all normal commercial passenger jets, even right opposite the Pope. These are modest arrangements for the leader of a world organization with more than a billion adherents.

On the second day in Brazil, Thursday, May 10, Benedict XVI came to a rally of young people held in the municipal stadium of São Paulo. Words can scarcely do justice to the excitement the presence of this delicate old man produced. The speakers' voices rang with heartfelt enthusiasm. Dancers and musicians exuded joy, and the exuberant responses from the tens of thousands in the stands said it all. After four young people spoke of the challenges they faced, in social life, the schools, the job market, and at home, they sponta-neously embraced the Pope in a group hug-huddle. That this gesture was decidedly not Bavarian and even less in accordance with papal protocol made no difference; the Holy Father beamed with pure pleasure. The music was all popular, as was totally appropriate for the occasion and the audience. It was a rally, not a liturgy. After the speeches, music and dance performances, there was a Gospel reading followed by the Pope's address to the young there in the stadium and in all of Latin America.

The theme was "Disciples, Missionaries of Christ," and the Pope called all of them, each of them, to elevate themselves and join the movement of the Church toward eternal life in God's love. He challenged them, exhort-ing them literally to make the very best of themselves: "Do not waste your youth!" "Christ is calling you to be saints!" He quoted from his first encyclical, reminding them that *eros* is love that reaches out toward the other and up to God, but if it is not coupled with *agape*, God's love, the love of self-giving, then it withers, grasps, and clings, pulling the lover down, enslaving him or her in the vicious circle of self-gratification that leads to nothing but disappointment, disil-lusionment, and unhappiness. The Church is not a monolith, but a movement. If she does not move hearts and minds, then she is doing nothing. And those who call themselves Catholic, young and old, should be doing the same thing. This is the New Evangelization, the springtime in the Church called for by John Paul the Great. This is the mission of Benedict XVI.

On Sunday, May 13, the final day of his journey, Benedict celebrated Mass, opened the 5th General Conference of the Episcopate of Latin America, and gave perhaps his longest speech ever before the gathered bishops of that region. In it, he said very clearly that the role of the Church was not in politics. The historical struggles in Latin America between military juntas and democratic movements, between obscenely rich oligarchs and the impoverished masses, are steadily working themselves out. The Church has less reason now than ever before to be politically engaged to insure the stability of the state, or to stand up against it in cases of extreme abuse. The Church now, however, should not give in to the attendant ideologies of "materialistic liberalism," just as she resists Marxism, in the form of liberation theology. What she needs to do is evangelize, evangelize, evangelize. She should not rely on organizations, structures, culture, and history. The days of 'national' Catholic cultures are slowly coming to an end. Instead she needs to proclaim her message so that people can make the free, clear, right choice to heed it. Benedict said when he returned to Rome,

> *I encouraged my brother bishops to advance and reinforce their commitment to the New Evangelization... [and] to reclaim everywhere the lifestyle of the early Christian community that is described in the Acts of the Apostles – a lifestyle dedicated to catechesis, to the sacramental life and to works of charity.*[6]

This means that they must declare, tirelessly, everywhere, and in spite of everything, "It is love that gives life."

The Church, said Benedict, must proclaim her faith that God is love, and through that truth, help to assuage the injustices and inequities that remain. She must be a force for peace; she must protect the individual as something inherently valuable, no matter how imperfect, weak, or poor. The Catholic notion of love and justice should uphold all good political and economic projects that are rational and positive for humanity. She stands for harmony and human solidarity.

The morning after the journey was over an American newspaper ran an article entitled, "The Pope Denounces Capitalism and Marxism." *Denounces?* In the text it claimed that "he raged with ... fire against

Marxism and capitalism." *Raged?* It is hard to imagine Pope Benedict railing against anything. Has anyone out there heard him raise his voice in anger? Even his most critical biographers do not cite a single instance. What he did say, in his usual measured tone, is that the main problem with putting all of human reason and faith into either capitalism or Marxism obviously entails a denial of the reality of God and therefore a divinely based morality.

This newspaper depicted the journey in terms of the Manichaean division of Roman Catholicism into liberal (good) and conservative (bad) camps. It said the trip "added to sense… that his papacy seemed to be moving closer to the conservative mold that Cardinal Ratzinger had embodied." The authors neglected to articulate what the features of that mold might be and how Ratzinger-Benedict ever departed from them. The most telling line has to do with the Pope's Sunday speech before the bishops: "Benedict remains, as ever, untethered to any set of views apart from his own." Such a statement shows how little such writers understand about Catholicism. The words that come from Pope Benedict's mouth are certainly his own, but the views are not. They belong to the many across time, the hundreds of millions of Catholics living *and dead,* clergy and laity, men and women, who have subscribed to the faith inherited from the apostles. Virtually any pronouncement the Pope makes has to be in communion with them. It is the same Church.

The Pope is not the absolute monarch over the Catholic Church, and certainly not in the way usually depicted in the media. The Pope *is* the absolute monarch over the 108-acre Vatican State, but the Vatican is only a state because it has to be, in order to maintain its independence from all the others. If it were not, then it would be under too much pressure from the Italian government, given its location. By keeping the Vatican a state, it can serve the Church throughout the world with minimal local interference.

SUMMER RECONCILIATION

In 2007, Benedict XVI continued his bridge building in other parts of the world, namely China. What to do about it? There the Catholic Church is divided between the Chinese Catholic Patriotic Association, the branch of the Church controlled by the government, and the underground, unofficial Church, which does not regard the Association as legitimate. While the underground is in full communion with Rome, the Association is not, officially at any rate, because the government selects and ordains the Association's bishops at its pleasure, without Rome's approval. Priests and bishops of the underground Church, however, are routinely imprisoned and abused in a number of ways. And the Holy See's actions have not always helped to ease the situation either; in the past it has recommended that the faithful avoid receiving the sacraments from Association priests. Certain Association bishops have been excommunicated. Both branches of the Church in China are suffering, according to Cardinal Zen Ze-kiun of Hong Kong, but the Association bows before the pressure while the underground chooses to resist. Both are trying to walk a tightrope; 85 percent or more of Association bishops later request to be acknowledged by Rome; they *want* to be in full communion, too. China may be much richer and more open than it was, but it is an error to say that there is religious freedom. The Vatican wants the Pope to have the final word in selecting bishops, as he does with the rest of the Church, but the Chinese government takes a dim view of that idea.

If I were a Chinese Communist, I would be suspicious, too. The very name of the Party is discredited all over the world. No one can seriously claim to be a Communist these days, in the Marxist sense of the term, without being held as a mild lunatic. It is normal to say in China that the Communist Party has abandoned Karl Marx but holds to "socialism with Chinese characteristics." Furthermore, history has shown that materialist, atheist, oppressive regimes (e.g., in Germany and Russia) cannot usually do much to foster the spiritual well-being of their people; if anything, they feel compelled to repress it. In 1979 the freshly elected Pope John Paul II made his first apostolic visit to Poland, was seen by half the population, and preached in favor of religious liberty and against fear. In the next year the workers' movement called Solidarity took shape, and the clock began to tick on the Iron Curtain in Eastern Europe. Not that anything quite like that could happen in China, being a totally different situation in many respects, where roughly 1 percent of the population is Catholic. But due to recent history, the members of the Communist government have reason enough to be a bit wary of the moral authority of a Pope.

In June, Pope Benedict issued an open letter to all members of the Church, the *one* Catholic Church, divided as she may be, in China. He exhorted bishops, clergy, and the faithful to bury their differences, forgive past wrongs, and treat each other with charity, especially in the areas where there are rival bishops and communities, one underground, the other with the Association. To the government, Benedict said that the Church in China is not a Chinese church, but a branch of the universal Church, and union with the Holy See is indispensable. All it really wants is religious liberty, the freedom to operate the way she does throughout the world. The Pope said he was open to full diplomatic relations and ongoing discussions about episcopal appointments, diocesan organization, etc. He asked all Association bishops not yet in communion with Rome to apply for recognition, just as he asked all those already in communion to be public about it. The Church can only prosper when she is not divided against herself. The Chinese government knows full well how to keep her weak. The question is if it will ever let her be whole and strong.

The initial response is encouraging. There was no widespread crackdown on Benedict's letter, the vice chairman of the Association invited him to visit China, and the government selected Joseph Li Shan to be the next Bishop of Beijing. Although there was no request for prior papal approval, Shan had been on a list of candidates to whom the papacy said it would raise no objection. Another ordination, that of Paul Xiao Zejiang as Coadjutor Bishop in the province of Guizhou, which took place on September 8, was even more promising; both the Vatican and the Chinese government gave their assent beforehand. Benedict's letter was an olive branch to the Chinese government. The Pope wants an undivided Church in China, and the Communist Party does not want a hothouse for antigovernment activity. Maybe this will be a win-win situation.

LITURGICAL "REFORM"?

Following on the publication of *Sacramentum Caritatis*, the word was out by the end of June: Benedict XVI had applied the seal of his approval to a *motu proprio*, a document coming from him directly, one that allowed for wider use of the Latin Mass, the so-called "Tridentine" liturgy that was more or less the norm from the sixteenth century until 1970. It is a simple matter, really, and not in anyway a "reform of the reform" that some had expected, dreaded, or ardently desired.

Pope John XXIII, the pontiff who convoked the Second Vatican Council, also issued a revised Roman Missal in 1962. In keeping with the established practice of the centuries, the main language of the liturgy was Latin, including a smattering of Greek and Hebrew words, allowing for the Gospel reading and homily in the vernacular. Vatican II neither scrapped this Missal nor wrote up another. The Council did promulgate the "Constitution on the Sacred Liturgy" in 1963, its first major document, which expressed the desire for a reform of the liturgy with greater use of vernacular, simpler rites, and "full and active participation" of the faithful. After the Council was over, under Pope Paul VI, a revised Missal was issued in 1970, the so-called *novus ordo* Mass that is said almost everywhere today, with its trademarks: free use of the vernacular and the option for the priest to face the congregation over the altar. This implementation of the new Missal gave some people the impression that the Tridentine Mass was abrogated, struck from the books, or otherwise done away with, to be replaced by the *novus ordo*.

For perhaps the majority of Catholics, this was a welcome change for any number of reasons; but many, it is fair to say, were appalled. These had loved the liturgy in Latin and were scandalized by the range of new abuses (usually in the name of "creativity") that accompanied the application of the *novus ordo*. A few of these people made the 1962 Missal their declaration of resistance, not only to the *novus ordo*, but to the Second Vatican Council as well. A small number of reactionary groups formed, the most prominent being the Society of St. Pius X, that rejected the 1970 Missal out of hand and condemned some of the Council's documents. The controversy came to a head in the 1980s, when its founding bishop, Marcel Lefebvre, started ordaining bishops on his own accord, which is a schismatic act. He and his followers were excommunicated.

Benedict XVI just wanted to clarify one very important point: there is only one Roman rite. There was and is "no contradiction" between the two Missal editions of 1962 and 1970. "In the history of the liturgy," he said, "there is growth and progress, but no rupture."[7] If you think about it, the issue of which language is used and where the celebrant faces is actually cosmetic, compared with the continuities in the prayers and structure of the Mass. Changes in languages and other nonessentials have occurred in the history of the Church, and they are certainly not revolutionary. The Catholic Church has sustained diversity in its liturgical rites, and about two dozen were celebrated at the Second Vatican Council. According to Benedict, one of the driving forces of the liturgical reform movement that culminated in the 1970 Missal was in part to get as close to the ancient Roman as possible. We should not forget that the earliest forms of the Mass were in Greek. There was a similar fuss when the Church shifted to Latin in the fourth century, when Latin was the closest thing to a common vernacular—at least closer than Greek. And, after all, the *novus ordo* can be said in Latin, though in most parishes there are precious few who want it that way.

What Benedict wants is unity in the liturgy. He pointed out that there had been no juridical procedure abrogating the 1962 Missal, but priests were not to use the 1962 without the express permission of his bishop. "In principle," he said, "[it] was always permitted." So as of September 2007, the *novus ordo* will be the "ordinary" form of the Mass, and the 1962 Missal will be the "extraordinary." They will constitute "two usages of the one Roman rite." Any priest can say either version on any day, except for the Easter Triduum when the *novus ordo* is to be preferred. The 1962 Missal is also good for baptisms, marriages, funerals, confessions, and anointing the sick. However, a number of bishops (particularly those in France) were worried that such a move would deepen the divide between the so-called "traditional" Catholics and the rest who unreservedly acknowledge the validity of the Second Vatican Council. The Pope, on the other hand, probably sees it as an opportunity to heal old wounds. But should he be proved wrong, his letter said that the matter would be reviewed after three years. It is very difficult to imagine a tsunami of popular support behind reviving a liturgy that almost no one would understand.

Not exactly earthshaking, is it? The media coverage, ever committed to finding fault lines in Catholicism, was painfully wrong. Once again, it depicted the Pope as a conservative or a reactionary set against contemporary liberal Catholics and the Second Vatican Council that was supposed to be a starting point for all good things. The Associated Press said the Pope was "reviving a rite that was all but swept away by the liberalizing reforms of the Second Vatican Council."[8] There was no mention of the fact that the Tridentine Mass was said, with Pope John XXIII's reforms, every day during the Council. The AP article totally misrepresents the liturgical reform movement leading up to and carrying through Vatican II; the writers mentioned none of the ancient precedents in support of what they depicted as liberalizing, modernizing changes.

It is incorrect to assert that loosening the restrictions on the use of the 1962 Missal is an act of opposition to the resolutions of Vatican II. Some major media writers do not seem to realize that the Council did not reform the liturgy per se but merely stated the guidelines by which it needed to be done. An Associated Press article alluded to various religious leaders who are concerned "that the move will lead to further changes to the reforms approved by 1962–65 Second Vatican Council."[9] Benedict's decree changes absolutely nothing in the reformed liturgy of 1970. The vernacular *novus ordo* is the form of the Mass he says, whether in his small papal chapel every morning (said in Italian) or at larger gatherings both in Rome and on his apostolic journeys. He does not seem to have celebrated by the 1962 Missal, at least not in public, during his pontificate to date. And what is meant by *"further* changes"? In what way has Pope Benedict XVI or his predecessor *ever* departed from the resolutions of the Council? It just goes to show that the media are bound and determined to create conflict, even where there is basically none.

⟶ AUSTRIA: SEPTEMBER 7–9

Toward the end of the summer, Benedict XVI made an apostolic journey to Austria, which was the nearest thing to a homecoming he could have wished for, being right next door to his native Bavaria. Since his childhood, he has been a lover of Austrian music (Mozart above all), culture, and Catholic identity. In 2007 he returned to Austria as Pope and pilgrim, to visit the Marian shrine at Mariazell for the 850th anniversary of her founding. In an interview on the plane, he said that he wanted to bolster people's faith and remind them that Jesus Christ should be their point of reference. In secularist relativism, which is gathering strength in Austria and everywhere else in Western Europe, there is neither good nor bad, so it is easy to lose one's way through life. The Pope's goal was to show the Austrians that Christianity brings more unity, hope, and pluck for the future than any other alternative. In recent years the Church in Austria has been rocked by homosexual scandals among priests and seminarians, and there is a definite sense that Catholicism has been in retreat.

Cold, unremitting rain drenched his three days in Austria. The bad weather, combined with extreme security measures and long hours of waiting, made the size of the crowds welcoming him and taking part in the events much smaller than normal. The Pope had a cold to boot. Deutsche Welle reported rather smugly, "The small crowds were jubilant, but the Pope's voice failed him," a gross exaggeration. While he read his addresses with no trouble, his voice did crack when he tried to sing his blessing.

The Pope's plane landed in Vienna, which was not originally in the plan for the pilgrimage. As in Bavaria, he went from the airport to the *Marien-säule,* a tall column topped with a statue of the Blessed Mother, erected in gratitude for preserving the city during a terrible war over three and a half centuries ago. The prayer he made encapsulates his message for the visit as a whole.

> *To you [Mary] I entrust the country of Austria and its people. Help all of us to follow your example and to direct our lives completely to God! Grant that, by looking to Christ, we may become ever more like him: true children of God! Then we too, filled with every spiritual blessing, will be able to conform ourselves more fully to his will and to become instruments of his peace for Austria, Europe, and the world.*[10]

Austria's and Europe's problems with rock-bottom birthrates, more and more abortions, rapidly aging populations, and social listlessness would be solved if people thought of God rather than themselves, following in his path rather than one's own, gladly becoming his instrument and not a solitary tool.

Benedict's speech in Vienna's Hofburg palace before members of the Austrian government and diplomatic corps is the clearest, most concise distillation of his thought about Europe and her sociopolitical woes I have ever read.[11] While he acknowledged the tremendous strides in economic and material prosperity that have been achieved in the last two generations, he warned against cutting off Christian roots for the sake of embracing materialist relativism. By way of support, he quoted Europe's foremost postmodern (non-Christian) philosopher, Jürgen Habermas:

He has stated: "For the normative self-understanding of the modern period Christianity has been more than a mere catalyst. The egalitarian universalism which gave rise to the ideas of freedom and social coexistence, is a direct inheritance from the Jewish notion of justice and the Christian ethics of love. Substantially unchanged, this heritage has always been critically reappropriated and newly interpreted. To this day an alternative to it does not exist."

Put another way: even if one is not Christian, there is really no choice but to agree with Christian values, particularly in the social, political, and cultural sphere.

The Pope also pled for children, saying that they should never be regarded as "a form of illness." Reminding his listeners that Europe was the place that first articulated fundamental human rights, the Pope said that it cannot be a place for abortion because abortion is a violation of the most basic right to life. Children *are* the future, he said, so young families need encouragement and support that will benefit society as a whole. He also spoke in favor of hospice care versus "actively assisted death," that almost invites abuse for the sake of cutting costs or making money. Finally, he exhorted Europe to use her immense economic power to work for good, against AIDS, poverty, and war throughout the world. While growing older in her population, Europe "must not give up on itself, [and] not become old in spirit."

At Mariazell on the following day, Benedict explained the meaning of a pilgrimage: quite simply, "setting out in a particular direction, traveling towards a destination." He then tied this Christian idea and practice to all of human history saying that all life is a pilgrimage toward a goal, toward God. Our lives have a "deeper purpose"; they are not random meanderings, ending at nothingness.

God can write straight even on the crooked lines of our history. God allows us our freedom, and yet in our failures he can always find new paths for his love. God does not fail. Hence [Jesus'] genealogy is a guarantee of God's faithfulness; a guarantee that God does not allow us to fall, and an invitation to direct our lives ever anew towards him, to walk ever anew towards Jesus Christ.[12]

Then he referred to his message from the day before in Vienna: Those who have faith must believe in truth; they cannot be resigned to failure or oblivion. "This attitude of resignation with regard to truth," he said, "lies at the heart of the crisis of the West, the crisis of Europe. If truth does not exist for man, then neither can he ultimately distinguish between good and evil."

How do we proceed? What is the way out of this crisis? How can we believe in truth when there are so many apparent reasons to dispense with the whole idea?

> *Truth proves itself in love. It is never our property, never our product, just as love can never be produced, but only received and handed on as a gift. We need this inner force of truth. As Christians we trust this force of truth. We are its witnesses. We must hand it on as a gift in the same way as we have received it, as it has given itself to us.*

Truth is, then, love, just as love is true. If we gaze upon Christ, the Crucified One, who gave himself to us in his suffering, and see his outstretched arms, we must see that they are "also a gesture of embracing, by which he draws us to himself, wishing to enfold us in his loving hands." The crucifix is a symbol of the ultimate gift of self for the sake of love. Christ Crucified tells us how to interpret the Ten Commandments. They are a Yes to God, family, life, love, solidarity, truth, and respect for others and their property. This, said Benedict, is the way forward.

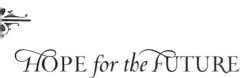

HOPE *for the* FUTURE

"Let us put it very simply: man needs God,
otherwise he remains without hope."

–*Pope Benedict XVI*, Spe Salvi

Just before Advent 2007, Benedict XVI published his second encyclical letter, *Spe Salvi,* about Christian hope and its power to save. Over a million copies were sold before Christmas, and the number of free downloads to date is anyone's guess. In the encyclical, Benedict asks the question, What must we hope? While science and technology have brought about innumerable improvements in material life, it still remains true that only Love can redeem man, give his life meaning, and make him better than he would otherwise be. While the whole story of the scientific advancement in Western civilization can be summed up in the progression from the slung rock to the nuclear warhead, there has been no corresponding development in morality. Love allows us to *live*, not just in a biological sense but in meaningful relationship to others—through giving, sharing, helping, and understanding. All of these acts of love help to free us from the selfish trap of ourselves. In this love Christians must have hope. This is faith.

Christians can never lose hope because of the simple fact that God became man to suffer *with* us as we do, let himself be crucified for our sins, and then rose from the dead. If you believe these things actually happened, then you can never really lose hope in the here and now, and beyond. We learn and practice hope not through therapy but prayer. When you converse with God, he listens. "Answers" come according to his time, not ours, and they come in many forms. Sometimes there may be movements of the heart and soul; often there is silence. And the timeless prayers of the Church are always there to help us when personal prayer is difficult: Our Father, Hail Mary, and the liturgy. The encyclical emphasizes putting hope into action through good works, maintaining hope in the face of suffering, and having faith in the Last Judgment (the reality of ultimate justice), and the prospect of joining completely the grace of God. The encyclical ends with a passionate exhortation to the Virgin Mary that she may guide us on our journey, like a star over the ocean, toward hope itself.

On the day of the encyclical's release, an article from Reuters said, "Papal Encyclical Attacks Atheism, Lauds Hope." The word *atheism* does not appear in the encyclical until four-fifths of the way through, where Benedict rightly explains it as an attitude of moral righteousness, "a protest against the injustices of the world and of world history." Outrage at the suffering in the world easily leads to the belief that there is no benevolent deity. Benedict certainly condemns murderous, atheistic regimes of the twentieth century, but the encyclical is scarcely concerned with atheism. It argues that there is no alternative to hope, as defined in the Judeo-Christian tradition. At the very beginning of the work, Benedict recommends, "A self-critique of modernity is needed in dialogue with Christianity and its concept of hope."

What does the future hold for Benedict XVI? Growing popularity seems almost guaranteed. In 2007 officials recorded that 2.8 million people came to see the Holy Father at papal audiences and celebrations at the Vatican and Castel Gandolfo, which broke a number of records. His pontificate is no longer a novelty on the world stage. People come to pay tribute to a man of great learning and wisdom, and to pray with him. He is perhaps the most educated leader in the world today and probably the best writer as well.

In his first three years as the leader of the Catholic Church, Pope Benedict has found his own pace, and he is doing nothing precipitously. He is not an old man in a hurry. All his decisions thus far have been carefully based on a life of study and service in the Church. And yet, in the words of Cardinal Tarcisio Bertone, the Vatican secretary of state, Benedict "is a volcano of activity."[1] Despite the burdens of his vocation, the Pope maintains his peaceful equanimity. "I have never seen him perturbed in meetings in the Vatican," Bertone said, "when he may have had reason to be. He is very kind."[2] I can add that in all the papal biographies I have seen that are critical or hostile toward him, not one could cite an instance of bad temper. One American journalist, however, said he saw Ratzinger roll his eyes . . . once.

A high priority for Benedict must be to complete and publish the second volume of his work about Jesus of Nazareth. There is little doubt that it will be as well received as its predecessor. In 2008 he will publish an encyclical about Catholic social teaching, and he may also write one about faith, and so finish his series of encyclicals on the theological virtues (i.e., faith, hope, and love) albeit in reverse order. In terms of a reform of the Roman Curia, something that Pope John Paul II generally neglected, there is talk that Benedict might establish some new positions where women can participate in the uppermost leadership of the Church more directly. The Pope will not convene a Third Vatican Council or anything of that nature, nor should any Pope, until history moves further beneath our feet than it already has in the last hundred years.

Benedict proclaimed the year starting from June 29, 2008 to June 29, 2009 as the "Pauline Year," in celebration of the great saint's 2000th (or so) birthday. During this commemoration of one of Christianity's greatest saints, Benedict will no doubt do everything in his power to continue to advance Catholic-Orthodox relations along the path toward eventual unity. In 2008 he will visit the Marian shrine at Lourdes in France, travel to the United States to deliver an address at the General Assembly of the United Nations and visit Washington, D.C., and fly to Australia to attend the Twenty-First World Youth Day. Benedict will probably try to keep this pace up as long as his energy and health permit. In the end, it is all in God's hands anyway.

What lies in the future of the Church as a whole? Few are better positioned to know than Benedict XVI. His prediction made in 1970 is just as good today as it was then, and in part, already confirmed in the intervening years.

The future of the Church can and will depend only on the strength of those who have deep roots and who live from the pure fullness of their faith. . . . It will be a spiritualized Church that does not rely on a political mandate and that curries favor with the right as little as with the left. It will be a difficult time for the Church. For the process of crystallization and clarification will cost her much valuable energy. It will make her poor, will make her a Church of the meek. The process will be all the harder because it will be just as necessary to root out sectarian narrow-mindedness as boastful self-will. It is safe to say that all this will require time. The way will be long and wearisome, just as was the way that led from the false progressivism on the eve of the French Revolution—which made it fashionable even for bishops to deride dogmas and perhaps, even, to let it be known that the very existence of God was not a certainty for them—to the renewal of the nineteenth century. But after the purification of these uprootings a great strength will emanate from a spiritualized and simplified Church. For the inhabitants of a totally planned world will be unutterably lonely. If God has completely disappeared from them, they will realize the extent of their terrible poverty. Then they will discover the small community of believers as something entirely new—as a hope that is meant for them, as an answer they have always sought in secret. Thus it seems certain to me that very hard times await the Church. Her own crisis has as yet hardly begun.[3]

Admittedly the world was much different in 1970 than it is now, but the realities remain the same. In 1970 the West was riding on the crest of a two-decade wave of unprecedented economic expansion, and just starting to plunge into its torrid love affair with sex, drugs, and rock 'n' roll, with universal relativism and aggressive secularism. Intellectuals committed themselves to Freud, Nietzsche, and Marx, and Western capitalist democracies set themselves firmly against the Communist East. Nuclear war was an ever-present danger, the regime of the Soviet Union had no end in sight, and the Church seemed to be falling apart from the inside.

Now the scene is very different. Communism is dead, or confined to silly regimes such as are to be found in Cuba and North Korea. The much-feared specter of a nuclear armed Iraq or Iran has yet to materialize. The opulent West continues to consume about half of the world's resources, though a rapidly industrializing China and India are increasing their claim. Intellectuals are beginning to move away from postmodernism—a flaccid, nihilist set of ideas, a hangover, more or less, after a one-night stand with Nietzsche and Freud—but there is no real sign that the scholarly establishment will turn in any better direction. The Church, however, while still taking in lots of water, is headed forward and not down.

One of Joseph Ratzinger's former students, Christoph Schönborn, now the cardinal of Vienna, has said that the Catholic Church is becoming less a *Volkskirche*, a church of nations, and more an *Entscheidungskirche,* a church of personal decision. In earlier centuries, it was a given that the Bavarians, the Austrians, the Irish, the Italians, the Poles, the Portuguese, and the Spaniards among others, were all Catholics. The Church was thoroughly embedded in these peoples' states, societies, and common cultures, so much so that many people from these groups did not really reflect or internalize the faith as it deserved. Nowadays the scene is very different. To be a believing, devout, "practicing" Catholic is to be a rebel against mainstream, postmodern society. To live the faith requires a decision by the individual, and people are forming new communities, based in faith, left and right. These people are Catholic because they want to be, in spite of all the forces arrayed against them. And those who do not want to be Catholic simply don't have to, without having to deal with any disadvantage—social, political, legal, or otherwise. The new situation actually has much to recommend it over the old, if we look at it in a positive light.

There are real signs of a Catholic rejuvenation. The dozens of new communities and lay ecclesial movements, such as the Community of Sant'Egidio, known for its successful peace negotiations in Africa and other war-torn parts of the world, and Regnum Christi, with its rapidly growing priestly order, the Legionaries of Christ, are expanding in the size of their membership and in the extent of their activity. Numbers of seminarians, priests, and religious seem to have bottomed out, and in places around the globe, show real, if modest, growth. Those orders that committed themselves to 1970s secularism continue to atrophy, getting little or no fresh blood to replenish their ranks, but orders that embrace the habit, real poverty, chastity, and obedience are getting vocations.

One of the many beauties of Catholicism is that it will never die as long as there are those who truly believe in it, and there need not be many. Those whose faith is clear, simple, and unsullied by the host of compromises requested by consumerist culture, will carry the Church forward, no matter what state she is in. Throughout the course of human history, we have seen the Church at her best when she is free from the state or struggling under its oppression. She was often at her worst when she was too snugly at the side of secular authority. She should always maintain her right to tell off all sides of the political spectrum when they violate human life, diminish human dignity, and trample on the truth of Christ's teaching. She is cash-poor; the Vatican operates on about a billion dollars a year, quite impressive for a world membership of 1.1 billion. But she is definitely house-rich; her cultural heritage in buildings, art, and other valuables is priceless.

There are signs of hope that Benedict XVI may be able to mend old and newer schisms. One of the more recent ones, with the Society of St. Pius X, might come about due to the Pope's having relaxed the restriction on the celebration of the beautiful and venerable Tridentine Mass. But members of the society will have to accept the authenticity of the Second Vatican Council in terms of Catholic tradition, something that they have basically forsworn. Although there are good grounds to be skeptical, there is always hope.

The same pertains to the Orthodox Churches. Benedict cannot be more forceful in his expressed wishes for unity, but as he readily admits, one cannot wipe away a thousand years with a slash of the pen. It will be no easy task for the patriarchs to accept a special role for the successors of St. Peter. Nonetheless, the trajectory set a half a century ago is still in charge; the only variation we can expect is the pace.

In terms of ecumenism with regard to the 600–700 Protestant churches and sects, probably not much will be accomplished, and not much should. Indeed the only thing that even puts these faith organizations into a single grouping is the fact that they are not Catholic or Orthodox. It is reasonable for the Pope to wait till they can agree on something, anything (theological, ecclesial, logistical, or otherwise) among themselves, before he should try to look for concessions for the sake of unity. The five-hundred-year-old rift in the ranks of the faithful is an integral part of the history of the modern era, and its existence is one of the things that has helped to make the Church more consciously Catholic.

History shows us that the Church is always in one crisis or another. As soon as she appears to pull out of one, she pitches headlong into another. In 1970 Cardinal Ratzinger spoke of "very hard times" ahead, and I would like to think that they have been weathered now, for the most part, until the next wave arrives. While numbers of the faithful—if the statistics are remotely reliable—are soaring in Africa, they are plunging in Latin America, to the advantage of Pentecostal churches. While the vestiges of Christianity in Europe are graying with the general population, the Church is seeing all kinds of activity in the United States. The state of the Church in South and East Asia shows an uneven balance sheet.

Catholic Christianity is demanding. It always has been and always will be. In many ways it cannot be reconciled with postmodernism. For all those who complain that the Catholic Church is boring or mean or unrealistic, they should bear in mind that the first concern of the Church is not people like them, hard as it is to say. The Church's first concern, in fact, is not people at all. It is God, as revealed to the world by Christ Jesus. If the Church does not do justice to God in his revelation, then she can never do justice to anyone on earth.

The Catholic Church cannot make concessions to the fashionable currents of the present moment, because in doing so she would cease to be Catholic. All the usual recommended accommodations, Benedict has written, are tantamount to turning away from the Cross. "The Christian Faith is a scandal for people of every age." Certainly the "secondary scandals" that have come to nest in the Church over the course of time—the Inquisition, the executions, warring Popes, venal bishops, pedophile priests—have to be assiduously cleared away, but the central scandal remains. The Second Vatican Council confirmed it, saying "Yes to the scandal of a love so exorbitant that it seems impossible." The Council tried to render the scandal of God in simple terms, but the demands remain just as high as before. Christians are obligated to give all of themselves, neither more nor less.[4] Anyone who says that the Council was meant to be revolutionary, that it was supposed to become tolerant and welcoming of worldliness, has got it completely wrong. "The Church's openness to the world means, then, that the demands upon the Christian are increasing, are becoming more urgent and total, not that they are decreasing."[5]

The only way to be a devout Christian is to embrace the process of conversion, and it is most definitely a process, not a mere event. What kind of process is it? "Of dying," says Benedict, a dying to oneself, to the lone, enclosed, imprisoned "I." And this conversion process is one of death by fire. In the words of Jesus, recorded not in the Bible but in the writings of Origen, "Whoever is near me is near fire." The Holy Spirit alighted on the apostles as flames at Pentecost. If you want to embrace Christianity, Ratzinger said years ago, you have to be willing to get burned. Catholicism is not about easy accommodations. In November 2007, Benedict exhorted a gathering of Italian university students to "go against the tide." In a consumerist, materialist society such as ours today, where so many people are obsessed with *seeming* and *having*," all Catholics need to remember that *being* is what truly counts. Being good and being loving sets you free.

Is there a final idea or single sentence that Benedict would want you to take away from an account of his life, career, and teaching? I don't know how he would respond, but here's my guess: "Love God. Try it, do it, you can, you *must*, because he is love itself. There is nothing more worthy in life or death. If you want to know how, just listen to Jesus Christ through reading, reflection, and prayer. He is there, *here*, then, now and always, and he is listening, and waiting lovingly for you."

Thank you for joining me on this journey. May God bless you.

AFTERWORD

If you would like to come see the Pope's homeland, please consider joining me on a summer pilgrimage in Bavaria, "In the Footsteps of Benedict XVI."

The journey will last nine to ten days, and we will visit the towns and cities most important to Benedict XVI in his youth: Marktl am Inn, Altötting, Tittmoning, Traunstein, and Salzburg. We will also spend time in Munich and Regensburg and see other beautiful sites such as the Chiemsee and the Bavarian Alps as we travel through the region. The Bavarian Pilgrimage Office is handling all the logistical arrangements in Germany, and one of the Legionaries of Christ will be on hand to lead the prayer sessions, celebrate the Eucharist, hear confessions, and provide spiritual guidance. I will be the guide for the bus and walking tours. I don't know of anyone who has come to this corner of the world and regretted it.

For more information, please see www.brennanpursell.com.

APPENDIX

A DAY *in the* LIFE
of the HOLY FATHER

by Edward Pentin, National Catholic Register *correspondent*

VATICAN CITY — Thanks to unprecedented access to the papal household, a clearer picture of Pope Benedict XVI's daily life at the Apostolic Palace has come into focus. Luigi Accattoli, veteran Vatican correspondent for the Italian newspaper Corriere della Sera, *recently was allowed to see daily life in the papal quarters in detail. And his verdict: It's a routine "full of tasks but also rich in moments of rest and reflection." Accattoli was granted permission to view a documentary about the Pope's daily affairs made by the Vatican Television Center. The documentary has not yet aired because the Vatican media agency is currently negotiating broadcasting rights with private television networks. According to Accattoli, the Holy Father meets many guests but they are mostly welcomed in formal, public ways "that don't impinge on periods reserved for work." In contrast to his predecessor, Pope John Paul II, an average day of the theologian-Pope is, Accattoli said, "one of less public activity but more time spent in study and writing."*

EARLY RISER. The papal day begins early. The exact time varies, but usually Pope Benedict XVI is up by 5 a.m. or slightly later. Before becoming Pope, Cardinal Joseph Ratzinger was always a morning person, determined to use the first part of the day for meditation and prayer. Now, he still begins his day in the chapel.

AUDIENCES. Benedict remains in his study until 11 a.m. Then, he takes an elevator to a lower floor in the Apostolic Palace to attend any public audiences scheduled for that day.

These audiences, which are managed by members of the Pontifical House-hold headed by American Archbishop James Harvey, are normally held in the Pope's private library or in a hall nearby. Usually the audiences are with heads of state, individual bishops, or groups of bishops. They can also include groups of priests participating in *ad limina* visits, or laity involved in the life of the Church. Wednesdays are an exception to this routine, of course, as that's when the Holy Father holds his weekly general audience, either in St. Peter's Square or in the adjacent Paul VI Hall.

MORNING MASS. Pope Benedict concelebrates Mass with his two secretar-ies, Msgr. Georg Gänswein and Msgr. Alfred Xuereb, between 7 and 8 a.m. in his private chapel. Somewhat modern and austere in appearance, the chapel was also used by Paul VI and John Paul II. Four *memores domini* (consecrated female members of Communion and Liberation who look after the private papal apartments) also attend and make up a small congregation. They are joined by the Pope's valet, Paolo Gabriele, but it's rare that visitors or friends are also present. The Mass is celebrated in Italian and one of the four *memores* reads the First Reading and the Responsorial Psalm. There's no homily but long pauses are provided for reflection and prayer, especially after each reading and after holy Communion.

PREPARING FOR THE DAY. Breakfast is served from 8 to 8.30 a.m., after which the Holy Father adjourns to his study in the papal apartments. On his table in his private study, which is rich in books, are two telephones—one landline, the other a cell phone. Benedict only uses his cell phone occasionally, when he wants to respond personally and directly to people, and only when calling those select few who know his number already.

One of the first tasks the Pope undertakes in his workday is sifting through the morning's newspapers. One of his two secretaries brings "an abundant selection" of newspapers and periodicals selected by an official in the Secretariat of State. The publications are bound in a green leather case with the words *Rassegna Stampa* (Press Review) printed on the front. Also brought to him is a selected amount of mail to read. One of his secretaries then gives a rundown of the day's agenda, noting people the Holy Father will meet and problems warranting his attention.

LUNCH. Lunch is served at 1:30 p.m., usually by Paolo Gabriele. Benedict always dines with his two secretaries, and it's rare he'll have a guest at table, in contrast to his more gregarious predecessor. Accattoli notes that in this

respect, this Pope has reverted to the "reserved nature of Italian popes." The food is Italian, while the drink is almost always freshly squeezed orange juice. However, wine is served on occasions when guests dine with him.

SIESTA. After lunch, the Holy Father, accompanied by one of his secretaries, walks for ten minutes on the terrace of the Apostolic Palace, which has a garden, vases of plants, and lemon trees. Then, passing near the Michelangelo cupola of St. Peter's Basilica, he then returns to his apartments, where he normally takes an afternoon nap for an hour to an hour and a half.

AFTERNOON. By 3:30 p.m., Benedict is back at his desk to prepare homilies and attend to documents. At 5, one of his secretaries brings mail that has arrived during the day, and documents to sign that have already been decided upon in other meetings with his heads of Vatican offices and other Vatican officials. Such documents are placed in a folder with the words "To be Signed by the Holy Father."

EVENING MEETINGS. From 6 to 6:45 p.m., the Pope has routine meetings in his private study. These are usually weekly and monthly engagements with senior Vatican officials, rotating among Cardinal Tarcisio Bertone, the

Vatican secretary of state, Archbishop Fernando Filoni, the Vatican's *sostituto* (official responsible for the running of the Roman Curia), Archbishop Dominique Mamberti, the secretary for Relations with States (the Vatican's foreign minister), Cardinal Giovanni Battista Re, the prefect of Congregation for Bishops, Cardinal William Levada, the prefect of the Congregation for the Doctrine of the Faith, and other key members of the Vatican hierarchy.

EVENING. From 6:45 to 7:30 p.m. in warmer months—and from 4 to 4:45 p.m. in winter — the Holy Father walks in the Vatican Gardens accompanied by his two secretaries. The walk passes along small, narrow paths and occasional steps. During his walks, he prays the Rosary. Supper follows the same form as lunch, and is served at 7:30. Afterward, at 8, Benedict has some time to unwind. He withdraws to a sitting room furnished with sofas and green armchairs, where he watches *TG1*, a popular Italian news program.

Compline (night prayers of the Liturgy of the Hours) follows in his chapel, and shortly after 9 p.m. the Pope retires to his bedroom, although he doesn't go immediately to bed. The lights of the three windows on the top floor of the Apostolic Palace, where his apartments are located, aren't generally switched off until 11 p.m. Benedict no doubt wishes to squeeze in just a little more time for reading and possibly writing before turning in.

Edward Pentin writes from Rome.
Photographs used with permission of Vatican Television Center

ENDNOTES

CHAPTER 1: FROM SMALL-TOWN BAVARIA: MARKTL AM INN

1. Quoted in Matthew E. Bunson, *We Have a Pope! Benedict XVI* (Huntington, IN: Our Sunday Visitor Publishing Division, 2005), 180.
2. Joseph Ratzinger, *Milestones: Memoirs, 1927-1977* (San Francisco: Ignatius Press, 1998), 9.
3. Joseph Cardinal Ratzinger, *Salt of the Earth* (San Francisco: Ignatius, 1997), 43.
4. The President's speech was delivered on the tarmac at the Munich airport on September 9, 2006.
5. *Milestones*, 7.

CHAPTER 2: A PILGRIM IN ALTÖTTING

1. Quoted in Stefan v. Kempis, *Benedetto: die Biografie* (Leipzig: St. Benno-Verlag, 2006), 33.
2. Papal homily, September 11, 2006. Italics are mine.
3. *Milestones*, 9.
4. Joseph Cardinal Ratzinger, *The Spirit of the Liturgy* (San Francisco: Ignatius Press, 2000).
5. Joseph Cardinal Ratzinger and Vittorio Messori, *The Ratzinger Report: an exclusive interview on the state of the Church* (San Francisco: Ignatius Press, 1985).
6. *Compendium: Cathechism of the Catholic Church* (Washington, USCCB Publishing: 2006), 54.
7. Catechism of the Catholic Church, 2nd ed., (New York: Doubleday, 1995), 272.
8. The phrase appears in both the *Compendium* and the Catechism.
9. *Spirit of the Liturgy,* 83.
10. Ibid., 148.

CHAPTER 3: IN THE LAND BETWEEN TWO RIVERS

1. *Salt of the Earth*, 44, 48.
2. Johann Nußbaum, *Poetisch und herzensgut* (Rimsting, 2006), 38.
3. Kempis, 61.
4. *Salt of the Earth*, 45–48.
5. Ibid., 44.
6. *Milestones*, 10.
7. Ibid., 11.
8. *Salt of the Earth*, 45.
9. *Milestones*, 11.
10. Kempis, 222.

[11] *Milestones*, 11.

[12] Ibid., 11.

[13] Quoted in Alfred Läpple, *Benedikt XVI. und seine Wurzeln: was sein Leben und seinen Glauben prägte* (Augsburg: Sankt Ulrich Verlag, 2006), 129.

[14] *The Ratzinger Report*, 166.

[15] *Salt of the Earth*, 27.

[16] Joseph Cardinal Ratzinger, *On the Way to Jesus Christ* (San Francisco: Ignatius Press, 2005), 38.

[17] Ibid., 34.

[18] "Begegnung in Rom," transcript of video conversation between Prof. Dr. Joseph Ratzinger and August Everding, Bayerischer Rundfunk, originally aired April 16, 1997.

[20] *Milestones*, 10.

[21] Ibid., 12.

[22] Ibid., 12.

[23] *Salt of the Earth*, 52.

[24] *Milestones*, 13.

[25] *Salt of the Earth*, 53.

[26] See "A Future Pope is Recalled: A Love of Cats and Mozart, Dazzled by Church as a Boy," by Mark Landler and Richard Bernstein, *New York Times*, 22 April 2005.

[27] *Milestones*, 14.

[28] *Salt of the Earth*, 52.

[29] *Milestones*, 14.

[30] Ibid., 16.

[31] Kempis, 56.

[32] Christian Feldmann, *Papst Benedikt XVI: eine kritische Biographie* (Hamburg: Rowohlt, 2006), 25.

[33] *Salt of the Earth*, 53.

[34] *Milestones*, 20.

[35] Joseph Cardinal Ratzinger, *Many Religions—One Covenant: Israel, the Church and the World* (San Francisco: Ignatius, 1999), 44–45.

[36] *Salt of the Earth*, 44.

[37] Feldmann, 21.

[38] *Salt of the Earth*, 51. Feldmann, 20.

CHAPTER 4: IN THE LAND BETWEEN TWO RIVERS

[1] *Milestones*, 22.

[2] *Salt of the Earth*, 46–47, 51.

[3] Ibid., 50.

[4] Kempis, 70.

[5] *Milestones*, 23.

[6] *Salt of the Earth*, 52.

[7] Kempis, 63.

[8] See Ian Kershaw, *Popular Opinion and Political Dissent in the Third Reich: Bavaria 1933-1945* (2nd ed, New York: Oxford University Press, 2002).

[9] *Milestones*, 26. *Salt of the Earth*, 50.

[10] AP article, 7 April 2006.

[11] *Milestones*, 25. Kempis, 74. "Joseph und die Hitlerjugend," *Süddeutsche Zeitung*, 25 July 2006.

[12] Ibid., 27.

[13] Steven Ozment, *A Mighty Fortress* (New York: Harper, 2004), 280.

[14] *Milestones*, 28.

[15] Ibid., 29.

[16] John Allen, *The Rise of Benedict XVI: The Inside Story of How the Pope was Elected and Where He Will Take the Catholic Church* (New York: Doubleday, 2005), 148.

[17] Interview with Professor Hans-Ulrich Wehler, *Der Spiegel*, April 22, 2005.

[18] See Volker Laube, *Das Erzbischöfliche Studienseminar St. Michael in Traunstein und sein Archiv* (Regensburg: Schnell und Steiner Verlag, 2006) for an investigation of the Pope's participation in Hitler Youth and the seminary's difficulties under the Nazi regime.

[19] *Salt of the Earth*, 52.

[20] Kempis, 102.

[21] *Milestones*, 34.

[22] Kempis, 106.

[23] *Milestones*, 36.

[24] Ibid., 37.

[25] Ibid., 39.

[26] Ibid.

[27] Ibid., 39–40.

[28] Joseph Cardinal Ratzinger, *God and the World* (San Francisco: Ignatius, 2002).

[29] Ibid., 253–54.

[30] Ibid, 421.

[31] Ibid, 125.

[32] Ibid, 126–27.

[33] *The Ratzinger Report*, 188.

[34] *God in the World*, 128.

CHAPTER 5: FROM BOY TO PRIEST: FREISING AND MUNICH

1 *Milestones*, 156.
2 These numbers are taken from Greg Tobin, *Holy Father Pope Benedict XVI: Pontiff for a new era* (New York: Sterling Publishing, 2005), 103.
3 Läpple, 16. These nicknames originated during the Gymnasium years according to Kempis, 7.
4 Feldmann, 30.
5 *Milestones*, 45.
6 Ibid., 45.
7 Kempis, 67–68.
8 See "Mit brennender Sorge," 14 March 1937.
9 Kempis, 19–20.
10 *Salt of the Earth*, 59.
11 *Milestones*, 47.
12 Läpple, 55-56; Kempis, 118.
13 Matthias Kopp, ed., *Und plötzlich Papst: Benedict XVI. im Spiegel persönliche Begegnungen* (Freiburg: Herder, 2007), 41-43.
14 Joseph Ratzinger, *Deutsche Tagespost*, December 23, 1971, quoted in Läpple, 81.
15 Läpple, 77.
16 Zenit.org, Code: ZE07040301.
17 Läpple, 51.
18 Kopp, 44.
19 *Salt of the Earth*, 55-56.
20 www.vatican.va: Papal homily, 15 April 2007: *Eucharistic Celebration on the occasion of the 80th birthday of the Holy Father*.
21 Kempis, 129-30. *Milestones*, 99.
22 Läpple, 46.
23 Donald J. D'Elia, "The Catholic as Historian: Witness in Every Age to Christ's Presence among Us," in Donald J. D'Elia and Patrick Foley, eds., *The Catholic as Historian* (Naples, FL: Sapientia Press, 2006), 10-11.
24 *On the Way to Jesus Christ*, 89-90.
25 Ibid., 88.
26 *Milestones*, 101.
27 The poem and the information for the passage about Bogenhausen come from the *Süddeutsche Zeitung*, August 31, 2006, except where otherwise noted. See Kempis, 136, for two more examples.
28 Läpple, 99. Kempis, 137. *Milestones*, 102.
29 *Milestones*, 107.

[30] *Altöttinger Liebfrauenbote*, July 2, 2006.

[31] *Milestones*, 113.

[32] Ibid., 114.

CHAPTER 6: NORTH, SOUTH, AND BACK AGAIN

[1] *Milestones*, 116.

[2] Kopp, 187.

[3] Ibid., 69.

[4] *Salt of the Earth*, 79.

[5] Kopp, 110.

[6] Kempis, 169.

[7] Kopp, 244–45.

[8] Kempis, 171.

[9] *Milestones*, 131.

[10] Joseph Cardinal Ratzinger, *Co-Workers of the Truth: Meditations for Every Day of the Year* (San Francisco: Ignatius Press, 1990), 173.

[11] *Milestones*, 148.

[12] See Avery Cardinal Dulles, S.J., "Benedict XVI: Interpreter of Vatican II," Laurence J. McGinley Lecture, 25 October 2005, Fordham University, 3–25.

[13] *Milestones*, 134.

[14] Feldmann, 7.

[15] Kempis, 178–79.

[16] Feldmann, 53.

[17] *Milestones*, 139. On the genesis of the work see, D. Vincent Twomey, S.V.D., *Pope Benedict XVI, The Conscience of Our Age: A Theological Portrait* (San Francisco: Ignatius Press, 2007), 16, note 8.

[18] Joseph Cardinal Ratzinger, *Introduction to Christianity* (San Francisco: Ignatius Press, 1969), 164.

[19] *Salt of the Earth*, 77.

[20] Ibid., 67.

[21] Läpple, 143.

[22] Feldmann, 55.

[23] See, for example, Stephen Mansfield, *Pope Benedict XVI: His Life and Mission* (New York: Tarcher/Penguin, 2005), 71.

[24] Kopp, 38.

[25] Mansfield, 8–9.

[26] Kempis, 192.

[27] Quoted in Alexander Kissler, "Verachtet mir die Pharisäer nicht!" *Süddeutsche Zeitung*, Feuilleton, 14/15 April 2007.

[28] *National Catholic Register* (December 3–9, 2006), 12.

[29] *On the Way to Jesus Christ*, 92.

[30] *Salt of the Earth*, 80.

CHAPTER 7: THE PLACE HE CALLED HOME: REGENSBURG

[1] Karl Birkenseer, *"Hier bin ich wirklich daheim": Papst Benedikt XVI. und das Bistum Regensburg* (Regensburg: Pustet, 2005), 9.

[2] Kempis, pp. 201–02.

[3] Läpple, 146.

[4] Kempis, 198.

[5] Birkenseer, 18.

[6] Twomey, 23–25.

[7] Birkenseer, 18.

[8] Kempis, 215.

[9] Birkenseer, 29.

[10] Ibid., 27.

[11] Ibid., 37.

[12] Mark Landler and Richard Bernstein, "A Future Pope is Recalled," *New York Times* (April 22, 2005).

[13] Feldmann, 61.

[14] *Milestones*, 150.

[15] The phrase apparently comes from Klaus-Rüdiger Mai. See Kempis, 40.

[16] "A Future Pope is Recalled," *New York Times* (April 22, 2005).

[17] Kempis, 24.

[18] Ibid., 207; Feldmann, 69.

[19] Kopp, 82.

[20] Kempis, 211.

CHAPTER 8: ARCHBISHOP AND CARDINAL

[1] Kempis, 197.

[2] *Salt of the Earth*, 79.

[3] *Milestones*, 152.

[4] Kempis, 215.

[5] Ibid., 219.

[6] *Milestones*, 152.

[7] Kempis, 220.

[8] *Milestones*, 153.

[9] Kempis, 222.

[10] Quoted in "A Future Pope is Recalled," *New York Times* (April 22, 2005).

[11] Feldmann, 77-79.

[12] Ibid., 80–81.

[13] *Süddeutsche Zeitung*, (August 14, 2006), 51.

[14] Feldmann, 82–83.

[15] *Süddeutsche Zeitung*, (August 14, 2006), 51.

[16] Feldmann, 74.

[17] *Süddeutsche Zeitung*, (September 9/10, 2006), 15.

[18] Ibid., (August 14, 2006), 51.

[19] *Salt of the Earth*, 82.

[20] Ibid., 83.

[21] Kempis, 223; Feldmann, 174.

CHAPTER 9: CALLED TO ROME

[1] *Salt of the Earth*, 83.

[2] Kempis, 252; Bunson, 157.

[3] *Salt of the Earth*, 85.

[4] Quoted in *Co-Workers*, 114.

[5] *National Catholic Register*, January 21–27, 2007.

[6] *Salt of the Earth*, 94.

[7] Feldmann, 95. For a more detailed and sympathetic account of these cases and more, see Paul Collins, *God's New Man: The Election of Benedict XVI and the Legacy of John Paul II* (London: Continuum, 2005), chapter 8.

[8] www.vatican.va, "Joint Declaration on the Doctrine of Justification."

[9] Quoted in Mansfield, 123.

[10] *Süddeutsche Zeitung* (August 16, 2006), 35.

[11] Feldmann, 97.

[12] *God and the World*, 93.

[13] Ibid., 457.

[14] *Salt of the Earth*, 94.

[15] Interview with Ray and Sue Glemser, January 11, 2007.

[16] *Ratzinger Report*, 98.

[17] Ibid.

[18] *God and the World*, 12.

[19] *Spirit of the Liturgy*, 83.

[20] Joseph Cardinal Ratzinger, *Truth and Tolerance: Christian Belief and World Religions* (San Francisco: Ignatius Press, 2003), 54.

[21] Ibid., 56.

[22] Both were written before he became Pope. The English translations appeared

shortly afterward.

[23] Joseph Cardinal Ratzinger, *Values in a Time of Upheaval* (New York: Crossroad, 2006), 52.

[24] Ibid., 111.

[25] Joseph Cardinal Ratzinger, *Christianity and the Crisis of Cultures* (San Francisco: Ignatius Press, 2005), 93.

[26] Kempis, 242.

[27] See Jürgen Habermas and Joseph Ratzinger, *The Dialectics of Secularization: On Reason and Religion* (San Francisco: Ignatius Press, 2007).

[28] Feldmann, 174.

[29] Läpple, 125–27.

[30] *Münchner Merkur* (January 5, 1989), quoted in Läpple, 123–24.

[31] Bernhard Hülsebusch, *Professor Papst: Benedikt XVI.—Neue Episoden & Erinnerungen* (Leipzig: Benno Verlag, 2007), 34.

[32] Allen, 146.

[33] Feldmann, 72.

[34] "Begegnung in Rom."

[35] Birkenseer, 28.

[36] Feldmann, 178.

[37] Kempis, 238–39.

CHAPTER 10: THE GUILLOTINE

[1] *National Catholic Register* (May 1–7, 2005).

[2] Harold James, "Empire and US: Power or Values?" *Historically Speaking,* March/April 2007, vol. viii, no. 4, 27.

[3] Kempis, 267.

[4] Bunson, 98.

[5] www.vatican.va, "Missa Pro Eligendo Romano Pontifice" (April 18, 2005).

[6] Kopp, 161.

[7] Stephan Kulle, *Papa Benedikt: die Welt des deutschen Papstes* (Frankfurt am Main: Fischer Verlag, 2007), 32.

[8] www.vatican.va, "Address of His Holiness Benedict XVI to the pilgrims from Germany" (April 25, 2005).

[9] George Weigel, *God's Choice: Pope Benedict XVI and the Future of the Catholic Church* (New York: HarperCollins, 2005), 149.

[10] See Weigel and Allen.

[11] Kempis, 26.

[12] *Süddeutsche Zeitung Magazin* (July 27, 2007), 8.

[13] Kulle, 42.

[14] Michael Collins, *Pope Benedict XVI: Successor to Peter* (New York: Paulist Press, 2005), 89.

[15] www.vatican.va, "First Message of His Holiness Benedict XVI at the end of the Eucharistic Concelebration with the Cardinal electors in the Sistine Chapel" (April 20, 2005).

[16] Collins, 90.

[17] Kempis, 19–20.

[18] www.vatican.va, "Homily from the Inauguration Mass of Benedict XVI" (April 24, 2005).

[19] See *Ratzinger Report*, 67–69.

[20] *Süddeutsche Zeitung* (August 23, 2006).

[21] Hülsebusch, 50.

[22] Janina Müller, heute.de (August 28, 2006).

[23] *Süddeutsche Zeitung Magazin* (August 23, 2006).

[24] *Süddeutsche Zeitung Magazin* (July 27, 2007), 10.

[25] "Begegnung in Rom."

[26] Kulle, 210.

[27] *Süddeutsche Zeitung Magazin* (July 27, 2007), 10.

[28] *Compendium*, xii. As Prefect of the Congregation for the Doctrine of the Faith, Cardinal Ratzinger oversaw the drafting and revision of the text. Much of it bears his mark in terms of ideas, approach, and phraseology.

[29] Kulle, 141.

[30] Feldmann, 197: Kulle, 137–38.

[31] *Deutsche Welle* (April 19, 2006).

[32] Kempis, 272.

[33] See Pope Benedict XVI, *God's Revolution: World Youth Day and Other Cologne Talks* (San Francisco: Ignatius, 2006).

[34] Feldmann, 176.

[35] Interview with Peter Seewald, *Süddeutsche Zeitung Magazin,* 27.

[36] Kulle, 236–37, 246–50, 313–16.

[37] www.vatican.va, "Papal address to Roman Curia" (December 22, 2005).

CHAPTER 11: RESCUING THE WEST – 2006

[1] This quote and the following from www.vatican.va, "Prayer to commemorate the victims of the Concentration Camp of Auschwitz-Birkenau" (May 28, 2006).

[2] *Süddeutsche Zeitung* (May 29, 2006), 3.

[3] *Süddeutsche Zeitung* (August 31, 2006).

[4] *National Catholic Register* (October 1–7, 2006), 5.

[5] See www.vatican.va, "Meeting with the representatives of science in the Aula Magna of the University of Regensburg" (September 12, 2006).

[6] *Süddeutsche Zeitung Magazin* (July 27, 2007), 10.

[7] Zenit.org, Code: ZE06122002.

[8] Ibid., Code: ZE07101204. Kulle, 164.

[9] *Süddeutsche Zeitung* (August 12, 2006), 41.

[10] Kopp, 28.

[11] www.vatican.va, General Audience (December 6, 2006).

[12] Hülsebusch, 94; Kulle, 190.

CHAPTER 12: THE MESSAGE OF LOVE – 2007

[1] Zenit.org, Code: ZE07010707.

[2] *National Catholic Register* (January 14–20, 2007).

[3] Homily, January 7, 2007, Feast of the Baptism of the Lord.

[4] *Vilsbiburger Zeitung* (January 22, 2007).

[5] www.vatican.va, papal homily, April 22, 2007.

[6] *National Catholic Register* (June 3, 2007).

[7] Zenit.org, "Pope Explains Norms on Missal of 1962," July 8, 2007.

[8] "Pope Removes Restrictions on Use of Old Latin Mass," Associated Press (July 7, 2007).

[9] Associated Press (June 28, 2007).

[10] www.vatican.va, "Prayer before the Mariensäule at Am Hof Square in Vienna," September 2007.

[11] www.vatican.va, "Meeting with the public authorities and the Diplomatic Corps at Hofburg Palace in Vienna," September 7, 2007.

[12] www.vatican.va, "Holy Mass on the occasion of the 850th anniversary of the foundation of the Shrine of Mariazell," September 8, 2007.

[13] *National Catholic Register* (August 5, 2007).

[14] Ibid.

[15] Joseph Cardinal Ratzinger, *Glaube und Zukunft* (Munich, 1970), 120–21, 123ff.

[16] *Co-Workers*, 167–68.

[17] *Co-Workers*, 174